# gotcha!

# gotcha!

## Tales from a Black-Belt Bounty Hunter

Joseph Laney and Cyn Mobley

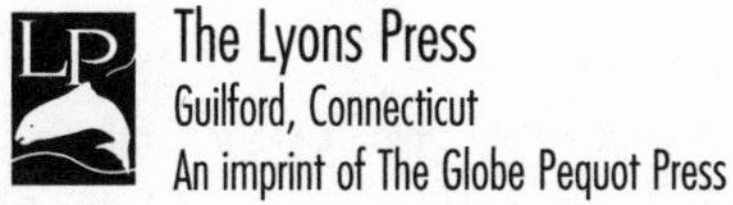

The Lyons Press
Guilford, Connecticut
An imprint of The Globe Pequot Press

The Lyons Press is an imprint of The Globe Pequot Press.

10 9 8 7 6 5 4 3 2 1

Printed in the United States of America

Book design by Mimi LaPoint

ISBN 1-59228-545-7

Library of Congress Cataloging-in-Publication Data is available on file.

I dedicate this work to my late sensei, Grand Master Harold Long, who taught me the skills to stay alive and to my wife, Debbie, who taught me the reason for living.

—Joseph Laney
7 January 2004

# foreword

If you like true crime stories, you're going to enjoy this book. Even if you don't normally read that sort of book, I think you're still going to get a kick out of reading about the odd, strange, and sometimes just downright dumb things that criminals do. They're the sort of folks you probably don't deal with every day, but you need to know that they're out there.

Of course, I've changed the names. In some incidents, the dates and exact locations have been altered so that there's no recognizable connection to any person, alive or dead. Other than that, it all happened just the way that I've described it.

Before I started writing this book, I used many of these stories as lessons for my martial arts students. Sometimes I told stories to emphasize the effectiveness of a particular fighting technique or to point out the importance of awareness as a self-defense measure. Other times, I used them to point out what wouldn't work or how easy most people are to kidnap.

Using street stories in the *dojo* (training hall) brings in a new dimension to traditional training. Most, if not all, martial arts students wonder whether what they're learning will actually work for them when they need it to. If they're studying our system, Isshinryu, it will. Isshinryu is a straightforward and effective system for practical self-defense.

It's one thing to tell my students that. It's another to show them how it has actually worked on the street. Additionally, we use the street stories to set up scenarios in the dojo, reenacting what happened, conducting some post-action analysis to figure out exactly why the techniques are so devastating or, in some cases, why they misfired. We also go one step further, working out countermeasures to each technique. Working with real-life scenarios means increased student confidence and more intense workouts.

Most of the stories about the folks I catch are just downright funny, and sometimes I'd find that students got so caught up in the story that we delayed working on the actual techniques. Since I enjoy telling a good tale, getting sidetracked is something I have to watch out for myself, as well.

The street stories developed a following across the South, and I was constantly being asked to retell one or another. In response, I started posting some of the shorter ones on my website. More and more people kept asking for updates or new stories, or wanted to talk over techniques, so I kept writing down more stories. I'd considered writing a book about the folks I'd chased and finally, at the urging of friends and family, started to organize one. But I made slow progress on it, and I had absolutely no idea what getting it published would entail.

One evening, I arrived early for my karate class and a prospective new student was stretching out on the floor. She wasn't exactly new to karate, as she'd studied for several years under my late instructor. Her name was Cyn Mobley.

Cyn had reached the rank of green belt before joining the United States Navy, and she had served on active duty and in the Reserves for twenty-four years before retiring as a commander. She returned to the Knoxville area and was interested in continuing her martial arts training. As we talked, I learned that Cyn was an accomplished writer and had authored more than twenty books, with one of them hitting *USA Today's* best-seller list.

Naturally, the subject of my future book came up. I asked her for some writing tips and suggestions about how to go about getting it published. She was extremely helpful but it quickly became clear that if I continued to attempt to write this book on my own, it would be at least the next millennium before it saw publication, if then. I was completely unprepared for the amount of work such an undertaking required.

Writing the stories down is different from telling them. I write like a cop and my stories read somewhat like police reports. They're accurate and to the point but lack what's needed to characterize the events in a way that keeps readers drawn to the story. That, along with the arduous task of putting together a book proposal, made it perfectly clear to me that, without Cyn, these stories would never make the transition from getting told to an audience to being in print.

Finally, I asked Cyn if she'd coauthor this book. After some discussion, we worked out some ground rules we could both agree on and started on a proposal.

This is how we worked it out: I wrote the rough draft for each chapter and forwarded it to Cyn, who went through it and added her special touch of magic. This method assured that the stories remained true historically but at the same time were "a good read." We passed the chapters back and forth via e-mail until we had a finished product that was both accurate and entertaining.

I want to thank Cyn for her patience with a novice and the lessons she taught me about improving my writing skills. Perhaps in future joint efforts, she can give the red pen more of a break.

—Joseph Laney

---

Joseph is a true Southern storyteller in the classic sense. His stories and characters immediately captivate any audience and have a depth of context and understanding that you don't often find.

The challenge of coauthoring a book like this is trying to capture the voice and feel of hearing Joseph tell the story in person. At first, I found that he would leave things out in the written version that I remembered in the original story. I sent back early chapters peppered with questions, asking what someone looked like, how it felt to be somewhere, what else he was thinking about. Some of these were things that his cop training would filter out before they got committed to paper—others, simply a necessity of making an oral story work on paper.

There were two things that I found really astounding. The first was the instinctive feel he has for story structure and flow, how to work in the various dojo scenes with the stories, how the two complemented each other, working together on more than just a surface level to make a point. In fact, the combinations are so multilayered at times that I sometimes—well, okay, fairly often—missed a connection that became clear on a second reading. He had the flow of each chapter worked out so well that even making a point on a deeper level didn't distract from the sheer entertainment value of the stories themselves. The words in the chapters changed—how the scenes were arranged did not. It already worked too well.

The second was that he was teachable. I've worked with many new writers who never make the progress he's made. By the time we were halfway through the book, he was already anticipating what questions I'd have about something and coming up with phrases and descriptions that truly stopped me dead. When he talks in the book about there never being an end to learning in martial arts—about there always being another level—he means it, and he carries that attitude over into the rest of his life, as well. Reducing his stories to paper is more than just rearranging sentences or words. It requires trying to understand what he sees when he watches someone's moves, the small cues he picks up unconsciously as a result of his expertise, sometimes things that seem entirely obvious to him that none of us would notice. It was a rare opportunity for a rusty junior *karate-ka* (karate practitioner) to cross-examine a master on virtually any subject, to get a glimpse of what it might mean to be a true martial artist, all with the justification that it was "for the book." Inspiring would be an understatement.

Much of it is still almost like magic to me. If I've been able to capture a bit of it for the reader, then perhaps Joseph will eventually forgive me for pestering him with so many questions. I know working on this book has advanced my own martial arts training far beyond where I would be otherwise.

For several months now, Sensei Laney has had a special rule in effect in the dojo sparring ring: no hard wristlocks or finger breaks on Cyn. No punches or other strikes that would impair her ability to write. No eye gouges. Not until the book is turned in.

Guess what? It's done.

I'm going to go pick up some extra ice packs tomorrow.

—Cyn Mobley

# gotcha!

# introduction

Jeremy Walker gets stopped for suspicion of driving under the influence of alcohol or drugs. While a conviction does carry a maximum sentence of a year in jail, he's most likely going to be sentenced to a weekend in jail and a few days of picking up trash along the side of the road, and get smacked with a hefty fine.

But what happens between the time he's first arrested and the moment he's sentenced? He's in jail waiting for arraignment and trial. Yes, Jeremy has a constitutional right to a speedy trial. But the time he spends in jail waiting for his trial will be longer than his eventual sentence, if he's convicted. Even worse, what if he's not guilty at all? This isn't good for Jeremy or the community.

Fortunately for Jeremy, there's an answer: bail. The right to post money or property as a guaranty for making court appearances is guaranteed by the sixth and the eighth amendments to the U.S. Constitution. Unless Jeremy is accused of a heinous crime or the court considers him a flight risk (and you can imagine all the arguments in court about that! What the heck is *heinous*, anyway?), he has the right to have reasonable bail set.

Bail also serves the public good. Almost every jail in the nation is grossly overcrowded. Without bail, the community would have to spend money better used elsewhere to build more jails—and high-security buildings are expensive to build and operate. Additionally, while Jeremy's sitting in jail waiting for trial, his family may need public assistance, since there are very few defendants who can earn a living while incarcerated.

Of course, if Jeremy has enough cash or real property, he can post the entire amount of the bond himself. But in most cases, Jeremy does not have enough cash on hand or room on his credit card to pay what the court considers a reasonable guaranty that he'll show up for his court dates. The bail bond company, or *surety*, steps into the gap to help, providing a bail bond that is somewhat like an insurance policy.

Bail is like buying any type of insurance policy. Jeremy pays a premium to use the financial backing of the bail bond company as a guaranty that he'll show up for his court dates.

For its part, the bonding company provides collateral to the court, and how much collateral it puts up determines the total dollar value of the bonds the company may write. The bonding company's collateral can be backing from an insurance company or property. These days, the courts require the property collateral to be in the form of certificates of deposit, which are held at the clerk's office.

Jeremy will probably spend his first few hours in custody being booked, fingerprinted, searched, and bored. At some point, he'll be formally charged (arraigned) in front of a magistrate or judge, either in person or via a video link. At the arraignment, Jeremy hears the charges against him, is advised of his constitutional rights, and enters a plea. The judge or magistrate will review the seriousness of the charges and Jeremy's background information: does he have a job, family, or previous record? Are there any facts about the case that make him a flight risk or that might qualify as a heinous crime? Based on all the information available, the judge or magistrate will set bail.

Then Jeremy makes his phone call. Depending on how long the processing and arraignment takes (and procedures vary dramatically from county to county, state to state), this may be the first indication anyone else has that Jeremy is in jail.

Most of the time, Jeremy will call his family or friends, and they'll either post bail or contact a bail bond company. Most bail bond companies have someone available twenty-four hours a day, and their telephone numbers are posted near the jail's telephones.

A bonding agent will ask Jeremy or his friends and family a number of questions and then decide whether Jeremy's a good risk. Sometimes the agent will require a cosigner to the bond or extra collateral from the client as security. Making the bond or refusing to make it is the agent's call.

If Jeremy's bail is a thousand dollars, the bond will usually cost him one hundred dollars. If the bonding company is property-backed, the agent will pocket about forty dollars and the bail bond company sixty dollars. If an insurance company underwrites the bonding company, the bonding fee is split equally between the agent, the bonding company, and insurance company.

Suppose the bonding company approves Jeremy's application. He's a free man, right?

Not exactly. Jeremy may be physically released from the county jail but he's still in custody. The bail bond company just takes over for the county.

The company may require him to check in with them and may set other conditions in the bail contract. If Jeremy breaks any of the terms of the agreement, like not showing up for his court date or failing to check in with the company, the company can revoke the bond and rearrest him immediately. In that case, Jeremy goes back to jail and the bail company keeps his one hundred dollars.

Jeremy will probably show up for court—most people do. But if he doesn't, the court will issue a conditional forfeit. The forfeiture is served on the bail bond company, giving the company 180 days to surrender Jeremy to the court or the forfeiture of bail becomes final. If the bonding company doesn't catch him in time, the company must pay the court the entire face value of the bond.

When a conditional forfeit is issued, the paperwork is turned over to the bail enforcement or fugitive recovery agent, the modern terms for what most people know as a bounty hunter. That's when I get to know Jeremy, first by reviewing his file (which contains a wealth of personal information I'll use to find him) and later by having the pleasure of snapping handcuffs on him.

Some bounty hunters like myself are in-house, meaning I work for one company. Others are freelance and work for several different bonding companies. Either way, the standard fee for catching a fugitive is 10 percent of the face value of the bond. Most larger bonding and surety companies use their own in-house recovery agents. The job is dangerous and there is considerable exposure to criminal and civil liability, even when the job is done right.

The bail industry and, particularly, bounty hunters have a bad reputation because of the actions of an unprofessional few. This is no longer the Old West, but sometimes the unprofessional few don't seem to realize that.

There is no federal law that defines the roles of bounty hunters. Until very recently, most recovery agents have relied on the 1873 United States Supreme Court Ruling in *Taylor vs. Taintor*:

> *When bail is given, the principal is regarded as delivered to the custody of his sureties. Their dominion is a continuance of the original imprisonment. Whenever they choose to do so, they may seize him and deliver him up in their discharge; and if that cannot be done at once, they may imprison him until it can be done. They may exercise their rights in person or by agent. They may pursue him into another State; may arrest him on the Sabbath; and, if necessary, may break and enter his house for that purpose. The seizure is not made by virtue of new process. None is needed. It is likened to the rearrest by the sheriff of an escaping prisoner. "The bail have their principal on a string, and may pull the string whenever they please, and render him in their discharge." Taylor v. Taintor, 83 U.S. 366, 372 (1873)*

In recent years, though, most states have passed legislation adopting provisions of The Uniform Criminal Extradition Act. The particulars of this law vary greatly from state to state but they all deal with the handling of out-of-state fugitives and some specifically to bail recovery. In 2000, the United States Court of Appeals for the Sixth District ruled that the constitution does not immunize a bondsman from local state law and that the bounty hunter must abide by the laws of the state they have entered.

In other words, the days of crossing state lines and *indiscriminately* kicking in doors and dragging people out are over. (Note the word "indiscriminately.") The bounty hunter had better know the law in each state he's in. That's why most bail companies and sureties have their own in-house professional recovery agents. The bottom line in the bail industry is money, and if the company gets sued or the recovery agent gets arrested, it's not making any.

I work full-time for a bail bond company in Knoxville, Tennessee, as a fugitive recovery agent—a bounty hunter. Unlike many recovery agents, I work alone. Getting to erase a name off my skip board after I make an arrest gives me a good deal of satisfaction.

I also operate and train in a karate school, more traditionally called a *dojo*, and I take teaching people to defend themselves seriously. I teach what works, techniques I use on the street every day.

Many people studying martial arts wonder if their training will serve them well in a crisis. This depends entirely on the training and the *sensei* (teacher). Most martial arts instructors have never been in a real fight. While generally that's a good thing—I approve of avoiding trouble whenever possible—a martial artist is a warrior. You can't train warriors if the only fights you've ever been in involved a lot of pads, gloves, and a referee.

On the street, there are no rules. No time clock, nobody pulling somebody off you if you make a mistake, no trained opponents—just predators. These stories are about that world.

All names have been changed to protect the guilty—and in some cases, the innocent, particularly me.

# one

Most people go through life blind, their senses dulled by the assumption that they're living in a civilized world. They've forgotten the most fundamental fact of life: we are predators.

Criminals understand mankind's predatory instincts. They depend on our complacency, our unspoken and unwarranted assumptions that the world is a safe place.

But there's a positive side to the predatory instinct, as well. There are those of us who acknowledge our basic nature, train it, and use it for good.

That's where I come in.

After a long month of chasing bail jumpers, I'd planned on taking the last weekend in June off. By Sunday afternoon, I was pretty mellow and feeling kindly toward my fellow man. I'd just lit the charcoal, intending to grill a few steaks for dinner, when my business cell phone rang. My wife, Debbie, gave me a resigned look. Without asking, she picked up the bowl of potato salad and took it back to the kitchen. She already knew what was going to happen to our plans for a quiet cookout.

The call was from one of my most reliable snitches, a guy I'd trust to rat out his own mother. He'd just gotten word Buck Carter had picked up a freelance contract to drive a semi to Knoxville.

Now, Buck Carter had been cluttering up my chase board for several months. He'd skipped out on two charges of aggravated assault and one count of assault on a police officer, and I'd worn out a fair amount of shoe leather trying to track him down. Seeing his name still on my chase board was starting to irritate me.

More important, the bail bond company had thirty thousand dollars riding on Buck's promise to appear in court, a promise he'd failed to keep. Since my fee is 10 percent of the bond amount, the chance to nail him was worth interrupting plans for a quiet Sunday afternoon.

According to his booking photo and data sheet, Buck was a big fellow. He had eighty pounds and four inches on me, and an ugly expression on his face that told me he considered himself a badass.

I wouldn't know until I saw him whether his size gave him an advantage or not. I did know that the assault on a cop meant he wasn't likely to come along peacefully when I flashed my badge at him.

You read a file on a guy like Buck, you know that this wasn't just an isolated incident. The assault, the jumping bail—it was part of a pattern. He started trouble and then he ran from it.

Sure enough, I was able to track Buck down by showing his booking photo to a few truck drivers who parked their big rigs at the large truck stop just outside of town. They all knew him—cops weren't the only ones he liked assaulting. After talking to the other drivers, my assessment of him as a badass changed a bit. He was a blowhard who used his size to his advantage. He didn't play well with others and his fellow drivers were only too willing to give him up.

My next call was to his employer's dispatcher. When I agreed to wait until after Buck had dropped off his trailer to bust him, the dispatcher told me where Buck would be on Sunday afternoon. Buck was hauling a load of frozen chickens, and the company would be most appreciative if the load wasn't left spoiling on the side of the road. I was glad to do it their way—no telling when I'd need their help again.

I found the plant Buck was delivering to and parked my van in a corner of the lot. He was supposed to be there at 3:00 P.M. and he was right on time. Just like the dispatcher had said, he was driving a big blue Kenworth with glitter decals on the side. Naked-lady mud flaps completed the décor.

Whatever else you might say about him, Buck was one hell of a truck driver. He backed up forty feet of trailer like he was parking a Toyota, with only one pull-forward adjustment before he was completely lined up. He stopped his rig flush with the loading dock. He left it running when he climbed out, to keep the refrigeration on.

The booking photo and data sheet hadn't been wrong, but seeing a guy on paper isn't like seeing him in the flesh. Buck *was* a big fellow, but I was willing to bet he'd packed on that eighty pounds he had on me chugging Budweiser, not working out. He wore faded jeans and a Budweiser T-shirt that stretched tight over a pretty impressive beer belly.

I reminded myself not to get overconfident. Heavy guys will surprise you sometimes. There's a fellow in my dojo who's built like Buck and he moves like a weasel. Give a guy four years of high school wrestling experience and it sticks with him.

The rest of what I saw was more encouraging. Buck took his time getting out of the truck's cab, moving like his back was bothering him. His six-foot five-inch frame was covered with biker tattoos and he had a long, oily-looking beard littered with crumbs of food. He walked heavily on his feet, oblivious to everything around him—like big guys are sometimes. It's like they think their size will carry them through anything. Fact is, most of the time they're right, and that fit with what his trucker buddies had told me about him. Buck was a big, nasty bully, but from the way he carried himself, I was pretty sure he wasn't a trained fighter. I'd be really pleased if he wasn't a big, nasty bully carrying a weapon. That always changes the odds.

I got out of my van and walked over to him, looking as small and unthreatening as I could. To do that, I have to feel small and unthreatening. Your attitude is always reflected in your body, and other people, whether they're aware of it or not, pick up on the cues. It's not easy when you're my size, but looking down when you walk and hunching your shoulders a bit goes a long way toward making you look harmless.

So does smiling. Guys like Buck, you don't usually have to sneak up on them. They already think there's nothing anybody can do to them. They're wrong and it's their overconfidence that gets them in trouble.

I stopped a little short of him, judging the distance carefully. I was just outside his reach, not so close as to make him uncomfortable but close enough that I could be inside his reach with a quick half step.

"Hey," I said in my best good ol' boy Southern voice. "You Buck Carter?"

He nodded, glaring at me. The booking photo hadn't really done justice to those little pig eyes of his. I pulled out my badge with my left hand.

As soon as he saw my badge, his nostrils flared and lips snarled. Those pig eyes turned wild. Then he made his big mistake—he reached into the pocket of his jeans.

I don't believe in fair fights. Before he could grab whatever he was after, my knuckles slammed square into his solar plexus with a punch.

Buck was used to being the one who started fights, and he was completely unprepared for the first two knuckles on my right fist trying to make contact with his backbone. His belly was loose and slack, his solar plexus exposed and vulnerable.

A rush of foul air spewed from his lungs as my fist sank deep. He would have spit out his tongue if it hadn't been attached to the back of his mouth. He bent over to puke. Helpful fellow that I am, I grabbed his ponytail and snatched him face down onto the asphalt. All the fight was gone out of him.

I had the cuffs on him before he was even able to breathe again and then I patted him down. I went for the pocket he'd been going for and pulled out a switchblade.

The knife was a beauty, a genuine Italian-made stiletto switchblade with a ball release on the cow horn handle. The thin seven-inch blade made a distinct clicking sound as it sprang open. The blade was clean, recently oiled, and sharp. Buck took better care of it than he did his beard.

Buck finished puking and rolled over on his side on the ground. His pig eyes were half shut and he was groaning. Buck wasn't used to hitting the ground like that. His beard looked nastier than it had before, and I just knew my van was going to stink from his being in it.

"Hey," I said. "You don't want to get booked carrying this, right? Just be another felony charge. Want me to hold onto it?"

"Yeah, man. Take it. It's yours."

The switchblade was quality craftsmanship and I was delighted that Buck had decided to donate it to my collection. I almost wore it out over the rest of the weekend playing with it.

By Monday morning, I'd grown so attached to my new knife that it felt like it was a part of me. I flipped it around in my hand on the drive downtown and slipped it into my pocket after I parked. It wasn't until I was walking into the courthouse that I remembered that some folks—that would be the police and the deputies that man the metal detectors—just don't seem to have the same appreciation for fine steel that I do. They've got this weird idea that the courthouse is a little safer when people don't wander around it carrying weapons.

I'd beg to differ. My world is safer when I'm carrying.

Fortunately, I didn't have to pass through any metal detectors to get to the clerk's office. If I'd had to surrender it, no doubt some deputy would have added it to his collection. That fine little bit of Italian steel already knew it was with someone who appreciated it and it was far better off in my possession. At least I knew how to handle it without hurting myself.

Three times a week I check the Municipal, Criminal, and Fourth Circuit Court clerks' offices. If a client of ours has failed to appear for a hearing or trial, there'll be a forfeiture waiting for me. It's a certified copy of the court's order, with a raised seal from the court on it. More than that, it's my authorization to find you, take you into custody, and get back the money my boss put up for your bail.

It's always slightly disappointing to find that all of our clients have been good boys and girls and made all their court appearances. No matter—something might come in from one of the other counties we service, and I had twenty-seven old names listed on my chase board that still had to be dealt with. Crime's a growth industry.

After I got in my car, I pulled out of the parking lot and turned left, heading for the Gay Street bridge that would take me back to the office. There had been no rain for weeks and the ground was cracked and hard. The leaves on the trees drooped from the layers of dust that covered them. There was rain in the forecast for the afternoon and the air was thick. The humidity made it seem like a sauna. I turned up the air-conditioning in the van and drove the mile and a half or so to the office.

Our office is a good deal classier than most bail offices you'll see. It was originally built as a pharmacy and has a long, high counter running across most of the back wall. What used to be the store area is a large open space, and light from the ceiling to floor windows in the front keeps it open and cheery. The beige tile is kept spotless, and the center area is filled with comfortable furniture as a waiting area. Matching rugs mark off each individual working area. Desks for the bondsmen—the folks who answer phones, take information from clients, and actually show up at the jail and spring our clients—line the walls. There's none of that cubicle business here. Because we're not always dealing with the crème of society, this arrangement allows the bondsmen to look out for each other.

The owner, Frank Gilmer, has a slightly larger desk with a more comfortable chair just to the left of the entrance. Looking at him, you'd never guess that he knew most of the prostitutes and pimps in a five-county area. He's a large man with a knack for dressing well. More important, from my point of view, he's got a well-deserved reputation as an honest businessman.

Frank's been in the bonding business for almost twenty-five years and he started this company. For the first few years he worked it by himself in a couple of counties. Now the company is in several East Tennessee counties and has about a dozen agents.

Frank looked up over his reading glasses as I walked past him. I shook my head to indicate we didn't have any new warrants at the courthouse and headed for my office in the back. I'm the only one with a private office and a separate phone line. A slab of one-way glass lets me keep an eye on things in the main room. Like I said, we don't deal with the highest class of people here.

I might have struck out that morning, but the agents from the other counties had checked their respective courthouses and brought in some new business for me. There was good news waiting for me in the form of two new files in the box mounted on my door.

Conditional forfeitures go first to Frank. Sometimes he can resolve the problem easily with a call to the right pimp or other regular client. If he can't, he swears a little and then tosses the files in my box.

I am his only chase man. I am the only one who works for the company who does not get people *out* of jail. My job is to put them back in.

My office is small, but that doesn't bother me. I'm not there much. My chase board is the first thing I see when I walk in. Large-scale maps of the area cover up wood paneling on the other two walls.

I settled down with a cup of coffee and started leafing through the files. I get all the forfeitures, even the ones that are too small to bother hunting down, and I read them all. Sometimes I'll run across one of the smaller fish while looking for a barracuda, so it pays to know their names and at least a little something about each one.

The first folder was a shocker. I couldn't believe Frank had actually made bond on the scumbag.

We had received a forfeiture on a man who had been charged with sexual assault on a child. His name was Wiley Smith. The warrant was out of circuit court. That meant Wiley's case had been through a preliminary hearing and he had been indicted by a grand jury. He failed to appear for his jury trial.

I saw Frank hang up the phone. I walked out and tossed the folder on his desk. "What the hell is this?"

Frank leaned back in his chair and looked up at me over his reading glasses. "What the hell does it look like? It's a folder."

I shook my head in disgust. "When did we start getting child molesters out of jail? You know how I feel about those sons of bitches." Usually we see eye to eye on what kind of cases are worth making bond on, and I couldn't remember the last time he'd bonded out a child molester.

Frank sighed. "Wiley and his boss swore he didn't do it."

"And you believe them?" It wasn't like Frank to be so gullible. We both knew the old joke—how do you tell when a client's lying to you? His mouth is moving.

"This one might be different. They said the girl's mother is setting him up for blackmail."

"Right. That's why he's running."

"Just find him." Frank said.

Wiley's boss, Ken Reynolds, was signed on the bond. He owned a salvage company in Morristown and he was responsible for the entire amount of the $25,000 bond, as well as all expenses incurred in the capture of Wiley. I figured he'd be willing to help me find Wiley. After mother-in-laws, cosigners who get burned are about the best source of information around.

After getting shuffled through a few office drones, I got through to Reynolds at his office. When he finally answered, I could hear heavy machinery in the background.

Reynolds's voice told me he'd grown up around here, so I didn't have a whole lot of sympathy for him. He should have known better than to believe somebody like Wiley. But after he talked a bit, I couldn't help but feel sorry for him. He was a good man, the kind of guy who carries over what he learned playing high school football to his office. If you were on his team, you were one of his, and it'd take more than a few charges written on a district attorney's charge sheet to change that.

With a guy like that, you can generally count on getting honest answers, so I went with the direct approach. "Why did you cosign his bond, Mr. Reynolds?"

"Please, call me Ken." he said.

Yep, he was a team fellow. That's the first thing you notice about them—they're always recruiting.

"I just don't think he did it. The mother of that little girl is trash."

Well, okay, no normal man can ever understand why another guy would do something like that, but that's not a reason to put up twenty-five grand. "That it?"

Please-call-me-Ken was quiet for a bit. I could almost see his face twisting up while he thought. Then he let out a heavy sigh. When he started talking again, the indignation was gone from his voice. "I was over a barrel. We had this big contract and without a crane operator, I was sunk."

"I can see that." I couldn't, but no point in telling him that.

Call-me-Ken sounded relieved that I understood his position. "I know it doesn't look good for him to have disappeared, but I think he's just scared."

"Disappeared?" I asked. "Only thing I know is he didn't show up for his court appearance."

There was another pause then Ken came clean. "When he didn't show up for work, I went looking for him at his trailer. The landlord said he moved out in the middle of the night."

Great. I knew what was coming and I was already getting pissed off. "How long ago was that?"

"About six weeks ago."

I bolted upright in my chair. "Why didn't you let us know? Now he has a six-week head start on us."

"I thought he would come to his senses and come back. I still think he will."

"You better hope you're right."

Having come clean with me, evidently Reynolds felt he was in a position to ask for a favor. "I want to ask you to do something for me."

"What?"

"Wait a couple of days before you start looking for him."

This from the man who stood to lose twenty-five grand? "Why?"

"Wiley's been going to church with me for six months now. I think the Lord's going to work all this out."

"Uh-huh."

"And a couple of the men who work for me are friends with him. I told them to pass the word I would pay for his lawyers and do whatever it took to help him."

Ah. On to more practical things. In my mind, that might be more likely to work than an appeal to Wiley's new-found faith.

"All I'm asking for is a couple of days," Reynolds said.

I didn't like it, but Reynolds was going to foot the bill if the court made Frank's company pay off the bond. Besides, it would take me a few hours to run through everything in Wiley's file and do some homework on him.

"I hope you're right," I said. I was pretty sure he wasn't. "I don't look for him to turn himself in. But it's your dollar. I'll call you in a couple of days. If he hasn't come in, I'm going after him."

"Fair enough," he said.

I hung up the phone and looked outside. It had started to rain. Large fat drops were coming down in sheets. I noted my conversation with Ken in Wiley's folder and filed it in my cabinet and added his name to my chase board.

The next bail-jumper file in my box was Freddy Latham. Freddy's file was from Sevier County, an area visited by people traveling to the Smoky Mountains and other scenic places in the area. The mountains and pristine forests of the national park draw people from all over the world. The surrounding tourist areas are crammed full with hotels, amusement parks, and outlet malls, as well as nightspots for those who like to party, all easy prey for criminals.

The criminals may be dumb but they ain't stupid. Like the bank robber who, when asked why he robbed banks, answered, "Because that's where the money is." Most of my runners from this county live somewhere else and have just dropped by to cash in on the tourists. Finding them usually requires a road trip.

Freddy was charged with domestic assault and resisting arrest when the police arrived at the motel. He pretty much trashed the room and picked up vandalism and public intoxication charges as well. After he bailed out, Freddy went home and never bothered to come back for his court date.

Most jumpers have been avoiding somebody most of their lives. I called all the contact numbers on the bond application and they had been disconnected. Even though the normal credit check and social security trace rarely provide current information, I always do it. Our clients are rarely rated with A-plus credit. There are usually dozens of collection agencies looking for them as well. This is how many of the less-hardened skips learn some dodging skills. They have been accustomed to avoiding bill collectors. Simple things like moving and not leaving a forwarding address, having utilities in somebody else's name, and giving false address information for vehicle registration are but a few. Not to mention having a post office box as a mailing address and an unlisted phone number. These techniques aren't very effective if somebody is dead set on finding you, but it works against most collection efforts.

Booking intake sheets are full of valuable information, not least of which is a picture of the skip. It's a black and white computer-generated printout that shows a front and profile shot. The intake sheet also gives vital statistics like height, weight, DOB, and hair and eye color. One of my favorite pieces of information is the tattoo description. They can change hair color, wear contacts, and gain or lose weight. The tattoo brands them for life.

I noticed something else interesting. The section that asks for gang affiliation was marked "Yes."

I called the sheriff's department in North Carolina, figuring they'd probably be familiar with my man.

"Hell, yeah, I know Freddy," the sergeant bellowed. "He went to school with my boy. What's he done this time?"

"Jumped bail."

The sergeant lowered his voice. "Aw shit. I ain't seen him in a while but he's around here somewhere. His momma lives up in Black Hollow."

"Does he belong to any gangs?"

"They think they're a gang but they're just motorcycle gang wannabes," he snorted. "The bunch he runs with all grew up here. Main kind of trouble for these boys is the drinking. Only people they ever really hurt is themselves with the fighting and the cutting. They only do that when they get drunk. Hell, they ain't real bad boys."

I thanked the sergeant for his help and told him I would probably be in his area soon to look for Freddy.

"Come by and stop in when you get here. We'll help you all we can. Just ask for Sergeant Philips," he said.

I decided to leave early the next morning. It was about a five-hour "road chase."

Usually I have a pretty good idea exactly where my jumper is before I go on the road. But this wasn't that long a trip and the phone leads were all dead ends. Sometimes you just have to be there.

By then it was almost six in the evening. I had just enough time to stop by the house and pick up my *gi* (karate uniform).

By the time I bowed in the front door of the dojo, my black belts had already started the lower-rank students on their assignments. The dull crack of bare knuckles pounding the *makiwara* (striking board) filled the room. Others banged shins and forearms on posts as part of their drills. This isn't stuff that you'll see in most dojos and it's not for everyone, but there's a reason behind everything we do.

Most instructors who teach self-defense have never been in a street fight. They teach tournament sparring. Very pretty stuff, lots of high kicks and wide stances and flashy moves. They have lots of belt promotions, detailed contracts, extra fees, splashy ads using models in trendy magazines, and a high turnover. They don't require their students to harden their bodies for combat for fear of losing them to other softer schools. On the streets, they're sushi.

The Steel Hand Dojo trains in the spirit of *bushido*—the warrior code. We follow the traditional ways, emphasizing conditioning the body to be used as a weapon. We train for survival—street fighting. We don't wear pads or equipment of any kind in our sparring, and we don't train for tournaments or to win trophies.

The regimen at my dojo is harsh but results in physical, mental, and spiritual growth. Every belt rank promotion is earned through blood and sweat as students, karate-ka, overcome their own personal barriers. In the old days, when a martial artist lost a fight, he died.

I stretched out in a corner of the room while watching my students work through their *kata* (form movement). Katas are the foundation for fighting and are a major component of the training. They teach the correct mechanics for generating a balanced, powerful attack or defense.

I'd just finished stretching out my hamstrings and was sitting with my feet together and legs in a V shape to work out my adductors and groin muscles (easier on forty-seven-year-old knees than doing the splits) when I noticed something odd. A little jerkiness in one student, a few moments off balance in another—what was it? The pattern started to emerge as I watched. Multiple symptoms, but one common cause—bad *mae geri* (front kicks).

We don't have many kicks in our system, and the ones we have are aimed low. Most times, if somebody tries to kick you on the street, they'll try to nail you in the groin. That's actually a big mistake. The groin area is naturally protected by the adductors and other inner-thigh muscles. And—although many men like to brag—it's usually a pretty small target.

It's also an easy kick to block—just rotate the leg in a bit and the kick will bounce off your thigh muscle. Sure, that hurts, but nothing like a kick to the groin. It's hardly going to slow me down.

Now, I'm not above taking a shot at the groin when it's presented. But Isshinryu karate, if practiced as an art, focuses on dissecting and dismembering the body. We study anatomy, the weak points in the body, and we focus on the mechanics of how and why people are able to move. When somebody tries to kick me in the groin, I know he's not a trained fighter.

Every movement you make begins with your feet. They're what take you wherever you're going. They're what enable you to come after me. If I can take out a foot, the lower the better, then I can pretty much do anything else I want to after that.

The best targets for a front kick are the front of the ankle, to damage the tibialis anterior tendon, or the inside of the knee, to tear the cruciate ligaments. Low kicks, delivered with proper technique, are crippling. And that's what I wasn't seeing in my students.

Faulty techniques are like a virus. If you don't correct them immediately, they spread and mutate. There was no telling how this one had started—a black belt, teaching and having a bad day, an injury that caused one student to compensate in a way that others started mimicking—it could have been anything. But because I was seeing the same problem in several students, it had to be addressed as a group. I stood up and walked over to the front and center of the room.

"Line up!" I commanded. Everyone immediately lined up facing me in rows according to rank, with black belts in front. "Several of you are leaning back when you throw your front kicks. And they're not snapping. Without correct posture and stance you're off balance and you're inhibiting your *ki*. You do that on the street, you're sushi."

Several of the newer students looked at me inquisitively. I stood relaxed and positioned, the knot of my *obi* (belt) just below my "one point," which is about two inches below the navel. "Ki is an internal energy that flows in the body along pathways that are called meridians. These pathways allow for the energy to flow to our vital organs. When we are not properly balanced, we disrupt our ki flow. At the same time, we want to disturb the ki flow of an attacker by striking certain points along the meridians. Those points are the same ones used in acupuncture. The same knowledge used to heal can also be used to destroy. Our katas teach us how to protect our points and how to target those on an enemy."

We went through the anatomy of the leg and foot again, focusing on the proper target points. Then I brought a beginner white belt to the front of the class and had her demonstrate the kick while facing one of the many mirrors that lined the wall. Her kick was weak and sloppy. I led her through the correct form and she slowly repeated the movement with me. After she had the form correct, I showed her how to add power to her kick.

"Don't just kick with your leg," I said. "Crunch your abdominal muscles as you scissor your legs and bring up the knee just before you extend the foot. Then snap it back with an attitude and set the foot back on the floor. I want you delivering that kick with malice aforethought."

She bit her lip and tried to remember everything I told her. She kicked. For the first time that evening, the sound of her gi pants snapping could be heard across the room. Her eyes got wide with amazement at the power she had generated. She bowed to me and went back to her place in the group.

I watched as the group worked on their snap kicks, correcting individual form. The virus was eradicated.

We ended the night's workout with everyone taking a turn in the ring, sparring with one of my black belts. I then sparred with the black belts. Finally, when everyone was sweating down to their bones, I had them line up. We performed one last kata as a group and then bowed out.

I had called my wife earlier and we decided to meet for dinner. Debbie had just gotten back from visiting her dad, who was living with her sister in Atlanta. She had lost her mother last year and her dad was in poor health. The many trips back and forth were tiring and we often ate out when she got home. There's a Cajun seafood restaurant close to the house and it's one of our favorite places. We talked over shrimp salad and creole before going home to bed.

The next morning, I gulped down a couple of cups of coffee and waited for the caffeine to kick in as I watched the early morning news. Debbie was still asleep as I finished dressing. I leaned over and gently kissed her cheek and quietly left.

It was a beautiful day. It had rained all night and the air was crisp and clean. The scenery crossing into North Carolina from Tennessee on I–40 was breathtaking. The clouds were low and formed a misty cover to the trees.

Asheville, North Carolina, is a long steep drive over the mountains. After leaving the interstate, I had another three hours of driving on county two-lane highways ahead.

When I got to the little town, I stopped and filled up with gas and checked the map for alternate exit routes. Always have a full tank of gas and a clear sense of direction before doing an out-of-town snatch. You never know when you might be in a hurry to leave.

Small town and rural jails have a feel all their own. This one was pretty typical. Two police cars were outside. The "dispatch area" was just a guy at a radio, and there were a few desks around for officers to fill out paperwork. A heavy steel door led back to the cell block area. It was open and some of the prisoners had their arms hanging out of their locked cell doors as they talked and smoked cigarettes. Not Mayberry, RFD—but not too far from it, either.

The dispatch area was unoccupied. Just then a door inside the dispatch office opened and a deputy walked out still drying off his hands. "May I help you?"

"I'm looking for Sergeant Philips."

"You found him. You must be the bounty hunter from Tennessee. Damn, you don't waste time." We shook hands and walked into the dispatch office. Another deputy walked in as we sat and talked.

"Have you seen Freddy lately?" Philips asked the deputy.

"Nope," he answered. "I heard he moved to the other side of the county." That's another difference in rural police work. You don't need snitches. Everybody knows everybody else's business. You need to find someone, you go ask a relative.

"You want us to show you where his momma lives?" Philips asked. I nodded. Philips told the deputy to let me follow him to Black Hollow. "After you turn up the hollow, it's the last house. You can't go no more. If you run into any trouble, just holler at us." I didn't bother to tell him my cell phone had long ago run out of coverage.

I followed the deputy down twists and turns of the winding roads, watching for anything that might make it difficult if I had to get out in a hurry. After about thirty minutes, we made one last turn and he stopped. I pulled up next to him and rolled down the passenger-side window.

"This is Black Hollow," he said. Of course, down in this part of the country, it's pronounced "holler." "Keep going till you can't go no more. It's the last house. You can't miss it." I thanked him and drove on. I looked back in the rearview mirror and saw the deputy turn around and leave.

I saw why they named it Black Hollow. The woods were thick. Trees hung over the road and at times made it look almost like a tunnel. The road seemed to go on forever and I passed a few houses before coming to a rickety wooden bridge. I stopped and got out to check it. It had a couple of planks missing. I held my breath and drove across it.

The asphalt road soon turned to gravel. The road narrowed down to one lane and I had to pull over to let a pickup truck go by. The driver gave me a friendly wave as he passed.

Five miles later—finally—I could "go no more."

Since I didn't know if my guy was here or how I was going to get him in the car, I slipped my handcuffs off my gun belt and put them in my hip pocket. No need to limit my options. The weapon, though—that was a different matter. I'm always armed. No matter how good your front kick is, my 9mm is tougher and faster.

The driveway led up to a large frame house sporting a fresh coat of paint. Somebody'd gone to some trouble, landscaping the yard with hedges and fruit trees, and there was a large vegetable garden in the back. Two new pickup trucks and a car were parked next to a big old satellite dish.

A large German Shepherd Dog was watching me from the end of his chain. I watched him for a bit to make sure the other end of the chain was really attached to the large oak next to its doghouse. I know German Shepherds pretty well, and they're about as protective as any dog you'll find, almost as much as a pit bull.

The dog watched me for a bit. When I got out of the car he went on full alert, and by the time I started toward the front door he was barking and lunging at the chain.

I knocked lightly and listened for footsteps. Whoever was inside already knew I was here—the Shepherd had made sure of that.

A mature heavy-set woman wearing a tank top and shorts answered the door. There was a cigarette hanging out the side of her mouth and she had a beer in one hand. She was hanging out of her clothes in several places and exhibited a number of tattoos. I guessed her to be in her mid-sixties.

It never hurts to be friendly. Sometimes it makes things go easier and at the very least, it throws people off their guard.

I gave the lady a nice smile. "Excuse me, ma'am. I'm looking for Freddy."

"I'm Freddie," she said.

Booking photos can be pretty bad, but they're usually not that far off. Not only was she too short and too heavy to be Freddy, but my extensive training in human physiology and the parts of her that were sticking out of the tank top and shorts told me she probably was the wrong gender as well.

I held up a picture of Freddy.

"That's my boy," she said. "He's named after me."

It figured.

"Why are you looking for him?"

I knew I was probably going to have to lie to her.

People ask if it bothers me to lie. I must admit that sometimes it does, when I think about it. But sometimes you ought to lie—if you're good at it—which I am. First, sometimes lying makes things safer. Second, it doesn't count as lying if you're lying to a liar. I wasn't sure which category this situation fell into, but I knew if I told her the truth, that chain wouldn't be on the Shepherd much longer.

When I was a police officer, I participated in many sting operations. We lured people in with false pretenses or set them up with bait for drug buys. There's no question that it's in everybody's best interest to have an arrest carried out as safely as possible, and that means you have to pick the time and the place for confrontation. I've tricked people back to Tennessee from as far away as Texas with the promise of getting them a new court date. As soon as they walked in the office I slapped on the cuffs. It saves us money and the arrest occurs on my turf.

Now, this lady had every reason to be suspicious of me. Here I was, a stranger, flashing a booking photo of her boy. I gave her my best good ol' boy smile and looked kindly straight into her eyes. She smiled back. I had pushed the right button and connected with her.

Reassured by my charming smile, she invited me inside the house and we sat down. There was a shirtless man sitting on the sofa breathing with oxygen. The tubes stretched from the canister to his nostrils. A cigarette was smoldered in the ashtray next to him. "I told you to turn off the oxygen when you smoke," she snapped. "You want to blow us up?" I started to wonder whether it was a good idea to have come in. "So why do you want my boy?"

I smiled again and kept my voice friendly. "I'm Freddy's bondsman from Tennessee. He didn't show up for court on a domestic violence charge."

"So you here to take him to jail?"

"No, ma'am. I've got a really sweet deal for him that'll get us all off the hook on this bail. If I can take back a notarized affidavit from Freddy and his wife that no assault was committed, the DA is willing to drop charges. It's really a sweet deal."

From her expression, I knew I wasn't going to have to explain how bail worked. This wasn't the first time her namesake had been in trouble and it wouldn't be the last. "What's the other choice?" she asked.

"Then I would have no choice. I'd have *to go back to Knoxville*"—I made sure she heard that part so she wouldn't think anything could go down today—"and take out a federal fugitive warrant. But that'd be stupid—all he has to do is sign this affidavit and it's all over. All the charges get dropped."

"Can he mail the affidavit to you?"

"No, I have to notarize it." Good thing I'd concealed the handcuffs.

She reached a decision and nodded. "I'll take you to him. I can ride with you and get Freddy to bring me back home. He lives in the sticks and ain't got a phone."

I smiled. "Great."

That's the interesting thing about mothers, no matter whether you're out in the sticks or in a big city. They worry about their kids when they're on the run. They know that if the cops catch their kid, things are more likely to go wrong along the way and somebody's going to get hurt. When I'm not lying to them, I make it clear to them that they've got a lot less to worry about if I find the young'un than if the cops do. They know I'm telling the truth and they talk.

We both got in my van and began the long trek back to the main road. "He's not a bad boy," she said. "He really doesn't beat her up bad. Only when he's been drinking. She needs to learn to leave him alone when he's had too much."

"Think he'll be home?"

"Yeah, he don't work. If he ain't home he won't be gone long. His old lady brings the kids home on her way from work. He really loves those kids."

Freddie wasn't joking about her son living in the sticks. It made her place look like Times Square. By this time, it was dusk. I made mental notes at each turn about how to get back to the main road. The thought of being lost while trying to make a hasty escape didn't appeal to me. Finally, we reached Freddy's trailer, and I wondered how they were able to haul it there.

"You can pull in the driveway," she said. "Freddy's car ain't here. Looks like Lori is back with the kids, though. He won't be long."

I looked down the driveway. There were three cars parked down the narrow, almost vertical driveway. One of them had a block under a front tire to keep it from rolling. If I parked in the driveway, it'd be easy to block me in.

"I think I'll park up here." I said. "My emergency brake is bad. I don't want my van to wind up in their living room." We both laughed.

I turned around and parked it at the top of the driveway facing back the way we'd come, then headed down the hill staying right behind her. I didn't think Freddy would shoot through his momma to get me.

There were several garbage bags full of beer cans strewn around the yard. A few single cans with bullet holes in them were scattered about. I could hear hard rock music coming from the trailer.

"Whose cars are these?" I asked.

Freddie was already panting and out of breath from the short walk. "The gray one is Lori's car. The other two belong to Freddy's friends. They stay here off and on."

I followed her around to the back of the trailer. I heard barking. A pit bull was chained close to a motorcycle. The bike was missing a tire and had part of the engine dismantled. A small child wearing only a diaper was playing in the dirt next to the dog. The young boy ran up to Freddie and she scooped him up.

"How's my little sweetie?" Freddie gasped. "Let grandma put you down now. We need to talk to your daddy."

I followed her up the short flight of steps to the porch at the back door. She stopped and tried to catch her breath. Lori came to the door before she got a chance to knock.

"Hi, grandma. Freddy ain't home. He went to get some beer. He shouldn't be long."

Lori was still dressed in her nurse's scrubs. She was wearing a name tag from a local nursing home and had a naked infant on her hip.

We both walked in. Nobody seemed to pay much attention to me.

It was a single-wide trailer with a full-sized pool table crowded into the middle of the living room. Two men in their mid-twenties were engrossed in the game. Both were of medium build with long straggly hair down to their shoulders. One of them was shirtless and his body was decorated with the names of old girlfriends and Harley-Davidson insignias.

A samurai sword hung on the wall along with other various types of martial art weaponry. Plastic doesn't take a good edge so I wasn't impressed. It was all cheap, fake, the kind of stuff you'd find in a novelty store. The rest of the wall covering consisted of WWF wrestling and NASCAR racing posters. Two huge stereo speakers were on either side of a sofa at one end of the pool table. There wasn't enough room to get around the table without squeezing past the sparse furniture.

On the other side was the kitchen. The sink was full of dirty dishes and the small table next to the wall was covered with empty beer cans. A few of them had fallen to the floor. The two sportsmen moved the empties out of their path with their feet as they positioned for the next shot. Nobody offered to pick anything up. I made myself comfortable on a lawn chair just inside the door.

Lori and Freddie sat with the baby. The floor vibrated with Ozzy Osbourne music.

After the shirtless player finished a shot, he looked at me. "You the one looking for Freddy?"

I wondered if it was the sergeant or the deputy that had tipped them off. Freddy might not have a regular phone, but every fool in the world has a cell phone these days, even out here. "Yeah, that was me. I'm here trying to help him."

"You going to take him to jail?"

"That's not what I'm here for. I just want to get a paper signed and get out of here."

"Why you wearing a gun?"

I looked at him. "Hell, aren't you?"

"Hell, yeah." he said. Just then he reached around and pulled a small revolver out of his hip pocket. "Ain't it sweet? It's a Smith."

"Sweet," I echoed. It was a Smith & Wesson Airweight, a nice little .38. My wife used to carry one. Even if it had been a piece of shit, you don't talk bad to a man about his gun, especially when you don't want him to use it.

He put the gun back in his pocket and lined up his next shot with his right hand. The other player lined up his shot, gripped the back of the cue with his left hand, and bridged the tip of the stick with his right, which was placed on the table. That told me this guy was a lefty. If they decided to come at me, I knew which hand each one would lead with.

The other guy never said a word, which made him more dangerous, as far I was concerned. Was he packing? Probably, and he wasn't talking. Bad combination. Like a good German Shepherd Dog, he wasn't gonna growl before he bit.

Just then the door swung open and Freddy walked in. He was wearing shorts and tennis shoes with no laces. His belly hung out of his unbuttoned shirt. His long greasy hair fell to his shoulders and it looked like he was sporting a week-old beard. He was about six feet tall and weighed in at around two hundred twenty pounds. He'd put on some weight since he'd been out of jail, no doubt the result of fine home cooking.

Or maybe not. He looked like he was on real good terms with the twelve-pack of beer he was carrying.

"Hi, Momma," he said, looking at me, not her.

He walked around the other side of the pool table and into the kitchen. He reached in his open shirt and pulled out a long barrel .357 magnum revolver from his waistband and laid it down loudly on the counter. He was definitely putting on a show for my benefit. His shirt gaped open, allowing me to get a good look at the tattoo of a dragon covering his chest. The other two stopped playing and stood on the opposite side of the table from me. He gently set the beer down next to the gun.

"I ain't going to jail," he said as he stared hard at me.

His momma spoke up. "Just listen to him, Freddy. He's here to help you."

"Like hell!" he screamed. There was a wild note in his voice that I didn't like.

The whole room tightened. I was no longer aware of the music. My eyes scanned back and forth between Freddy and his two buddies. I watched their hands. If anybody moved suddenly, I was going to draw my weapon. I don't do that unless I'm ready to use it.

But maybe I could head off a confrontation. I leaned back and relaxed, letting my body posture defuse the situation. They had no way of knowing that I'm a lot faster when I'm relaxed than when I'm tight. At the same time, I kept my gun hand close to the holster. "Look, I have an affidavit for you and Lori to sign. As soon as I take it back and file it at the courthouse in Tennessee, the charges will be dropped.

Otherwise, there will be another warrant on you and the local law will come get you." I watched his eyes to see if there was a hint he knew this was bullshit.

Lori jumped in with, "Please baby, why not? Aren't you tired of running? I'm sick of this."

Freddy turned toward her and exploded. "Shut the fuck up. It's your damn fault anyway." He turned his attention back to me. "So why you wearing the fucking gun?"

I laughed. "That's just in case you don't want to let me out of here. Hey, buddy, I'm just the messenger. I really don't give a shit if you sign it or not. Either way, I'm leaving here alone. But I'm telling you it's a sweet deal. You get out of the charges without it costing you a dime and we get off your bond. It's over."

He thought for a minute. "And we can sign the papers here? I don't have to go nowhere?"

I looked him straight in the eye. "I got the papers in the van. We do it all right here."

Freddy pops open a beer. "Why the fuck not? Let's do it. Get the papers."

"Smart thing to do, buddy. I'll be right back."

I walked out the back and heard the billiard balls banging around as soon as I walked out. Dusk had come and gone and it was dark, with no moon.

I made my way up the driveway and located Freddy's car. Luckily, he parked it behind the rest of the vehicles, blocking them in. His car was parked at a very steep angle. It would be impossible to push it out of the way.

I reached the top of the driveway and retrieved two tire deflators and a cheap penknife from my large equipment bag in the van. After quietly closing the cargo door, I opened the side sliding door and pulled out my small equipment bag. I found my roll of duct tape and laid it close to the door. While keeping an eye on the trailer, I positioned my leg shackles close to the roll of tape and laid out another set of handcuffs. Leaving the side door of the van open, I made my way back down the driveway.

It's this part of the job I thrive on. The adrenaline was pouring at this point. The time right before the snatch is always surreal. I felt like I was floating when I walked. I could hear everything. My vision seemed panoramic and my nostrils were filled with scent. I have been unable to achieve this level of awareness any other way. I was a predator.

I screwed the tire deflators on the front and back tires on the driver's side of Freddy's car. The hissing of the escaping air sounded like sirens to me but there was no reaction from the trailer. I guess Freddy figured that he had enough buddies and firepower to back him up so he wasn't particularly worried about me.

I leaned inside his open car window and stuck the penknife in the ignition then worked it back and forth until it broke off inside the switch. There was no way any of the cars in the driveway were going anywhere for a while. I left my business card on the front seat and I walked toward the trailer.

The dog knew something was up even if the people didn't, but he just lay there and looked at me with eyes wide and ears up. Maybe he didn't mind so much if ol' Freddy disappeared for a while. It's a sad state of affairs when a pit bull is smarter than the folks that own him.

I swung open the door and they all looked at me. I was shaking my head. "Hey Freddy, you got a fucking flashlight? I dropped my damn notary seal under the van. I can't find it." My mind was racing. Was it going to work?

Freddy laughed. "Yeah, man. Hang on." Freddy searched through the kitchen drawers and pulled out a small yellow-handled flashlight.

I immediately turned around and walked back down the steps. It worked. Freddy came outside.

"Here, shine the light for me on the ground so I don't bust my ass." I said. "I'm a city boy."

Freddy laughed again and led me up the driveway. "Come on," he said, leading the way.

I followed him past the row of parked vehicles as he shone the light on our path. As we passed the passenger side of his car I got ready in case he noticed it leaning slightly from the two flat tires. He kept walking.

He was breathing heavily by the time we reached the top of the driveway. As he walked closer to the van, I timed his steps with mine. When we got even with the side door and as my left foot stepped forward, I was in range. Time seemed to stop.

I slammed my right forearm into the back right side of his neck in an upward direction and drove my right knee into his tailbone. The contact of the forearm strike was to the back and side of the neck just below the occipital bone. This meridian point is known as gallbladder 20. The electrical disruption to the brain caused by this technique will knock most people out. He was already starting to fold when my knee lifted him off the ground. That threw his pelvis forward and his head back toward me, exactly where I wanted it. My right arm wrapped around his neck until the bend of my elbow was at his windpipe.

He dropped the flashlight and it hit the ground. I brought my left arm up and placed my right hand inside the bend of my left elbow. My left hand was balled into a fist and placed at the base of his skull. He was bent over backwards and I had him in a full-blown sleeper hold. All of this took about a second and a half.

In law enforcement circles, the sleeper hold is also known as a carotid restraint. Most agencies won't let their officers use it because it's fairly easy to kill someone if you don't know what you're doing.

The biggest problem is that most agencies get a very limited amount of unarmed defensive training. Applying this technique incorrectly or for too long can be dangerous. It's very effective because it cuts off the blood supply to the brain and causes unconsciousness in a short period of time.

Just as I had him locked, I expanded my chest. I kept his windpipe in the bend of my elbow to avoid crushing it.

The sudden viselike grip on each side of his neck by my bicep and forearm was applied right below his carotid sinus. He started to struggle but the force of the forearm blow to his neck combined with being bent over backwards had rendered him helpless long enough for the sleeper hold to take effect.

He had no sooner reached up to grasp the arm around his neck before I felt his grip weaken. Just then, he went limp. I immediately released him. Had I held the choke on him any longer he might not have revived. It was vital to let go just as he passed out. At the same time, I knew I didn't have long before he would wake up.

I eased him down and rolled him over as I pulled the handcuffs out of my hip pocket and cuffed both hands behind his back. Reaching inside the van, I grabbed the duct tape and made two wraps around his head covering his mouth.

He twitched as I quickly searched him. He was waking up. I found a knife in his pocket—not nearly the same quality as that sweet little Italian switchblade—and tossed it in the weeds. I tossed the pack of cigarettes from his shirt pocket on my front seat.

I pulled out the leg shackles and quickly locked them around his ankles while bending his legs up. I fastened the chain of the shackles to his hand restraints with the extra pair of handcuffs. Freddy wasn't just restrained—he was hog-tied.

Freddy shuddered and his eyes popped open. He was awake but disoriented. I heaved him into the back of the van as I glanced at the trailer. Everybody was still inside and unaware of what had just happened. I pressed my remote control and the electric side sliding door was closing as I climbed in the driver's seat.

Freddy started to thrash. The duct tape muffled his screams.

I started the van and slowly pulled away with the lights off. After I rounded a curve a short distance down the road, I turned on the headlights and gave it the gas.

Freddy was thrashing harder and his gagged screams were louder. I pulled over and quickly opened the sliding door. Pulling out another set of cuffs, I fastened him to the floor. I grabbed his hair and pulled his face close to mine.

"Now listen, asshole. You're going to be still and shut the fuck up. If I have to stop again, I'm going to stick my Taser up your ass and barbeque your balls."

I didn't even have a Taser, but the threat worked. He lay there quietly with his eyes wide open as the reality of his situation began to set in.

When I got to the main road, I opted to leave a different way and not go through the same small town where the sheriff's department was located. The next county was not far up the highway. This would mean an additional couple of hours before we reached the interstate, but since somebody had tipped off the folks at Freddy's trailer, the sooner I was out of the county, the better.

When I reached the interstate, the cell phone came into coverage. There were no messages on the voice mail. I pulled into the back lot of a truck stop and parked.

"Okay, Freddy, we have about four more hours on the road. If you behave yourself, I'll make you more comfortable. If not, you can ride like this the whole way. It makes no difference to me." I turned off the van and put the keys in my pocket. I got in the back with him and slowly peeled the tape off his mouth. He cursed as it pulled at his beard.

"Okay, man, you fucking got me." he said. "I won't try anything. My legs and back are cramping." I kept his shackles cuffed to the floor and released the restraints that had him hog-tied. He straightened out his legs and moaned as he stretched.

"Get up on your knees." I said. After locking a belly chain around his waist, I warned him again. "You're still cuffed to the floor. I'm going to take off one of the cuffs so you can bring your hands around to the front. Don't fuck with me Freddy. If you do, this bad day will get a lot worse."

"I ain't trying shit," he said. He brought his hands around and I ran the cuffs through the belly chain and locked him back down. He was then able to scratch or handle any personal function he needed to perform, and there was at least one personal function I had no intention of helping him with.

"You need to piss before we hit the road?"

"Hell, yeah," he said. "I'm about to bust."

I pulled the van behind some of the big rigs and helped him out. He hobbled over behind a trailer and relieved himself as I watched. His knees were wobbly and it looked as if he might collapse. It was a combination of what had happened to him physically and the fading effects of him experiencing an adrenaline dump. He was spent.

With most jumpers, getting caught is a relief. Most of the time, they've jumped bail because they're scared or stupid. Sometimes you run into plain old scumbags, but those are rare.

Think about what it's like to be on the run. You know somebody's looking for you. You hear about them from your family and friends, if you're still in contact with them. You know any second, anytime, anywhere, somebody's going to take you down.

Getting it over is a huge emotional release for them. When the shock wears off, the relationship between the hunter and the hunted starts to change. We talked about kids, cars, music, and what would happen to him when he got back in jail. I gave him a few pointers for survival. Even though he talked calmly, his hands shook. Freddy wasn't going to admit it, but he was scared.

Just after crossing the Tennessee state line, the cell phone rang. A rough female voice asked, "Is this the bondsman?"

Ah, Freddy's momma. She'd found the card I'd left in his car. "Yeah."

"You goddamn lying son of a bitch. Where's my Freddy?"

"He's with me. You want to talk to him?" I handed the phone back to him without waiting for her to answer. I sure didn't want to talk to her.

"Hello, Momma," he said. He sounded a lot younger than the tough guy who'd walked into the trailer. "Yeah, I'm all right. He did what to the car? It doesn't matter. He was just doing his job."

They talked for about ten minutes. Freddy's buddies had walked several miles to a friend's house. They went back and picked up Freddie senior and took her home.

"Just wait there, Momma. I'll call you collect from the jail and let you know when I can get out." He hung up and handed the phone back to me. "Thanks, man."

Thanks from a guy I'd had in a sleeper hold a few hours before. It's a little like what hostage negotiators call the Stockholm Syndrome. I knew he had now completely resigned himself to his fate. It happens more times than not. They want to hear from me that it's not going to be so bad. I usually try to reassure them that things will be getting better. The calmer I can keep them, the better, whether it's true or not.

I pulled into an early morning fast-food drive-thru before we got to the jail. It would be his last decent meal for a while. I parked in the lot while he ate and lit a cigarette for him when he finished. When he took his last puff and put the butt in his drink cup, I started the van and drove to the jail.

We went right in the front door. His shackled feet only allowed him to hobble along slowly. I escorted him into the secured intake area and handed my paperwork over to the jailer. The officer gave me a receipt and took my restraints off Freddy and handed them to me.

Freddy stuck out his hand and said, "No hard feelings."

I reached out and shook his hand before they took him back. "No hard feelings. Good luck, Freddy." If he jumped bail again, I knew he wouldn't be my problem.

# two

By Wednesday I'd logged a half dozen arrests. Wiley Kent was never far from my thoughts, but the bread and butter of the bail business is the small bond. Hookers, drunks, and drug addicts clog the court system, and a good agent will write twenty or so small bonds in a day. It's not uncommon to have twenty thousand dollars a week in forfeits just on the small bonds. That's serious money, and it's my job to make sure we don't pay it—by rounding up the jumpers.

Like most other jobs, the work isn't over until the paperwork is complete. Most times it's just a matter of writing pertinent information on the skip's folder and making sure a receipt from the jail is in hand. I make copies of each folder for my personal records and enter the information into my own database.

It isn't unusual for me to save my paperwork and then get caught up on data entry for my personal arrest records once a week or so. Each skip has his picture scanned and inserted into the record and that process takes time. Then I generate a report of all my arrest records to give to the company bondsman so he won't bond out people I'd had to chase down in the past.

Even with that information in hand, sometimes mistakes are made. It's easy to understand how one could slip through now and again because my arrest database at the end of June had eight hundred ninety-six entries.

Most of our clients aren't renowned for their honesty. Many of them swear on the lives of their children that they really were in court or that the court clerk made a mistake. I hear a lot of lies, but I'm used to them.

Occasionally, the court does make a mistake. There was a young fellow named Tom something-or-other who was out on a one-thousand-dollar bond for driving on a suspended license. I'd talked to him on the phone a couple of times and he told me that his court date wasn't until next week. He said he had the paperwork to prove it.

Yeah, right.

I told him I believed him and that I could get him a new court date. All I needed to do was meet with him and notarize a paper for him. That's my standard line and it's worked more times than I can count. There's something about being a notary that makes you sound so harmless.

Tom agreed to meet me at a convenience store to get his paperwork "notarized." Since his license was suspended, he had to wait at work for his wife to pick him up before he could meet me. Usually I would have just gone to his job site and grabbed him, but I was transporting another prisoner to a different jail while I was talking to him. I picked the rendezvous point to be more convenient for me. I decided to let him drive all the way across town. He told me they would be in an old blue pickup.

I got to the meeting place about fifteen minutes early. It was one of those franchise convenience stores that sells self-service gas. Cars pulled in and out of the pump area, and there was a steady flow of people moving through the store. I pulled into a shaded portion of the parking lot away from the store traffic. This store was right off an exit of the interstate. The area was known for its suburban neighborhoods. People working downtown stopped here for last-minute items on their way home. It was mostly the cappuccino and SUV crowd.

I started to get in my predator mode again. It had been switched on and off several times over the last few days. Sometimes it's much harder for me to turn it off. Although this seemed to be a pretty routine setup, you never know. There's no way to predict how someone will react to being arrested. It only takes one mistake at the wrong time to kill you. The best approach is to quickly eliminate a jumper's options and confront him on your terms.

I raised my hand out the window when I saw Tom's truck pull into the store parking lot. His wife was driving and there was a baby strapped in a car seat between them. They were a young couple, in their early twenties. She parked on the passenger side of my van and got out first. She was wearing a waitress uniform. Her name tag said "Sue."

Tom leaned over the car seat and unbuckled a happy, healthy-looking baby boy dressed in a blue outfit. Tom got out of the car with him and carried that little baby like he was a carton of eggs as he walked around to the van. He stood next to his wife as she fished through her purse.

The first thing I had to do was get him away from that baby. There was no way I was trying anything while he was holding a child.

I rolled down the passenger window and clicked open the electric side door. "How you folks doing? Fine looking boy."

"Thank you," they both said, smiling.

Something was already feeling wrong to me. Like I said, most jumpers are scared or stupid and Tom didn't feel like a man who was watching over his shoulder for someone to grab him. He was relaxed, moving confidently, and didn't have any of the jitteriness I'd come to associate with most bail jumpers. Still, a warrant is a warrant, and the court said we owed it a thousand dollars.

"Go ahead and get in the van, Tom," I said. "We can do the paperwork in here."

Tom kissed his son on the head and handed him to Sue.

Tom climbed into the van. He wasn't what I would call dirty. He was soiled and sweaty from honest work, sure, but there was just one hard day's worth of dirt on his clothes. The T-shirt underneath his coveralls was clean, if frayed. He smelled of sweat, but not the old sweat stink of jail. His hands were scrubbed but their stained roughness showed the wear of labor.

I knew from his file that Tom was a carpenter and that he built houses. His short blonde hair was bleached from working in the sun. His tan face was calm and he seemed to be more concerned about his wife and child standing in the heat than his situation. Tom and Sue were almost oblivious to everything except their family. I knew there was no way this guy was running.

Sue had the baby on her hip as she handed me some papers through the window.

"Thank you so much for helping us. We can't afford for Tom to miss any more work."

Tom shook his head. "Yeah, that's how all this started in the first place."

I usually don't care about the story, but I have a soft spot for babies. I closed the sliding door and turned up the air-conditioning. He didn't seem to notice he was trapped.

"What's this all about?" I asked.

Tom leaned toward me as he started to speak. That was unusual, too. Most of the time, if somebody's got something on their conscience, they lean away. I actually prefer that, since it lets me set the distance between us.

"I was late paying off a fine for a speeding ticket. I didn't even know they suspended my license. I got pulled over one morning driving to work and they arrested me. I got a letter in the mail from the state about a week later telling me about the suspension."

"Why didn't you pay your fine?"

"I *was* paying on it. We just had the baby and money was tight. I got the money now. I was going to pay it off when I went to court. Then you called and said I missed my hearing."

I looked through the papers and saw that the letter from the state was dated after his traffic stop. I read the standard form that notifies the defendant of his court date.

Bingo. Everything about him made sense now. He hadn't missed his court date and the court had issued the warrant by mistake.

I turned around and looked at Tom. "I came here to arrest you."

He clenched his teeth as his whole body tensed. I could see Sue clutching the baby. Her eyes were filling with tears.

I turned around as I opened the sliding door. "But I'm not going to. Take your family home and we'll call you when we get it straightened out."

Tom let out a sigh of relief, as Sue cried.

I suddenly felt tired. The adrenaline had been spent for the day. I needed a good workout at the dojo to clean out the pipes.

Frank was still at the office when I went back to finish up the paperwork. I told him about Tom's case and he said he would take care of it first thing in the morning. He called Tom and assured him we could straighten it out with the court.

Tom paid his fine and I never had to deal with his case again.

As I drove to the dojo that night, I thought about Tom and how I'd known he was telling the truth. A lot of it had to do with the fact that he hadn't been afraid of me. He'd had no hesitation about meeting me with his wife and baby and he hadn't looked nervous when I'd talked to him. It was about fear. It's an issue each of us faces in the dojo.

My dojo is carpeted and surrounded by mirrors. Two heavy striking bags hang from the ceiling. In one corner, tape on the floor marks off our *kumite* (sparring) area. It's a square fifteen feet on each side, with two sides against walls. That boxed-in corner has taught many students a valuable lesson.

If you get trapped in the corner, you have to fight your way out. Corners teach awareness, not only in kumite but also in life. If you get caught unaware and in a bad position, you have to fight harder. Being smart and being in tune with your surroundings will win, if not prevent, most conflicts. It's a lesson in life survival.

I was working with a young green belt on his sparring. He could generate a good offense, but his reflexes got the better of him when pressured and he kept turning his head away each time I attacked.

Controlling reflexes is a problem each student faces along the way. The green belt had been in the ring with me many times. He knew I wasn't going to seriously hurt him. But at the same time he knew when I hit him it was going to sting. I threw a series of punches, pausing between each one, waiting for him to notice what he was doing wrong. The frustration in his eyes told me he got the point.

"You know that you can't see the attack when you're not looking," I said. "You've got no chance of blocking the punch if you look away, and it won't hurt any less because you don't see it."

"I know, Sensei," he said. "I can't seem to help it."

"You *can* help it. Everybody experiences fear," I said. "But you can't let it control your behavior. Remember the meaning of *zensho*: live completely and die without regret. Everybody experiences fear. Being scared is allowing that fear to control your behavior. Face up to your fears and control your actions in a way that will benefit you. By doing so, you learn to channel your emotions in a positive way. The pain of being hit is only physical and temporary.

"Avoiding challenges affects your spirit and stays with you. Not facing the threat will not make it disappear. It's like the child pulling the bed covers over his head to hide from the boogeyman in hopes it will go away. It never goes away; instead it remains like a cloud hanging over you. Face your fears head-on and make them go away. Don't avoid life. You owe yourself more than that."

"Yes, Sensei," he said as he bowed.

Everyone has some type of issue that needs improvement. These come to the surface in the dojo, under pressure. Each student makes a choice, whether consciously or unconsciously, either to confront his fears and reflexes and improve or to live hobbled by them.

The first step to change is recognizing those bad reflexes and beliefs. The second step is deciding to change them.

I deal every day with people refusing to face their problems. They choose to run from the law instead of resolving the issue and getting it behind them. These people are simply delaying the inevitable and a dark cloud hangs over them. They have to constantly look over their shoulder and wonder if this is the day that they will be caught.

Many are relieved when they're captured, because their physical incarceration has released a spiritual imprisonment. But since they didn't release themselves, they learn nothing from the experience. They'll never make their boogeymen disappear that way.

The ones who choose to change and continue training improve. By the end of the evening, my green belt had made progress. He began to unchain himself from his fears and face the situation. The result for him was getting hit less and fighting better. The spiritual tools he was developing would serve him well the rest of his life.

I sparred with each student, with my black belts being the last ones in the ring. With the lower-ranked belts, the teacher is for the most part a punching bag. It may seem to the student that they are really fighting, but the lesson is kept at their level by design. Toward the end of each sparring session, the student is pressed to a level that is slightly beyond his capability. Only by raising the bar can real improvement be made. The tricky part is knowing how high to raise it for each individual.

With the black belts, the lessons are more like tweaking and fine-tuning a well-oiled machine. With the lower ranks I can make my point by simply using my speed or by exploiting their clumsiness. That doesn't work with the black belts. They're usually faster than I am and well balanced. The bumps and the bruises don't heal as fast as they did twenty years ago. But experience wins out over speed—being able to recognize my sparring partner's intent a split-second faster than he can see mine makes the difference.

The sessions with the black belts are more mental, more like a chess game. Don't get me wrong, it's rough, but the techniques are calculated and surgical. I have one advantage that I am not above using if I am getting swarmed by these younger, quicker black belts. Over the years, they have all been hammered by me at one time or another. This tends to create a slight intimidation factor. Not so much as to be noticed by others but just enough to give me a timing advantage if I need it. A lot of instructors won't admit to using this as a means of staying on top. I prefer to regard it as another mental obstacle that I'm trying to teach my black belts to overcome. At least that's the line I'm sticking with.

I bowed to my senior student after our match and instructed him to take everyone through another round of sparring. I bowed again and left the ring covered in sweat.

The cleansing effect of a workout is amazing. Nothing comes close to it, not strength training or running marathons, and I've done a lot of both. In the dojo, in the ring, you sweat all the way down to the bone.

I went home feeling great. Debbie had supper waiting and we ate and watched the news as we both got caught up with each other's day. We were looking forward to our son coming home in a couple of weeks from California. Joey had ten days of predeployment leave from the Marine Corps. My daughter-in-law and grandson had come back ahead of him and were staying with her parents until Joey arrived. This would be his second six-month deployment aboard the USS *Peleliu.*

The next morning I called Ken Reynolds. He said that he was tied up until Monday, and we arranged to meet at his office. I told him I wanted to interview his employees who were friendly with Wiley. He agreed. Ken gave me Wiley's last known address and it matched the one I had in his bail application. I decided to drive out and talk to Wiley's ex-landlord. There was the possibility that he had left something behind that might lead me to him.

Before I left I called Detective Pete Finchum, who was prosecuting the case against Wiley. He was a detective with a city police department that was in the same county I had previously worked in as a deputy. We knew each other. I always get good cooperation from my old contacts.

"What can I do for you Joe?" Pete asked, after we'd caught up on some small talk.

"You're working Wiley Smith?"

"Yeah, I was wondering when you would call. Looks like he hit the road."

"Looks that way. His boss doesn't think he did it."

"Bullshit," Pete barked. "The son of a bitch confessed."

"What?" I said, clenching my teeth. My grip tightened on the phone as I listened.

"Yeah, he was in the process of failing his third polygraph when he confessed. He gave it all up. Even admitted it wasn't the first time. Guess he didn't tell the boss that, did he?"

"Hell, no, he didn't," I said.

"I figured he ran," Pete said. "A couple of months ago the mother of the girl he molested called me up and said Wiley threatened to kill them. I told her to take out a warrant on him. When they went to pick him up on that charge, he was gone. She got so scared they moved to Bristol. They're laying low. It wouldn't be his first time."

"First time for what?" I asked. I didn't like this at all. Seemed like everybody knew more about my jumper than I did, and I was getting real irritated at Ken Reynolds. What else was he holding out on me about?

"Oh, didn't you know? Wiley did time for killing his brother in-law. Cut him in half with a shotgun. The sheriff up there had to track him down with bloodhounds. Found him hiding in a cave or some shit."

"This just keeps getting better and better," I said. "Thanks for the info, buddy. Let me know if I can do anything for you."

"No problem," he said. "I hope you catch the bastard."

After I hung up, I printed out a computer-generated map to Wiley's former residence. I looked through my files for any cases that would also take me to that general area, in order to save some road time. I located a file belonging to Leon Fisk. The notes on the folder indicated he was probably in Greeneville, which was only about thirty miles from where I was going.

Wiley's last known address was outside the little town of Bean Station, which is about a thirty-minute drive from Knoxville. It's a sleepy little town where everybody knows their neighbors. Older people sit out on their front porch, waving as cars pass by. It used to be the type of place people would want to raise their kids.

In many ways it's still a better place to live than in the city, but the drug culture has found its way out here, as well. It's not as rampant as in the city, but the small country towns have lost much of their innocence. Instead of the urban epidemic of crack cocaine, the drug of choice out here is Oxycontin, a powerful painkiller.

The map led me outside the city limits to a section of the county where residents are known to be less cordial. A gravel road led to Wiley's last known address. I drove up the long driveway to a brick house. The driveway continued around the back and ended at a trailer that was supported by cinder blocks. Rain had washed away the earth under some of the blocks, which caused the trailer to lean precariously.

An older man was sitting under the carport of the house in a lounge chair next to a parked truck. He seemed to be just looking out across his property. I raised my hand and waved as I got out of the van and approached him. "How you doing?"

"Well, I ain't dead yet. Not bad for an eighty-five-year-old man with cancer," he answered. It was now clear why he was so absorbed with just his surroundings. He was taking in as much of the essence of life as he could. The simple things tend to be overlooked until one is faced with losing them. He was a man in reflection. I introduced myself and he told me his name was Junior.

"If you're here looking for Wiley, he's long gone," he said. "The law has done been here and so has Ken Reynolds."

"You know Ken?"

"Everybody around here knows him or knows of him," Junior answered. "He probably owns half the county."

I nodded my head. "Yeah, Ken told me he came out here. What can you tell me about Wiley?"

"Nothing much to tell," he answered. "He come up here about two years ago and wanted to rent that trailer. I told him it wasn't leveled and didn't have no water or electricity. He said he didn't care and that he had a kerosene heater. He stayed up there about two years and always paid the rent on time. Ain't much else to tell except that he up and left about two months ago. Didn't say a word. One morning he was gone and the law came up here looking for him the next day."

"Did he ever have company?"

"Only that trashy cousin of his and her kids," he answered. "You know, that one that said Wiley messed with her young 'un."

"She's his *cousin*?"

"Yeah, she came here a lot with those kids," he answered. "Pure trash. Why, she came down here one day and dropped her drawers and offered it to me. I wouldn't stick my pecker in there for nothin'. I could smell her from where I was sitting. She never kept them kids up either. They had to take them out of school cause they was covered with lice."

Junior leaned over and spit into a can. Tobacco juice had started to run out the corners of his mouth. "You mind if I have a look in the trailer?" I asked.

"Help yourself. Just be careful. The floor is rotten in places."

Concrete cinder blocks had been stacked to make steps leading up to the front door of the trailer. The door was about five feet off the ground and I had to restack some of the blocks to climb inside. The entire trailer was leaning to the rear with trash and debris having gravitated on the floor toward the back wall.

The stench inside the trailer was overwhelming. Car parts and piles of soiled clothing littered the interior, and I could see the ground in places through holes in the floor. There was an old mattress lying on the floor in one of the two bedrooms. The other bedroom was his trash dump. Garbage bags were piled on each other and filled the room. Flies buzzed in swarms and some of the bags had been torn open by varmints.

I knew what had to be done and dreaded the thought. Poking through the debris of anybody's life is unpleasant, but Wiley's was going to be worse than most. His crime, his skip, his trailer—consistent filth was his trademark.

I put on a pair of latex gloves, held my breath, and dragged several of the bags to the front door. No way I was working inside the trailer. I tossed them outside.

I slit open the bags with my knife and spread the contents of the garbage bags out. You could almost see the stink rising off them, polluting the air his landlord had been enjoying. Junior hobbled up the driveway as I started to examine the garbage.

Postmarks on some of the soiled envelopes told me that I had opened some of the bags that he must have used about the time he left. There wasn't much information in any of the letters: mainly collection notices and bulk mail advertisements. Wiley liked Natural Ice beer and Copenhagen tobacco. Those were the only beer and tobacco brands in the garbage.

Junior wheezed as he approached. He sat on a stump next to where I was picking through the bags. He leaned over to spit every few minutes and peered over the mess I was making.

In one of the bags I found an envelope that contained some pictures. One of them showed Wiley standing next to a car that was parked in front of the trailer. "Is that Wiley's car?" I asked.

"Yep, Ken Reynolds gave him that car so he could get back and forth to work. That's what he's driving. The vinyl roof is tore pretty bad on the other side. You can't see it in the picture."

"It's nasty as hell in that trailer," I said. "How could anybody live like that?"

"That's just Wiley," Junior said. "He was living in a tent before he moved in there. Dirt never bothered him. If he sat down here right now, he'd leave a greasy spot. He told me one time that he rode around the country in boxcars and lived off garbage for six months."

Not what I wanted to hear. Drifters are the hardest to find. They usually cut all ties to their family and friends.

The wind blew the pieces of paper that were scattered about. Flies were starting to follow me out from the trailer to the relocated garbage. "You got something I can put this mess in?" I asked.

"Don't worry with that. My boy will be home soon. I've been after him to pick up around this trailer anyway. Just leave it."

I handed him a card and thanked him for his help.

That was the last time I saw Junior. His son called two weeks later and told me he died. He found my card taped to his father's refrigerator and wanted to tell me that he was going to junk the trailer.

While I wasn't happy about learning Wiley was a drifter, at least I had more information than I did before. Knowing some of Wiley's personal habits and tastes, not to mention having a picture of his car, was invaluable.

I stopped at the few beer stores in the area. They all knew Wiley, but hadn't seen him in a long time. Not a good sign.

I'd done all I could do around there for the time being. I noted the important facts of the day on Wiley's folder and put his file in my briefcase and him out of my mind. There were more men to hunt. You have to learn to compartmentalize the cases. No matter how bad you want to catch a skip, you can't let it distract from the other cases. Sometimes you can think too much. Sometimes you can force too hard. Sometimes you have to just get out of the way and let things happen.

Driving is good for that. I just place it in the back of my mind and forget about it as the miles go by. Many times an idea will surface when you just get out of the way. I started the van and began the thirty-mile drive to Greeneville.

I have yet to catch any rocket scientists, but my next jumper looked particularly dense. Leon Fisk was a twenty-two-year-old white male, married with two kids. Leon failed to appear on a theft charge on a five-thousand-dollar bond.

Leon's picture showed eyes looking up in a vacant gaze toward the one long eyebrow that stretched from one side of his forehead to the other. His mouth gaped open, and I could not help but feel this was his constant expression.

His looks were backed up by his actions. Leon would comb the parking areas of shopping centers looking for receipts for purchases that people had either dropped or thrown away. He would then go into the stores and locate the item that matched the receipt. After that, he would take the item up front for a refund as if he were returning merchandise he had purchased himself.

Who knows how many times Leon got away with this ploy? It caught up with him one day when a plain-clothes security guard noticed Leon and thought he was acting suspiciously. Judging from what I already knew about Leon, it wouldn't have taken a Sherlock Holmes to spot that this guy was up to something. Stealth did not appear to be Leon's forte.

The guard decided to watch him and noted Leon was empty-handed. The not-so-crafty thief took an item off the shelf and walked straight to the refund counter. By the time Leon left the refund counter with his money, they were waiting for him. Leon was busted.

I'd already done my homework and had an idea where he was headed. Unlike Wiley, Leon didn't strike me to be smart or able enough to cut all connections to family and friends. If I was right, he needed somebody to tell him when to get out of the rain.

His former landlady told me, "He's a piece of work. I knew he got arrested. I suspected him of breaking into some of the cars parked at the apartments. Never could prove it. He left in the middle of the night owing me a month's rent."

"Any idea where he might have gone?" I had asked.

"He told some of the other tenants his mother was in Greeneville. You can't miss his car. It's a little white Toyota. He spray-painted orange primer on all the rusted spots. It looks like polka dots."

In the past, a public records search meant a trip to the courthouse, or at the least a telephone call to the appropriate department. Today almost anything can be researched on the internet. Many municipalities now have websites that allow easy access to public records. There are internet subscriber services that also have this information in databases.

With just a few keystrokes I was able to find out the name and address of Leon's mother. Her name was Betty Fisk and she owned property in Greeneville. A few seconds later the printer spit out a map that took me right to her front door.

By the time I arrived in Greeneville, I'd planned out my approach. Leon wasn't the brightest flare in a roadside kit, but he was big. If he had a longer reach than I did, I'd need to get in close, fast, and stay inside his punching range. Depending on how fast he was or whether he had any training at all as a fighter, that might be the trickiest part.

Thanks to my printout, I found the road to Betty Fisk's house easily. After I turned on her street, I started checking out the addresses and knew the house would be about two blocks down on my right. It was a quiet neighborhood that had patches of woods separating the homes. I waved to an older couple going on their late afternoon walk as I drove slowly down the street. Most of the houses were about twenty years old and were well kept. People were out mowing their lawns and washing cars. Kids and dogs romped in their yards with sounds of barking and laughter.

As I got closer to the location, there were fewer houses and nothing but a wooded area to my left. Not wanting to draw attention, I sped up and drove past Betty's house. Just as I went by, a funny looking polka dot car caught my eye. I continued down the road looking for somewhere I could park and keep an eye on her house.

In the south, churches are more of a community center than they are in any other part of the country. Even the smallest community has at least one big brick building that's used by a variety of community groups as well as for church activities. Their parking lots are rarely unoccupied and usually make excellent surveillance points. Nobody notices a poor sinner stopping in for some moral support.

Sure enough, there was a nice church just two hundred yards from the Fisk residence. I was even able to park in the shade and still have an excellent view of her property.

I took out my binoculars and scanned the property. The car in the driveway definitely matched the description of Leon's vehicle. Two older-model cars were parked by a garage to the left of the driveway. The house itself was not as well kept as most in the neighborhood. It was badly in need of some paint and the yard was cluttered with lumber and other material. The front door was about three feet off the ground. There was no porch or steps. The door was open and I could see a light shining through the screen door.

Two small children were playing in the backyard, both of them trying to ride the same tricycle. Finally, one of them got bored with that and went exploring in the grass that needed mowing. I couldn't see all the way around the back of the house.

I let my seat back a little and watched the residence. There was no way to know if Leon was actually home, but waiting is something I'm used to doing.

After about thirty minutes, my patience paid off. A white male appeared from around the back of the house and walked to the polka dot car.

I zoomed in and focused my binoculars on his face. There was my man.

I glanced down at his jailhouse picture for reassurance, and there was no mistaking that dull appearance. Leon was about 5 feet 7 inches and about 195 pounds.

Leon looked like he'd just woken up, with his full head of black hair sticking out in all directions. An oversized T-shirt covered his dumpy physique and fell well below the waistline of his baggy shorts. His muscles looked slack and he walked stiffly and off-balance, as though he had no real consciousness of where his body was taking him. I could almost hear his knees crack when he bent over to tie the laces on one of his tennis shoes.

Leon walked around to the driver side of the car, reached inside the open window, and retrieved a pack of cigarettes off the dash. He lit one up then sat on the hood of his car and watched the kids as he smoked. He had no idea I was watching him.

Time to make friends. I put the seat back up and started the van. My arm was hanging out the window and I turned up the radio as I eased into the driveway. I had a CD of Stevie Ray Vaughn vibrating the doors as I rolled up with a big old smile. I was leaning back in the seat and felt like I didn't have a care in the world. My demeanor was relaxed and the van rocked to the music as I pulled up behind his car.

Leon turned around and looked, and I waved at him as my smile grew wider. I kept the van running with the music turned up. My hand tapped the outside of the driver's door in time with the beat. He smiled at me and slid off the hood of his car and walked toward me. He kept the same happy expression as he got closer. I turned off the van and the music stopped.

"How you doing?" I asked, smiling as I raised my hand again. Rocking up the driveway with the good ol' country boy approach worked.

"Not bad," he said. "What's up, man?" He stopped just to my side of the van and dropped his cigarette on the ground. Leon ground the butt into the dirt with his shoe as I slowly got out. All at once, Leon was looking at a man standing in front of him who was wearing a badge and a gun. The smile left his face.

"Hello, Leon," I said. "I'm with your bonding company. You didn't go to court for us. You're under arrest." He just stood there, trying to think, the process clearly painful for him. His eyes were staring at the one long eyebrow that stretched across his forehead. It didn't appear anybody was home.

"I'm not Leon," he said finally. "He ain't here."

"Where is he and who are you?"

"I'm his brother and I ain't seen him."

"Who's inside the house?"

"My wife and my mother." He was incapable of thinking very far ahead. His stupidity along with the sudden shock of the situation left him at a loss.

I decided to play along with him. I don't like making arrests in front of children. Watching a parent being physically restrained is terribly traumatic for them. The pronounced sadness and grief of a crying child begging for his daddy not to leave always hangs over me like a dark cloud. Intellectually, I know it's not my fault. The parents know they're fugitives and set up the situation by being with the kids. But the kids suffer enough with parents like that. If I can avoid adding to their pain, I do—sometimes I don't have a choice.

"I want to talk to your mother," I said. "Take me to her."

I followed Leon around to the rear of the house. The backdoor was open and we walked up the steps into the kitchen. Betty was at the sink and turned around when we came in the house. She watched her son walk straight through the kitchen. Her eyes got wide when she saw my badge and she followed Leon into the living room.

I was standing in the doorway between the kitchen and living room, about eight feet from Leon. He stopped and stood completely still in the middle of the room.

Betty grabbed his arm. "What's going on?" she asked.

Leon didn't say a word. He just stood there.

Betty got right in his face. "Leon, what the hell is going on?" she screamed.

All of a sudden Leon's brain must have switched on. He shoved his mother out of his way and he ran toward the front door. The screen door slammed against the side of the house as he burst through it. He jumped down to the ground, ran across the yard, crossed the street, and into the woods.

I was right behind him. The little fat boy couldn't run very fast and I wasn't worried about him getting away. The woods were thick.

Then we hit a thicket of briars. Thorns ripped at my clothes, face, and arms. Now I was pissed. He had about a ten-yard lead on me and I was closing.

"Stop, Leon, or I'll shoot," I yelled. Leon turned and looked at me but kept running.

*Smack.* He ran right into a pine tree. The impact spun him around and he landed face down on the ground.

"Don't you fucking move," I said, as I tried to hold back my laughter. He put his hands behind his back without being told. I was fighting back the chuckles as I cuffed him.

The left side of his head and ear were scraped from the pine bark. His left arm and knee were also bleeding slightly. I told him to turn over on his side and I helped him to stand up. I reached between his cuffed hands and grabbed the waistband of his shorts in the back. If he tried to run again, he was going to get a wedgie from hell.

We walked the fifty yards or so back through the woods. When we got to the road I saw Leon's wife standing in the front yard with a child on each hip. She must have been in one of the bedrooms. I stopped before we crossed the road.

"Get those kids in the house," I said. "They don't need to be seeing this." She turned and walked out of sight with the children. Just then, Betty came running around from the back, a cordless phone in her hand.

"You fucker!" she screamed. "You goddamn fucker! What the hell are you doing to my boy? You son of a bitch! You fucker!" She kept ranting nonstop while pointing the phone at me like a gun. "I'm calling the sheriff!" she said. "You goddamn fucker!"

"Call them," I said. I led Leon to the van and secured him inside with leg shackles. His wife came back outside without the kids.

"My poor baby," his wife cried. "Can I give him a hug? Please, sir?" I took out a first-aid kit.

"Yeah sure," I said. "Here, clean him up a little with this." She cleaned his scrapes with peroxide and applied some antiseptic. Betty disappeared back into the house.

"Can I smoke a cigarette before I go?" Leon asked.

"Yeah," I answered. "But your wife has to hold it for you 'cause I'm not taking the cuffs off." She lit a cigarette for him and held it while he puffed. After he finished, I let her give him one last hug then said, "We have to go." She stood there and waved at him as we backed out the driveway.

I backed out onto the street and started to drive past the house when I heard Betty screaming again.

"Stop you fucker! You better stop you goddamn fucker!" She ran across the yard and into the street. I stopped and she came up to the van with the cordless phone in her hand. "I got the sheriff's department on the phone! Now you've had it, you son of a bitch!"

I took the phone from her. I could barely hear the party on the other end over her nonstop cursing and yelling.

A sheriff's department dispatcher identified himself and asked, "Who is this?"

I told him who I was and why I was there. He told me to go on and get out of there. "One thing," he added. "I know those people. They're crazy as hell. Betty's cousin is a magistrate. You know how these little counties are. This might not be over."

I thanked the officer and pitched the phone back to Betty before I drove off. I didn't think any more about it. I drove the forty minutes to the county jail that needed Leon.

Not a bad day at all. I uncovered some useful information on Wiley, caught Leon, and would still be home for supper on time.

I got home early enough to spend some time with Debbie. We ate supper and went to bed early.

Around 11:30 P.M., the phone rang. It was Frank, the owner of the bail bond company. "Joe, I got bad news."

"What is it?"

"That boy you arrested tonight–his mother took out warrants on you."

"What the hell?"

"I spoke to the captain up there. He's a friend of mine," Frank answered. "The boy's mother is related to a judicial magistrate. She swears you threw her against the wall and pushed down some kids."

"That's bullshit," I yelled, now fully awake. "I was never close to those kids and it was the boy who shoved his mother." Beside me, Debbie stirred uneasily.

"Don't yell at me. I know it's bullshit. That doesn't matter and you know it. The fact is there are warrants out for you."

"Son of a bitch."

"I told my friend you would turn yourself in first thing in the morning. I'll have an agent waiting on you. You won't be there any longer than it will take them to book you. This is all part of the game. Goes with the territory."

"I still don't believe this shit."

"What are you bitching about? I'm the one who's going to be paying the lawyers to get you out of this. Just forget about it and go back to sleep. Call me when you head out in the morning and I'll have an agent waiting."

"Yeah, go back to sleep. Like that's going to happen." This was the first time someone had actually followed through on a threat to take out a warrant. Even though I knew it was bullshit, it took me a few hours to get back to sleep.

I took my time getting up the next morning and ate a leisurely breakfast with Debbie. As we finished, I turned to her and said, "Well, time to go to jail." Then I called Frank and told him I was on my way.

The jail in Greeneville is right next to the courthouse in the middle of town. The federal courthouse is just a few blocks down. I walked into the lobby of the jail and saw our agent. He stood with me at the reception window as an officer approached.

"Can I help you?" the officer asked.

"I'm here to turn myself in," I said. "My name is Joseph Laney. You have warrants for me."

"Yes sir. We have been expecting you," he said. "Have a seat and an officer will be right with you."

I liked his manner. Professional, courteous, with none of the flack you sometimes get from small-time police officers who feel like bail enforcement officers are encroaching on their territory.

A few minutes later a sergeant came out and walked up to me. "You Joseph Laney?"

"I am."

"Mr. Laney, I am serving you with three warrants for assault and one for criminal trespass. The bond for all charges is five thousand dollars." He read the warrants to me. "Any questions?"

"No, Sergeant. Want me to empty my pockets before you take me to booking?"

"Hell no," he said. "Let's just get this over with."

The agent turned in the bond for five thousand dollars at the window as I went downstairs. They took my picture right after collecting my fingerprints. I sat at the booking officer's desk drinking a cup of coffee as she typed in the answers to some general questions. When the booking procedure was completed, I got up and left.

Thinking about having time taken away from a weekend at home over a total lie really pissed me off. The court date was set for next month, which meant more wasted time on this silly matter. The only thing I looked forward to was my lawyer's cross-examining Betty. Thoughts of her squirming on the stand ran through my head while I was driving home.

There is a funny thing about the truth—it comes out the same way every time you tell it. A story filled with lies will always fall apart. Betty didn't have a chance of making her story stick.

As I drove back through the mountains, a thought occurred to me. If I failed to appear for my court date, *I* would be a bail jumper.

Would Frank send me out to track myself down?

# three

Monday morning, I called Ken Reynolds to confirm our appointment. He said he would have his two employees present who were friends with Wiley. The rest of the morning was spent "phone chasing."

I locate the majority of my skips through phone work. Before the agent gets somebody out of jail, a bond application must be filled out. All immediate family members, current and former wives and in-laws have to be listed. Ex-spouses and mother-in-laws (ex or not) are usually quite eager to stick it to the jumper. Other friends and family members a lot of times don't want to see the skips get in more trouble or don't want to see them hurt.

Of course, sometimes everybody lies. You have to read between the lines and ask the right questions. It takes a feel—a touch. I don't think you can teach it; it's instinct.

Wiley had listed a brother named Bill Kent and given a Morristown address. There wasn't a phone number shown for him. A directory search indicated the brother had an unpublished number.

Not a problem. I fell back to my internet subscriber service. My source sells information. Unpublished listings and physical addresses linked to post office boxes are his specialty. He can also look for utility service in somebody's name or run a check on toll calls from a telephone number.

In fewer than five minutes I had Bill Kent on the phone. He was less than helpful.

"I don't know where Wiley is," he said. "And if I did, I wouldn't tell you anyway."

"Don't you know what he did?" I asked. "That little girl is going to be messed up for the rest of her life."

"Wiley told me he didn't do it. But if he did, so what?"

"Being a sorry bastard must be a Kent family trait," I said.

"Don't fucking call here again." The next thing I heard was dial tone. He had hung up.

I did a reverse lookup on Bill Kent's phone number and printed a map to his house. A records search showed he owned another property on the other side of Morristown. I decided to check out both locations on my way to meet Ken Reynolds.

I drove to Bill Kent's house first. He lived at the end of a cul de sac in a middle-class neighborhood. Some kids were playing basketball in the street. The houses were close together with small yards. It was the type of neighborhood in which nothing goes unnoticed.

I parked in the driveway of a house with a for-sale sign in the front yard. The grass had grown tall. The bare windows gave an inside view of the empty dwelling. An elderly lady next door was working in her garden and looked over at me from her hunched-over position. Her attention went back to her flowers as I wandered around the property trying to look like a buyer.

Next door to the Kent house was a man in the driveway working on a classic car. It was a beautiful baby blue 1954 Mercury Monterey Tudor complete with lake pipes and fender skirts. The hood was up and he was leaning over the engine. No one seemed to pay any attention to me as I strolled past the Kent house.

The shade-tree mechanic saw me admiring his car as I walked up. The 256-V8 engine was spotless and shined as bright as the polished chrome on the grill. He could tell I appreciated quality cars, and he showed me the interior, which was done in top-grain leather. He let me sit in the car and rest one hand on the three-speed shifter with overdrive, as I showed him a picture of Wiley. The smell of the leather and the feel of the ball shifter in my hand were intoxicating.

"That's Bill's brother," he said. "He came around here a lot, but I haven't seen him in months." I told him about the charges against Wiley and gave him my card. He told me that if he saw my man he would call. The disgusted look on his face left no doubt he would help. At least I knew of another place Wiley Kent was not hiding. An important part of finding someone is finding where he's *not.* I thanked him and looked back longingly at the car as I left.

I drove to the other side of Morristown to the other property owned by Bill Kent. It was a lower-middle-class neighborhood. The houses were much older and many of them were vacant. Trailer parks and low-rent apartments bordered the little community. I turned onto the street of the property and immediately saw Wiley Kent's car. My heart jumped through my throat.

It was a short dead-end street. I stopped and parked about four houses away. The car was parked in the yard. It had been backed into some hedges so the license plate couldn't be seen. There was no doubt it was the car in the picture found in Wiley's trash. I started to get pumped.

It was the last house on the street and I could see that there wasn't an electric meter installed. The house looked like it was being remodeled. There was no mailbox or trash can. I scanned the car, using the binoculars. The lawn had been freshly cut but grass and weeds had grown up around the tires and bumper. It hadn't been moved for a long time.

I placed my clip-on holster in the small of my back and walked toward the house. A little black dog came right up the edge of his yard. He barked and ran around as I passed his territory. The front door of the house was padlocked from the outside. I walked around the house and peered in each window. There was no furniture, clothing, or trash. Building material and tools were lying about on the floor. Wiley was the type of person who would have left behind signs that he had stayed there. This was a cold trail.

After checking out the house, I went over to the car. It was locked and I looked in the windows for any clues. The floorboards were cluttered with Natural Ice and Copenhagen cans. I walked around to the back of the car and wrote down the license plate number.

An older man from across the street saw me checking out the car and came over. I showed him a picture of Wiley.

"Yep. That's one of the Kent boys," he said. "Miz Kent died a few years ago and left the house to the boys. Bill Kent's been fixing it up. I hope they don't move back in."

"Have you seen Wiley here?" I asked.

"I ain't seen him in years. That whole family is trouble."

"How long has this car been here?"

"It's been parked there for a couple of months," he replied. "I woke up one morning and it was there. Didn't see who drove it. They must have parked it in the middle of the night, because I get up early."

I thanked the old gentleman and gave him my card. He agreed to call if he saw Wiley or if somebody moved the car.

"Just don't tell anybody we talked," he said. "Those Kents are the type that would burn a man's house down. They're mean people."

"Don't worry. Anything you tell me stays confidential."

I went back to the van and connected my laptop computer to the cell phone adapter. A tag search showed the vehicle was indeed registered to Wiley. As expected, the address on the registration came back to his abandoned trailer. It was looking more and more like Wiley had left the area.

My notes were starting to fill up the front side of Wiley's folder. I decided to start a separate sheet for logging the leads. It was an omen of things to come. This would be the first of many sheets. I called Ken Reynolds and told him I would be at his office in fifteen minutes.

A tractor-trailer truck pulled out of the gate as I drove in. Its large open bed was piled high with twisted steel. Rusted beams and tailpipes stuck out in all directions. The trailer was low on the axles with the weight of the load. The driver stopped when I flagged him down and he pointed to the building where Ken had his office.

There were mountains of junked cars stacked into rows that covered acres. Trucks filled with salvage waited for their turn on the scales. The sounds of screeching metal pierced through the van windows as a crane ripped and lifted an old car from a stack. Its huge jaws opened and the load crashed into a compactor. The metal frames groaned as they were being crushed into cubes.

The violent symphony surrounded me when I got out of the van. The air was thick with a brown, rust-colored dust mixed with diesel fumes.

The quiet air-conditioned reception area was like an oasis. A heavy-set woman in her middle forties sat behind the reception desk. She peered up over her reading glasses as I approached her. After I gave her my name, she told me that I was expected and pointed down the hall. A row of fluorescent lights lined the ceiling, like the white stripes of a highway, and stopped at an open door at the end of the corridor. The carpet was worn and a man looked up from his desk as I passed his closet-sized office.

As I walked toward the end of the hall I could see Ken Reynolds sitting at his desk. There was another man standing in a corner of the room to my right. Instinctively, my peripheral vision scanned each of the inside walls as I passed through the door. There was a large crucifix hanging on the wall behind Ken's desk and a Bible lying on a table between two chairs where I was standing.

Ken stood up and walked around from behind the desk and we shook hands. He was a tall redhead in his mid-sixties with a broad smile. His shirt was hanging out of his loose-fitting jeans and the thick dust from outside covered his boots. He leaned slightly to one side, which told me he had back problems.

The man in the corner was staring at me, and I made sure his hands were in sight. I didn't acknowledge his attention by looking directly at him and acted as if he weren't present, ignoring his overt attempt to establish dominance in the room. He began to pick his nose with his right hand, which did not go unnoticed.

"This is Bob," Ken said. "He's a local bounty hunter I've hired to help us find Wiley."

"Oh," I said.

Bob was at least six-feet four-inches tall and had a large gut that hung over his camouflaged pants. His web belt sported a knife and scabbard. He crossed his arms in front of his tank top as he leaned against the wall. Unfortunately, his attempt to appear casual didn't quite work, as he was a bit too far away from the wall to pull it off. That shifted most of his weight to his right leg, the one closest to the wall. The resulting imbalance contradicted the impression that he was trying to convey, that he was prepared to react instantly to any threat. Additionally, his dominant shoulder was pressed against the wall, limiting his range of motion. Since he had no concept of where his own body was, he would have a hard time connecting his fist with any part of mine.

Up until that point, I'd ignored Bob. But I wasn't going to let Ken make him part of the team.

I turned my head to look at Bob, straight and hard. He wasn't expecting it and he wasn't up to the challenge. He immediately shifted his eyes toward the floor and tilted his shaved head slightly downward as he wiped his picking finger on his pants. If he'd been a German Shepherd Dog, he'd have been rolling over on his back to expose his belly. I knew what kind of a man he was; one who'd gotten by on size and intimidation. But he didn't have the heart for a real fight.

While letting out a slight sigh, I nodded my head, acknowledging his submission. Ken appeared to be unaware of the unspoken exchange.

With Bob out of the way—although Ken didn't know it yet—I turned back to Ken. "It's your money. But I work alone."

"Bob is the sheriff's nephew," Ken said. "He lives here local and I figured he could keep his eyes open for us. I've offered a $5,000 reward for Wiley."

"You paid him?" I asked.

"Five hundred dollars," Ken answered.

I turned and faced Bob again. "And just how many people have you caught?"

He looked down again. "A few."

"That's what I thought. I can't do anything about Ken throwing his money away. If you have information that will help find Wiley, then you can earn some more money. Otherwise, stay out of my way. Say goodbye, Bob. Ken and I need to talk."

Ken looked at him and nodded. "It's okay, Bob. We'll talk later."

Bob gave me a quick look as he started to walk out. The closer he got to the door the more macho his posture became. Distance often increases confidence in those unsure of their commitment. By the time he reached the door his shoulders swayed as he was in a full strut. He tripped over the carpet just as he looked over his shoulder at me with an indignant sneer. I just shook my head as he stumbled slightly and continued on as if nothing happened.

I see this type of behavior in the dojo all the time. It's all about distance and commitment.

My karate school is part of a gym. We have to pass through a room full of weight lifters to get to the dojo. You can smell the testosterone in the air steaming off the packs of huge guys scattered around the room. They're relaxed while they're in their own little groups, but when one of them has to pass by the other packs alone, his posture changes. His shoulders hunch up around the ears and you can almost see the hair on the back of his neck bristle as he eyes himself in the mirror. Except for the lengthy admiration of his own reflection, he is unaware of his behavior.

In the beginning, some of the packs showed dominant postures toward my students as they walked past on their way to the dojo. The weight lifters would stand rudely in the way of the door and intentionally be slow to move out of the way, giving my students condescending looks. The other pack members would stare mockingly at a slightly built black belt as he walked by and would whisper among themselves.

I teach my people to be aware of—but not to acknowledge—this sort of posturing. Never let them know that you notice it—that tips your hand. Like two dogs facing each other, there's no doubt when the fight is about to begin. It's stupid to announce your intentions.

Most of that juvenile behavior changed right after some of them decided to test the waters outside of their pack to verify their machismo, no doubt at the urging of those with slightly more brains. A few of the weight lifters strutted into the dojo. They limped out.

Now they don't stand in front of our dojo door: they open it for us. I thought about those big guys and their painful exits from my dojo as I watched Bob's awkward departure.

Ken sat behind his desk as I walked over and closed his office door. I took a seat in one of the chairs on either side of the table that had the Bible placed on it. "All answers to all questions are in that good book," Ken said. "The Lord will work this out."

"I believe that to be true," I said. "But the Lord helps those who help themselves. You said some of your employees were friends with Wiley—where are they?"

"They're in jail," he answered. "I didn't know that, when you called this morning. They were arrested last night in a drug raid on a methamphetamine lab. I think the dope crowd is behind hiding Wiley and that's one reason I hired Bob. He can get me in the jail to talk some sense into these men."

I told Ken about finding Wiley's car and my feelings that he had left the area. Wiley had been seen at several of his regular haunts up until about two months ago. Nobody had seen him since, and his only known means of transportation was abandoned in that same period of time. "Whatever you do, keep everything I just told you confidential," I said. If drugs are involved, you better be careful and don't trust anybody."

Ken agreed and said he would call me first if he heard anything. He knew he stood to lose a ton of money, but there was no doubt in his mind that everything would work out. He planned to visit his two employees at the jail later and minister to them.

On the drive back to Knoxville, I thought how I hoped that Ken's willingness to help others would come back to him. I knew we would need all the help we could get.

When I got home, Debbie was on the phone with Joey and the kitchen was filled with the aroma of supper. He was flying in from California in a couple of days and the house was abundant with homecoming decor. Stacks of pictures we had taken over the years were laid out and arranged on the dining room table. The spare bedroom we used for clutter collection had been straightened up and made cozy. Fresh towels in the extra bathroom and a refrigerator full of calories left no doubt that Joey's arrival was imminent.

Debbie handed the phone to me when she finished talking. He sounded good and was looking forward to coming home. Debbie and I spent the rest of the night looking through some picture albums in bed before going to sleep.

My cell phone woke me from a dead sleep at 2:00 A.M., and my voice was groggy and hoarse when I finally found and answered it.

"Hey man, this is Peanut. You there?" said the voice at the other end.

Peanut was his street name and he was one of my snitches. Paid informants are worth their weight in gold, and Peanut had come through for me before.

There is a whole chapter dedicated to the use of spies in the *Art of War*, by Sun Tzu. Snitches are usually one step ahead of the law themselves and most are out on bond. They're part of the street crowd and go unnoticed while looking and listening for anything that might make them a buck or two. Peanut was particularly valuable because he lived in one of the more notorious housing projects.

"Yeah, Peanut, I'm here." I sat up on the side of the bed and cleared my throat. "What's up?"

"Your boy TC is with his lady right now," he said. "They just went inside. He parked his blue Caddy around the corner."

TC was a thirty-four-year-old male who jumped bail on drug and weapons charges. He was a known pimp and had done time in the penitentiary for attempted murder. There were more warrants out for him in another county for assaulting a police officer and evading arrest. I had been looking for him for several months and heard he was in Atlanta.

"Peanut, you sure he's there?" I asked.

"Yeah, man, you know I always been straight with you," he answered. "I seen him walk in the door and he ain't come out. We got the same deal, right, man?"

"Yeah, Peanut. You'll get your money, just like always. After I catch him. Just be sure you call me if he leaves before I get there. I don't want to spook him and make him run by hitting the place if he's not there."

"Yeah, man, I know," he said. "Be cool man. Later." I got up and splashed cold water on my face before throwing on some clothes. It was a muggy night and the sounds of crickets chirping filled the darkness as I checked to make sure all needed equipment was in the van before driving off with a hastily made cup of coffee.

Of the dozen or so housing projects in Knoxville, this was one of the worst. One-way and dead-end streets divide the many buildings. Waist-high iron fences quadrant off different areas of the sparse landscape. During the day, crack dealers and pimps man the street corners that have been duly allotted according to who is alive and not in jail. The echoing warning of "Five O" (which comes from the old television cop show) can be heard when a police cruiser on patrol approaches. The alarm travels up the streets and the once-crowded corners empty as the vermin crawl in their holes, slithering back out when the coast is clear. At night, the police don't patrol here and only answer in force to emergency calls.

I've been in housing projects from Detroit to Miami and the only difference in any of them is how many acres they cover. They're all governed by the law of the jungle. There are good people who live there but they strive to get out, especially for the sake of their children, before they're engulfed in the drugs and the crime.

The projects have their own version of the neighborhood watch program, and I knew that once I drove in the clock was ticking. Another problem is actually a testimony to the way our tax money is spent on quality construction. The bomb-shelter-like brick buildings are divided into anywhere from two to eight apartments. The windows are covered with a thick wire mesh screen and the solid steel doors are secured by both locks and dead bolts. I've witnessed a police SWAT team consisting of several beefy officers holding a battering ram bounce off doors like these.

Working in the projects takes a special touch and specialized tools. One device is called the "door spreader." The original idea was not mine, but the one I use has been modified from the first ingenious prototype. It's a ten-ton hydraulic jack that has been mounted horizontally on a stand that supports it from the floor. Extensions are welded on the base and piston ends of the jack. The uniform construction of the local housing projects enables this tool to be of universal use, requiring little if any adjustment. The floor stand is of the exact height to position the jack extensions inside the door frame between the lock and dead bolt. The jack spreads the door frame wide enough apart that the bolts on both locks are clear. You can push the door open with one finger with very little noise. Most of the time the frame springs back to its original state with little or no damage once the pressure on the jack is released. It is, however, not a lightweight tool, since it weighs about thirty pounds.

One drawback to not having a partner is the possibility that the skip will run out the back door just as I come in the front. That, among other reasons, is why forced entry is not the preferred method of catching runners. Once you enter a residence forcibly, there's no turning back. The liability and risk factors multiply tremendously and you can usually reduce both of those with a little patience. If somebody goes in a building, sooner or later they're coming out. It makes much more sense to wait and catch them in the open.

But surveillance, particularly by a white guy, is not an option in the projects. That's why I built the "shin stopper." It's a one-ton hydraulic jack that has the same extensions as the "door spreader" but not the floor stand. When the jack is pumped between the door frame, it creates a steel bar across the opening that would stop a Mack truck.

The steel bar is placed at the back door about mid-shin level. Any lower and they might simply step over it or only trip over one foot. Any higher, and they bounce off it back into the house, allowing them to regroup and jump over it. When a runner hits it at mid-shin level, it sends them head over heels onto the concrete landing outside. They're usually quite vocal when their shins hit the bar, thus announcing their attempted escape. The introduction of their head to the concrete subdues them long enough for me to run around to the back of the building and execute the arrest.

As I entered the projects, silhouettes emerged from between the buildings trying to signal me over for a drug sale, only to disappear back into the shadows when I kept going. Many people from outside the projects have regretted coming here for such a transaction. The draw of the cheap thrill is often used as bait to lure in the prey. If the potential buyers are lucky enough to escape with their lives, it's often after they've been robbed or had their cars stolen out from under them.

TC's lady lived in a building that was at the end of a one-way dead-end street. The roads snake around the buildings like a maze. It's vital to know them like the back of your hand to keep from being trapped like a rat.

The road directly behind TC's building had an outlet for escape and also allowed me to park close to the entrance. Peanut had not called me back, which meant TC was still inside. I turned off my lights and drove the last block to the building.

I grabbed my equipment and hurried to the back door with the heavy load, knowing full well that the van was probably already being targeted. The back door was at the bottom of a short set of stairs, and after securing the shin stopper, I quickly made my way around to the front door. There was no way of knowing what was going on inside. The heavy steel screens blocked all sound and light. After positioning the door spreader inside the frame, I slowly started to pump the hydraulic jack while taking out my gun.

Each stroke spread the opening a little more. I watched closely as the bolts on the locks cleared the strike plates on the frame without a sound except for the creaking hinges. I crouched down low in a combat shooting position, braced my gun on the jack extension, and pushed the door open.

Inside it was pitch dark, but there were sounds coming from the back of the apartment. My entry appeared to be undetected so far. I crawled under my tool and slithered inside the darkness on my belly.

While creeping further inside, it became apparent that TC and his lady were heavily engaged in the bedroom. The loudness of their enthusiasm more than masked any noise I might have made.

Many would opt for night vision equipment in this situation, but darkness is my friend. I prefer using it instead of avoiding it. If a light is turned on while you're wearing infrared goggles, you're blinded. The techniques I use have worked for centuries.

*Kusanku* kata teaches the principles of surviving and fighting in the dark. The kata teaches you how to slowly and quietly feel your way through darkness.

It also teaches you the tactical advantages of staying low. First, any light that does filter in will do so from above, outlining your body if you're standing upright. Second, people naturally reach straight out in front of them as they stumble through the dark so they're more likely to touch you if you're upright. A person who stays low remains in the shadows and is unseen.

My breathing was controlled. The long slow inhalations and exhalations enabled me to hear all sounds. I could hear a fan whirring in between the howls from the bedroom. Sounds from outside were beginning to creep in the open door and I slowly pushed it closed with my foot.

I continued in a low crawl through the living room and turned the corner into the hall. All the apartments in these buildings had the same floor plan, and I knew the layout well.

It sounded like two cats were fighting in the bedroom and TC and his lady grew louder by the second. If the headboard kept banging against the wall much longer, the whole bed was going to collapse.

I crawled past the bathroom to my right and stopped just outside the open bedroom door. My eyes had adjusted to the low-level light that filtered down from the nearly-opaque windows.

Their excitement intensified even more and it seemed like a good idea to let them conclude their business, which might make him a little more passive. I lay there and waited as I listened to the exchange.

"Oh shit, baby, shit baby yeah, give it to me."

"You my woman. Yeah baby, here it is, oh shit, yeah."

Sure enough, after a few more howls and screams, they fell silent except for some labored breathing. All of a sudden the bed creaked and two feet hit the floor. A female announced, "I gotta go pee."

Not good.

I was lying between the bedroom and bathroom doors. The floor vibrated as the footsteps got closer and my mind raced. I rolled up on my right side and flattened out against the wall. My objective was to become the wall.

She passed right by me with heavy thumping footsteps. I've often wondered how loud she would've screamed if I'd reached out and grabbed her leg.

My feet stuck out just past the bathroom door and she tripped slightly over them. The groping woman must have thought she had tripped over something other than an intruder's feet and she cursed as she went on into the bathroom. After hearing her sit down and then the anticipated tinkling sound, I rolled back over to my stomach and inched just inside the bedroom door.

I decided to wait until she flushed before making my move as he might think it was her coming back into the room. After hearing the familiar *whoosh* sound. I stood up and turned on the bedroom light.

"Damn, baby," he said while covering his eyes. "Why you fucking do that?"

"I'm not your baby," I said. I snatched the covers off the bed, leaving him lying there naked.

He jumped and dropped his hands from his squinting eyes and found himself staring down the barrel of my 9mm. I saw a 25-caliber automatic lying on a small table that was close to his head. I quickly grabbed it and slid it in my belt as I cocked the hammer back on my gun.

"Roll over on your stomach and put your hands behind your back," I screamed. "Do it now! Right now! Fucking *move!*"

TC complied about as fast as I have ever seen anybody obey a command. He immediately rolled over and placed his hands behind his back. I gently let the hammer down on my gun and reached for the handcuffs.

Just as I got his last hand cuffed, all three hundred pounds of his lady friend walked in the bedroom door. She stood there for a minute, butt-naked, displaying her 56DDDs, with her mouth wide open. For a split second I stood there gaping back at her and hoped I wasn't going to go blind. Years of martial arts training can't prepare you for everything.

All of a sudden she started screaming while jumping up and down and waving her hands. Rolls of flesh rippled and the mammoth breasts rotated in wide circles as she bounced, and the fat hanging down from the backs of her arms flapped about as she continued her tirade. It was not a pretty sight.

I knew right then that I wasn't going to die that night. God would never let me leave this body with that sight burned on my retinas.

I shackled TC's feet and sat him up on the corner of the bed. I screamed at the berserk woman to shut up or I would take her to jail, too. It was a total bluff. I dropped the clip out of his gun and ejected a round out of the chamber before throwing the weapon under the bed.

"Be cool, baby," TC said. "This motherfucker's crazy. Put on some clothes, cover yourself up."

"Please do," I said. "Just keep your hands where I can see them. Then sit over there and shut up." She put on a robe and sat in an overstuffed chair in the corner.

"What about me?" TC asked. "I got to put on some clothes."

"The bed sheet will do. I'll wrap it around you."

"That ain't right man," he said. "That ain't right."

I wrapped TC up like a mummy in the bed sheet and walked him into the living room. After placing him on his knees, I took down the spreader. I let him get up long enough to walk to the back door so I could retrieve the shin stopper. I then led him outside.

As expected, a neighborhood watch committee had gathered around the van. I lifted up his sheet and chained the door spreader and the shin stopper to TC's handcuffs. If things went south outside, he would have to try escape bare-assed and dragging about fifty pounds behind him.

Time to flush that little idea out of his head, just so he wouldn't start feeling more confident with his neighborhood watch around him.

TC jumped as he felt the cold muzzle of my 9mm pushed into the side of his neck. I wanted everybody to see it.

"If any shit starts, TC, you'll be the first one shot," I said quietly. "You feel where I got it? It's angled so the bullet will exit out the side after it breaks your neck below the C3 vertebra. It probably won't kill you but you'll be paralyzed from the neck down. Don't fuck up, TC, or you'll have to find somebody to wipe your ass for you for the rest of your life. Let's move."

As we made our way toward the van, the group of three started to spread out with their obvious leader staying with the vehicle. He stood like a general directing his troops on maneuvers. They all wore baggy pants and long oversized T-shirts that no doubt concealed weaponry. One of them took position at the top of the stairs as the other fanned out to what would have been a clear line of fire. This group worked in concert like a pack of wolves cornering prey.

For a second, I was mentally in the corner of the sparring ring in the dojo, with the three of them between me and the way out. Only now, the stakes were a lot higher.

"What it is, TC?" said the one at the van. "What it is, man?"

"Back off," TC yelled. "This motherfucker's crazy. Don't fuck with him."

"He ain't shit, man. What it is?"

"I fucking telling you," TC screeched. "You don't know what this motherfucker just did. Back off or I'll fuck you up when I get out."

I could feel TC starting to shake and halfway expected him to empty his bladder. He was trembling so much the chains were rattling. Just ten minutes earlier, TC had been skinny-dipping with his lady. Now he wasn't sure whether he was going to catch a bullet from me or from his buddies.

We continued toward the van and TC drooped from the weight he was carrying. "Hey, man," he said. "This shit weighing me down. The cuffs cutting into my wrists, man."

Reaching down with my left hand, I grabbed the chain and lightened his load as we kept walking and started up the steps to the van. The vigilant member of the local neighborhood watch standing at the top of the stairs started to ease his hand toward the front of his shirt.

Just then, one of the three men in the street said, "Five O." I turned my head slightly and saw two police cruisers turn the corner headed our way. The trio suddenly vanished into the darkness. I holstered my weapon and opened the electric side sliding door with the remote control. I sure was happy to see those blue beacons of light that rotated on top of the police cars and bounced off the surrounding buildings.

The officers got out of their vehicles and walked up and looked in the van as I secured TC in the back. "So you got TC," said a sergeant. "Who fired the shots?"

I looked around at him. "There weren't any shots fired, at least not here."

"We got a call reporting shots fired on this street."

TC chimed in. "This motherfucker's crazy, man. The son of a bitch stuck a gun in my neck, threatened to shoot my ass. Get me away from him, man."

The sergeant chuckled and looked around. "Yeah, TC, yeah, whatever." He turned back to me. "So which hole did you drag him out of?"

I pointed to the back door, which was still open, and told him about the woman inside. He sent the younger officer to check it out, who reported back that nobody was inside. The big gal had apparently made a stealthy escape out the front. Pretty impressive for a woman that size.

After the sergeant reported in on the radio, I followed them out of the projects. It was still about a half-hour drive to the county detention center. When I got there, vehicles loaded with prisoners were lined up waiting to get in the sally port. A paddy wagon was right in front of me and I knew it would be a while before it was my turn. The late night and early morning hours are usually a busy time here.

Finally, the large steel garage door rattled open and I drove into the sally port. Everybody stays in his vehicle until the door closes back and the area is secure. All the doors in the intake area are operated by master control and are computer interlocked to prevent more than one door at a time from being opened.

I handed the corrections officer my arrest report before opening the side door to get TC out of the van. The officer's eyes got wide when he saw TC wrapped in a sheet. "Looks like you got somebody out of bed."

TC didn't say a word. He knew that now was the time to keep his mouth shut.

TC knew the routine. He went straight to the wall by the desk and waited for the officers to remove the restraints. They removed the sheet and had him "assume the position" after taking off the cuffs and shackles and handing them to me. After a quick orifice search, the officers handed him back his sheet and led him away into the holding cell to await processing.

With receipt in hand, I got back in the van and waited for the exit door to the sally port to open. The door rattled open, revealing a hint of dawn approaching, and I drove off.

About ten minutes down the road, the cell phone rang. It was Peanut.

"Hey man, you got your boy."

"Yeah, Peanut. Your money will be waiting for you at the office."

"How about a little something extra for the effort?"

"What are you talking about?" I asked. "We have a set deal."

"I know, I know," he said. "But I was watching the whole time and I'm the one who called the law. They always come when somebody reports a shooting. You looked like you might be in a bind. I couldn't let anything happen to my man."

"I had it handled," I said. "But I guess you have it coming. I'll make sure you get a little extra this time." I knew he was more concerned about not getting his money if something had happened to me rather than my well being. In any case, it would be good insurance for later on down the road if I did find myself needing some help.

"Go by the office tomorrow afternoon, Peanut. It'll be waiting for you."

"Cool, man. Pleasure doing business with you. Later."

I called and left a message on Frank's voice mail and told him to have Peanut's money ready. Always pay your snitches—they're worth their weight in gold.

# four

Even the horrifying memory of TC's naked girlfriend couldn't distract me from the one thing that was on my mind constantly: our son, Joey, was coming home.

Joey is a Marine and at that time was assigned to the 15th Marine Expeditionary Unit embarked on the USS *Peleliu.* He'd made sergeant in only three years and had already decided to reenlist for another four. This week he was starting three weeks of leave just before a six-month deployment.

Life in the Marine Corps is tough, especially for a married couple. This would be Joey's second deployment. He'd missed last Christmas, the birth of his own son, and would be gone this Christmas as well. My grandson is the spitting image of his father, who is not only our only son, but also our only child.

During Joey's younger years, he'd turned to Debbie first with his problems. She was a natural as a consoling mother and it was her shoulder he cried on. I was the disciplinarian, especially during those trying teen years.

Sometimes her instinct to comfort clashed with my inclination to make Joey toe the line. We both wanted the same thing for him, and between our perspectives, we achieved some sort of balance. Joey has grown into a man who is comfortable in his own skin and knows who he is.

Over breakfast, Debbie and I made our plans to meet at home before going together to the airport to get Joey. Even though it was still two days before his arrival, our enthusiasm grew each time we went over the arrangements.

I was especially looking forward to taking Joey on a chase with me. He enjoyed the hunt as much as I did, but there was more to it than that. It gave us some time alone together and that was increasingly important to both of us.

Joey was no longer the child who ran first to his mother when he had something on his mind. He was married and had a child of his own. More and more often, he had things on his mind he didn't want Debbie to worry about, questions about the realities of married life, dealing with the prolonged absences and the normal growing pains of any relationship.

His duties in the Marine Corps were something else he didn't want Debbie worrying about. Joey was assigned to a TRAP (Tactical Recovery of Aircraft and Personnel) team responsible for rescuing downed pilots over enemy territory. We knew this deployment would take him to the Persian Gulf and that with combat missions overflying Iraq, there was a good chance he'd have to go in to pull out a few pilots. Little did we know what was to come in the following months.

Sometimes Debbie felt as if Joey were shutting her out, and it made her sad. In retrospect, I don't know which would have been tougher for her, worrying about him or her sadness over misjudging why he was being evasive.

I'd finished breakfast and was just about to walk out the door on my way to the office when my cell phone rang. The office phone stays forwarded to me and the caller ID showed me it was Ken Reynolds. I let it ring a few more times before answering it.

"Good morning Ken. How are you?"

Just-call-me-Ken paused, apparently caught off guard by my knowing who was calling. Finally he said, "Good morning Joe. I'm fine, thanks."

"What can I do for you?"

"I have a guy you might want to call. He's a reserve deputy with the sheriff's department up here. He has some information about the drug crowd that Wiley hangs with and thinks they may be hiding him out."

Ken told me the deputy's name was Homer and gave me a number to call. I took down the information before asking Ken the obvious question. "What does Homer want out of this?"

"Nothing. He just wants to help. Homer works the traffic crossing at the middle school in the area, so he sees a lot of people coming and going."

I let out a sigh. "Have you paid him any money?"

"Just a few bucks," Ken said. "He said he could meet you this afternoon after all the buses have left the school."

I thought for a minute and decided it might be worthwhile. With Joey's homecoming on my mind, I could use some easy work. How intense could interviewing a school crossing guard be? "Tell Homer I'll meet him at the middle school at four o'clock." Ken agreed and after I hung up I called Frank and told him I was going to Morristown.

I arrived at the middle school a little before three o'clock, in time to watch Homer in action directing traffic at the crosswalk. He was a short, scrawny little man. His shoulders were pulled up tight toward his ears and he was slightly hunched over. As each car approached his turf, he scampered into the street blowing his whistle and holding up a stop sign. His gait was jerky and unsure. He reminded me of a squirrel crossing the road that couldn't make up its mind which way to go.

There was a small badge pinned to his baggy shirt, which swallowed his thin frame. The tiny .32 revolver he wore holstered through a belt on his jeans looked almost like a toy. I wondered whether it was loaded or if he carried a single bullet buttoned in his shirt pocket. He was wearing a sheriff's department cap that was pulled down tight almost covering his eyes. His face was drawn so tight it almost looked like he had a permanent smile. You didn't have to study him long to realize he was not happy.

I got out of the van and waved at him once. He looked in my direction. He gestured back to acknowledge me, and I got back in the vehicle and waited for him to finish directing school traffic. After the last school bus pulled out, Homer walked across the street and got in his car, a white Ford Crown Victoria, clearly a retired police car sold at a county auction. It still had the spotlight fixed on the driver side door and the roof was rusted where the emergency lights were once mounted. He had a blue light, which was probably bought at surplus store, stuck up on the dash.

Homer lit a cigarette and started the car, then pulled a U-turn right in the middle of the road and sped up to where I was parked. So much for being discreet.

Homer pulled up right next to me and rolled his window down. "You the bounty hunter?"

I nodded. "I am."

"You can leave your van parked here and ride with me," he said. "I got something I want to show you. No need risking anybody seeing your vehicle." Homer raked a pile of clutter off the seat onto the floorboard to clear a place for me to sit on the passenger's side of the front seat.

Ah, Homer had a plan. That worried me a bit. "Where are we headed?" I asked as he put the car in gear and pulled away from the curb.

Homer glanced at me, but looked away to avoid eye contact as he spoke. "We're going to my daughter's house. I think Wiley is working for a fellow by the name of Red Crawford, making methamphetamine. Red made moonshine for years and got into the meth a few years ago. It's easier to make and get away with. I've been keeping an eye on him." His gaze kept darting back and forth as he talked and his hands fidgeted on the steering wheel as he lit another cigarette.

It suddenly occurred to me why Homer was getting involved. He was a reserve deputy. A wannabe. This was his chance to get into something big. Homer wasn't just snitching—he was working a case. I felt around behind me in the grimy car cushions for the seat belt.

We started to drive and his nervousness was making me uneasy about riding with him. I tried to make some small talk with the hope of getting him to relax. "So, Homer, you lived here all your life?"

"Sure have. My dad was a preacher. The church is next to my daughter's house. You'll see it."

"So, your folks are still around close?"

"No. My mother run off right after I was born. The old man raised me and my brothers. He died five years ago."

"That must have been hard for him," I said.

He started to get a little more unsettled and twisted in his seat as he spoke. "He made us toe the line all right. That's the trouble with young 'uns today—nobody takes a strap to them anymore. Yes, sir, too many crybabies these days."

Homer's face tightened even more and I decided it would be a good idea to change the subject. "What makes you think Wiley is working for Red Crawford?"

Homer lit another cigarette. "They worked together for Ken Reynolds. Wiley helped Red make moonshine and grow pot. Everybody knew that. Everybody except Ken. My brother saw Wiley and Red riding in Red's truck last week."

We pulled into the front yard of a white frame house with a large covered front porch. Next door to the house was a parking lot that led to a church. A driveway circled around the old brick building and back to the street.

On the other side of the driveway behind the church was a steep hill. Actually, it was the start of a one-hundred-yard climb that ended at the top of a wooded ridgeline. At the crest of the ridge was a five-strand barbed wire fence.

Homer shut off the car and looked around nervously. "My wife's car is here. Let's hurry inside so nobody sees you."

He opened the front door and we walked straight in. His wife and daughter were sitting on the sofa talking and suddenly went silent as we entered the room. The daughter looked as if she had been crying.

"What's the matter?" Homer asked.

"Nothing," his wife answered. "Woman talk."

The two women got up and went into a bedroom and closed the door behind them. Homer shook his head. "They grow up too fast. She used to be my little girl and would come running when she was upset. She and the wife fought like cats and dogs while she was younger. Now she don't even talk to me."

Although Homer's theories on child development were sure to be fascinating, I had work to do. "What did you want to show me?"

Homer walked over to a window and opened a curtain. "Red's farm starts at the top of that ridge behind the church on the other side of the fence line. He has about thirty acres over there. If you parked in the driveway behind the church, nobody could see you. Once you get to the top of the ridge you can look right down on Red's place. There's an old garage a few yards from the house. That's where I think they're making the meth."

"Why don't the local officers investigate it?" I asked.

"They haven't been able to get enough proof to go in. There's only one road into the farm and there's a gate that stays locked."

I looked at Homer. "Well, I don't need proof. Looks like I need to go exploring."

We hurriedly got back in Homer's car and he peeled out of the driveway. It was a cloudy day and it was darker than usual for that time of day.

Homer's driving had not gotten any better, and I was looking forward to getting back to the van. He had just lit another cigarette when I noticed his eyes darting back and forth to the rearview mirror.

He sat up straight in his seat and gritted his teeth. "That son of a bitch behind me has his bright lights on."

Before I could turn around and look, Homer slammed on his brakes. The car behind us almost rammed us.

I wasn't amused. "Damn, Homer. What the hell are you doing? Whatever happened to a little stealth here? This guy's not fucking with you."

Homer thought for a minute and stomped the accelerator. Our heads snapped back as we peeled off down the road. The driver of the car was making sure to stay well behind us, but Homer couldn't get the high beams off his brain.

He rolled down his window to toss out his cigarette and I saw an idea dawn on his face. It was the first time I saw anything but a tortured expression on Homer. He almost seemed to be smiling. While lighting another cigarette, Homer reached and flicked the switch that turned on the spotlight. Then he reached outside the window and tried to point the light toward the car behind us. If he hit the right angle, he'd blind the driver.

"Homer, what the fuck are you doing?"

He didn't hear me. The glazed look in his eyes told me I was in trouble. The spotlight would only turn so far and Homer was flashing cars coming down the road in the opposite direction. His face was turning red as he wrestled with the light. Each time he tried to jerk it around a little further, the car swerved. Once we stopped, I was going to choke the shit out of him.

Just then, we swerved again and my side of the car clipped a mailbox. The noise snapped Homer out of his daze and he let go of the spotlight. He hadn't even noticed that the car was no longer behind us. My guess was the other driver stopped to let the maniac in front of him go on down the road.

He pulled up next to my van and I got out without saying a word. I didn't trust myself enough to stay within striking range of him. When I slammed the passenger's side door, the loosened passenger side mirror fell to the ground. I started to pull away and he stuck his hand out his window to stop me. Against my better judgment, I rolled down my window to see what he wanted.

Homer leaned out the window. "I'll keep Red under surveillance and keep you advised. Let me know when you're coming up to recon the farm." I didn't say a word and threw up my hand as I drove off.

The big day was finally here. Our daughter-in-law and grandson had arrived weeks earlier, as Joey was on mini-training floats, which prepare the troops for the long time they will be aboard ship. We all met at the airport and were waiting at the gate when he got off the plane.

I spotted Joey in the crowd long before I could see his face. He has a natural confidence in his walk. His wife and child ran to him and the reunion was long overdue. Debbie hung back until those hugs and kisses were exchanged then she threw herself at him. Then it was my turn to wait.

It was nice to have a full house. Things felt comfortable. It was like going back in time to when we were raising a family. But then again, we still were.

Debbie had taken off from work for a week and was content cooking in the kitchen and visiting with the kids. My grandson, who was just approaching his second birthday, decided he didn't like a particular dish and opted to deposit it on the floor. Joey took exception to this behavior.

"Take it easy on the boy," I said. "He's still just a baby."

Joey looked up at me, not believing he heard what he heard. It was just then I realized that the mother and father role reversals were more than just the child growing older. So was I.

With some coaxing, Joey agreed to accompany me to the dojo for a workout. He had started in karate at the age of eight and was promoted to black belt at twelve. Debbie was also a black belt under Grand Master Harold Long, and much of our time spent together as a family was in the dojo.

Our household in those days could have been taken from the script of one of the old *Pink Panther* movies staring Peter Sellers. Just like Inspector Clouseau's servant Kato, whose job it was to spring surprise attacks at unexpected times, our home was definitely a place to stay on your toes. Nobody was above or beneath setting traps and launching sneak attacks.

Our recreation as a family unit might seem violent to some, but it was in fun and nobody got seriously hurt. It was only after we progressed to weapons training that we decided to tone things down at the home front. It wasn't that we were hurting each other—I just got tired of hauling destroyed furniture down to the dump.

Joey was about to be separated from his family for six months and he had his own priorities, but he knew how much going to the dojo with him meant to me. As he dug out his old gi and black belt, I could see him getting a little more enthused.

I was surprised his gi still fit him. Joey had bulked up quite a bit from weightlifting. He had stayed active in karate up until his middle teens, when he got involved in sports as well as the other distractions that occupy a young man's mind. He kept working out but not on a consistent basis. Debbie continued to teach and train up until her arthritic back and hands prevented her from being able to spar.

We bowed in and I introduced my son to the junior belts. My black belts already knew Joey and they'd all sparred him from time to time when he was in town. We warmed up a little and worked on a couple of katas. He had to think a little at first but the movements quickly came back to him.

Practice does *not* make perfect—*perfect* practice makes perfect. That's the reason the first repetitive movements a karate student learns are so simple. You're working to eradicate the bad movements before moving on to instilling the right way to move. Only after you've performed enough repetitions of correct movements to cancel out the bad habits can you really start to learn.

The younger you are when you start to learn to move correctly, the fewer bad habits you have to overcome. I can almost always tell when someone has started martial arts training at a young age. Kids who start young, like Joey or my senior black belt, who started with me when he was eleven, have fewer bad habits to unlearn.

This doesn't just apply to karate. Think of an adult you know who has bad posture. Telling him not to slouch might make him momentarily straighten up, but it would take a conscious mental effort on his part. By the time he's an adult, he's done too many repetitions the wrong way. He's practiced bad posture too long to easily correct it. Now, if someone had started him off properly when he was a child, it would have taken far fewer repetitions to eliminate the negative and instill the correct posture.

Despite his early training, Joey hadn't been a regular in any dojo for a while. I knew his timing and his control would be off, so I decided that he'd spar only with my other black belts. No point in anyone getting hurt, not when we had so little time together.

I paired him up with Steve, who was a relatively new black belt. Steve is fast and takes no prisoners in sparring. He's also tough and I knew he'd provide the right amount of challenge for Joey while still being able to take whatever Joey dished out.

The two combatants bowed to each other and I started the match. Joey stepped back with his right foot into *seisan* stance, which loaded his power hand. This was home to him, a safe place. They circled, sizing each other up. Joey could tell that his timing was off and decided to stay put and counter Steve's attacks for a while instead of initiating them himself.

He should have known better, especially against one of *my* black belts. Steve stepped in and threw a lightning-fast back fist aimed at Joey's head. Joey blocked it but left his midsection open. I could see the follow-up technique coming even before Steve threw it, a reverse punch to the ribs. There was a solid *thump* as Steve's knuckles found their target. Joey and Steve touched fists and nodded to each other, acknowledging the hit. Joey would have a bruise the next day to remind him of what he should have remembered—that the first technique was usually intended to set up the second one.

Bruises aren't uncommon in my dojo, although I know many dojos that allow little or no actual contact during sparring. But Isshinryu karate training, when taught the way it was meant to be taught, hardens the body and turns it into a weapon.

Many schools have abandoned that philosophy, primarily for commercial reasons. It's difficult enough to find people who are willing to work out hard and break a sweat on a consistent basis. When you add bruising, banging, and bleeding to the mix, the field of those willing to participate narrows down considerably.

But sacrificing traditional training to make a profit is a treacherous mistake. The ability to withstand being hit is a vital part of martial arts training. Real karate operates on a completely different level than just some self-defense class. A martial artist trains to fight other martial artists. Odds are there will be licks swapped between the fighters. Sometimes it boils down to just one left standing.

Joey had learned that when he was young, and while he undoubtedly felt Steve's punch, he didn't let it affect him. Well, except that he was irritated at being scored on.

With the first contact out of the way, both men started to relax a bit. The pace quickened. Short combinations of one or two punches or kicks gave way to hard sparring. They closed in on each other and fired off combination after combination, testing each other, probing for weaknesses, taking advantage of openings almost before they were there. The whack of forearms blocking punches and the thud of knees jamming kicks were interspersed with solid thumping sounds as techniques slipped past the blocks and scored.

The match took on its own rhythm, its own life. Both men quit planning their moves, emptied their thoughts, and let training and instinct dictate their moves. Like a dance, the two fighters moved in violent concert. Sweat ran down their faces and their soaked gi jackets clung to their backs. They gazed at each other through swelled eyes and blood trickled from cut lips as they exchanged attacks.

Then Joey threw a hard roundhouse kick. It connected with Steve's knee. Even the white belts across the room, supposedly practicing kata but really trying to watch without looking like they were watching, heard that distinctive crack of a bone breaking.

The pain in his foot woke Joey from the trancelike state he'd been in. His expression changed and I was gratified by what I saw. His timing might be off, he might have forgotten a few moves in his katas, but there was one thing he knew for certain.

You've got two choices when you get hurt: you quit or you get mean.

Most large commercial schools won't go down the road that leads to understanding that fundamental principle. The reason is that most people will quit when faced with the reality of true martial arts training. You don't make a lot of bank deposits if you can't keep enough students to pay the bills.

By most modern standards, the retention rate at the Steel Hand Dojo is appalling. Corporate bean counters would be horrified by how many people quit when the sparring gets serious.

That's fine with me. The people who stay can fight.

Joey grew up training the hard way. He knew how to get mean. (Of course, in his case, he does have a slight genetic predisposition for that particular trait.)

Joey's face grimaced as he set down his injured foot and then his expression changed. I'd seen that look before, the one where emotion fades from his face except for his eyes. The intensity and fire in his eyes could have burned a hole through steel. His shoulders settled down as he slowly exhaled and consciously relaxed. I knew what was coming next.

All at once, Joey exploded, unleashing a barrage of hard, powerful techniques. The onslaught sent Steve reeling into the corner, struggling to cover up as a furious series of punches smashed through his attempted blocks.

Joey changed pace, catching Steve with a foot sweep and knocking him off balance. Steve stumbled, which threw his head forward, lining it up perfectly for an already-chambered punch. I saw it coming and so did Steve. His eyes widened as what was actually just a split second must have seemed like an eternity. He was staring at a loaded fist, and there was nothing he could do about it.

Joey fired the punch in hard and—just as quickly—pulled it short. Steve nodded in appreciation of Joey's control. They bowed to each other and embraced.

There is nothing quite like the respect and admiration that two warriors have for each other after a hard contest of skill. Both men were spent.

Several minutes before, the junior-ranked belts had given up all pretense of doing anything else and had clustered around the edge of the ring, moving around occasionally for a better view. They all learned something from watching the match, and even the youngest and juniormost belts knew enough to appreciate what they'd seen. The ability to launch a vicious retaliation and curb it with control at the appropriate time showed balance. For junior belts, what Joey and Steve did was almost like magic. The more senior belts could almost taste the time they'd be sparring at that level themselves.

Joey was limping as we started to leave the dojo. I said, "Let me see your toe."

He stuck out his foot then immediately pulled it back as he looked at me. "I don't think so."

Ah-ha, something else he remembered: my fondness for checking for broken bones by wiggling the injured part. Almost everyone in my dojo knows better than to admit that something hurts, and the ones who don't learn that lesson quickly. There's nothing like poking on a bruise to make it feel better after I quit.

I laughed as I turned out the lights. "Let's go home and ice it down," I said, suggesting my standard remedy for just about every training injury.

Joey and his family stayed with us the first week he was back. They were now about to share some time with my daughter-in-law's family, who live in the next county. Before they left, Joey wanted to go on a chase with me. I had already pulled a case file that wouldn't take us far from home, and we planned to go hunting his last day here.

Her street name was Peach and she was a prostitute. Peach was a repeat customer. We'd bonded her out a number of times and this was not the first time she had failed to appear. It was, however, the first time she hadn't turned herself in after missing a court date.

After they're arrested, prostitutes usually spend a couple of days in jail and then bond out. They show up for their court date and plead guilty and are sentenced to time served. It's just business, an occupational hazard.

Sometimes they're so high on drugs when they're arrested that they don't even know what day it is, much less when they're supposed to be back in court. But when they do sober up and realize that they missed their hearing, they usually turn themselves in. For them, going to jail is just a normal part of life, and the last thing they want to do is upset their bondsman. Once that happens, no bonding company will take a chance on them, and being locked up puts a damper on their business. Either way, they're not usually skips.

The few who do run are a pain to catch. Bonds for prostitution are low, so it's not cost effective to spend much time looking for them. Since they stay someplace different almost every night, they're hard to find. They're not hiding from me—it's just their lifestyle.

The normal tactics for finding them don't work well. Most of them have cut all ties with their families. Fact is, most prostitutes ran away from abusive homes when they were young and survived on the street the best way they could. Every single prostitute I've dealt with was sexually abused as a child. They live in a constant state of imbalance because their perception of life was warped early on.

Since they normally aren't in contact with their families, prostitutes use other prostitutes for their references on their bonding applications. Same problems finding them.

On the other hand, prostitutes make decent enough snitches. Given what else they'll do for twenty bucks, snitching is no big deal.

While most of the information I get from prostitutes is reliable, it's a question of timeliness. In cases that involve other prostitutes, the hooker is usually gone by the time I get there. Given the low bail amounts and the degree of difficulty, it's usually not worth my time to track down a prostitute who's skipped bail.

But this case was slightly different. Peach's pimp was a charming fellow nicknamed "Kid." He'd jumped a ten-thousand-dollar bond held by another bail company, and they were looking for him. I called the other company and they agreed to pay my fee if I caught their man. That made Peach worth looking for.

Kid had been in and out of the penitentiary since he was seventeen. He had joined the Aryan Brotherhood while in prison. To say he had violent tendencies would be an understatement. His professional resume included numerous weapons charges, robberies, and assaults. Needless to say, we considered Kid to be armed and dangerous. I'd be prepared when I met him.

If you want to cruise Knoxville looking for paid companionship, Magnolia Avenue is the place to start. The four-lane road starts a downtown run for four or five miles past the zoo and into East Knoxville. Then it splits and heads into suburbia.

There's too much police presence on Magnolia itself, so most of the hookers offer their wares along the side streets and alleys that run off Magnolia. Along these back streets and side roads, you'll find the crack houses that these people use as temporary residences.

Joey and I packed up our gear and drove downtown. I'd already decided that we'd wait in a parking lot where Magnolia intersects with downtown. It's sort of like having a favorite fishing spot on a creek. The parking lot has two exits, which would keep us from getting trapped.

More important, most of the folks cruising Magnolia would have to pass right by us. It was a good place to stop and check our gear before we started hitting the side streets.

I had pictures of Peach and Kid clipped to the dash for quick reference. Peach was a skinny blonde in her early twenties, but she looked much older. Years of smoking crack gave her a haggard look. She had a tattoo of a rose on her left calf.

Kid's head was shaved and he was six feet and about 175 pounds. He had a heart with the initials "AB" in it with daggers through it tattooed on his left shoulder and a swastika on his right forearm. Other Aryan Brotherhood symbols covered his body, but I was only concerned with the ones that were visible.

After we were assured that our gear was in order, we pulled out of the lot slowly and drove down Magnolia. Joey had an Ithaca model 37 12-gauge shotgun with a pistol grip stock held between his knees. It was loaded with alternating 00 magnum buckshot and number one buck. He had one shell chambered, with seven more rounds in the magazine. Strapped to the shotgun was a sling that held another thirty rounds.

I had my trusty 9mm, which had a fifteen-round clip and one in the chamber. There were two extra magazines that held fifteen rounds each on my belt. The equipment bag in the back seat held several more boxes of ammunition, along with chemical agents and other various tools of destruction. We had enough armament to start a small war.

It was a beautiful day. The sun was out and there was a slight breeze. It would be getting hot later, and midday heat always chases the crackheads inside. They disappear from late morning until sunset.

I drove at a snail's pace down Magnolia. Joey looked down the side streets to the right and I kept an eye on the ones to the left.

How many dads get to drive down a city street with their sons while heavily armed and looking for trouble? Legally, I mean. Life just doesn't get any better than that.

We'd checked out about two blocks of side streets when I noticed a red Ford F-150 4x4 pickup truck barreling down on us from behind. It was jacked up with over-sized tires and chromed out from top to bottom, including a roll bar. A decal spelled out FORD in huge letters across the top of the dark tinted windshield. The driver slammed on the brakes just as he got to my rear bumper.

We continued down the road at about ten miles an hour, still checking out side streets. The red Ford truck stayed glued to my bumper, the chromed grill filling my rearview mirror. The oversized tires elevated him considerably, and the sun glinted off the chrome grill pipes through my back window.

It wasn't like he couldn't have passed us. We were on a four-lane road and there was very little traffic. Nobody was in the lane next to me. We were going so slow he could have gotten out and walked past us.

Joey occasionally glanced at the rearview mirror but otherwise stayed focused on the side streets along the right side of the road. I tried to watch the left while still watching for signs of trouble from the truck behind me. It bothered me that I couldn't see the driver at all.

This kept up for about a mile, then this idiot started swerving back and forth. He would dart out into the passing lane then back behind me. Each time he swerved, he came closer and closer to my rear bumper. It was becoming increasingly difficult to concentrate watching the side streets and other traffic.

Was it someone I'd arrested in the past? My van was fairly well known in the area, and I've caught a lot of people in this section of town. Most of my skips don't hold a grudge, but I have had a few reunions that weren't cordial.

This kept up the entire length of Magnolia Avenue. Big Red stayed glued to my bumper, even when we stopped at traffic lights.

When we finally reached the point at which Magnolia split, the truck pulled to the left and eased up slowly along the driver's side. I shot Joey a look—I didn't have to tell him what to do. He crawled into the back of the van, unlocked the side door, and placed his hand on the handle in case he needed to quickly slide it open.

The truck inched forward. I heard Joey click off the safety on the shotgun. I took my weapon out of the holster and placed it on my lap. Only then did I roll down my window.

Just then, the passenger-side window of the truck rolled down and a man with a head full of gray hair leaned over from the driver's side of the truck and gave me the one-finger salute. His face was beet-red and he was screaming at the top of his lungs. "You shouldn't be on the road you damn idiot. I ought to kick your fucking ass."

He spun his tires and sped off down the left fork of the road. I looked back at Joey and we both burst out laughing.

I pulled over into a parking lot and Joey got back in the front seat. We both shook our heads and laughed some more. Without further incident, we made a few more passes up and down Magnolia until it started to get hot and we called it a day.

Joey's visits always go too quickly, and knowing I would not see him for at least six months made me want to hang on to every second. He and his family spent their last two nights in Tennessee at our house and we drove them to the airport. Our daughter-in-law and grandson were staying here with her parents while he was deployed. The women were crying as Joey and I hugged goodbye. Debbie took a picture of our grandson waving goodbye to his father as he boarded the plane.

The house was far too empty when we got home. Despite my resolution to take some time off, I decided to go into the office for a while.

There was a message waiting for me from Kid's bonding company. He was in jail in middle Tennessee, charged with murder. I called the officer on the case.

No point in looking for Peach. She'd been brutally beaten to death and her body left in a sleazy hotel room. I erased her name off my chase board. Kid and Peach were about the same age as Joey and his wife.

I wished I had found her in time. Now her life was worth nothing more than the death certificate I had to turn in to the court to relieve us of her bond.

The next morning found me up early. My preliminary hearing in Greeneville was set for nine o'clock that morning. Answering Betty Fisk's complaint that I'd roughed her up while arresting her son, Leon, was more than just annoyance—I had better things to do than sit in a courtroom all day. The only bright spot in the day was remembering how Leon ran into the tree, but even that didn't make up for the fact that I had better things to do than drive to Greeneville and listen to her lie.

Like I said, the truth has a funny way of coming out the same each time you tell it. There was no doubt in my mind what the outcome of the hearing would be.

After making the hour and a half drive to Greeneville, I parked behind the courthouse. The front steps ended at a large oak door. The door was open and led into a lobby. Trails worn in the wooden planks of the floor led to county clerks and other offices.

In the middle of the lobby was another flight of stairs with thick oak casings and handrails. The stairs were solid but the years of traffic caused the steps to groan like an old man in pain as I made my way up toward the courtrooms.

I spotted my attorney, Sherman Shikes, waiting at the top of the stairs. He's a tall man, lanky, and he stays in shape putting miles and miles on his road bike. He's got a full head of hair streaked gray along the sides, a wide grin, and a firm handshake. His eyes pierce you as he talks and he can go from friendly interest to stabbing inquisition in the space of a second. He's a natural-born politician who radiates that intangible quantity known as presence. He walks into a room, everyone notices him.

Sherman was a hot commodity these days and was known as one of the best criminal defense attorneys in several counties, with good reason. He'd just gotten an acquittal for his client in a widely publicized murder case in Sevier County. Sherman represented clients in many high-profile cases both in state and federal court. He's not only good—he likes winning. Has to, no matter whether he's trying a case or riding his road bike.

Sherman didn't come cheap. As I've said, Frank was a good man to work for.

I've known Sherman for a long time. Back when I was a deputy sheriff in Sevier County, we were on opposite sides of the fence, so there's always an underlying note of good-natured competitiveness between us. I like to remind him that he lost or pleaded every time he represented someone I'd arrested. Conversely, he'd remind me that he made more money than anybody did, no matter which way the verdict went.

As I approached, I saw Sherman slap what I took to be another lawyer on the back. "See you in court, Judge," he said.

I waited until the judge was out of earshot, then asked, "Was that my judge? Hey, nice suit."

Sherman gave me a squinty look, acknowledging my smart-ass tone. "Yeah that was *your* judge. And thanks, it's merino wool."

I looked over his shoulder at the stairs and saw Betty Fisk entering the courtroom. Something in my expression must have changed, because Sherman moved to position himself to block my view of her. "Is that the woman who took out the warrants?" he asked.

Betty looked like she'd been dragged through a catfight. She sported a shiner and her face was scratched all over. Her Coors Light T-shirt hung down to her thighs, covering up some of her soiled jeans. The smoke from her cigarette clouded up around her uncombed hair and reminded me of foggy swamp.

"Yeah, that's the bitch," I said. "I don't see her worthless son, though."

Sherman grabbed my arm and pulled me to the side so that our backs were to her. "I know how pissed off you are about having to come up here over this bullshit. But I'm telling you—don't even look at her. You let me do *all* the talking."

I smiled at him. "Whatever you say, Sherm. You're the only one making any money today."

I did as instructed and sat down in a chair in the back of the courtroom away from everybody else. The first thing I did was check out the other people in the courtroom to see if there was anyone there I'd arrested before. Lucky me—no old clients, just potential new ones.

The courtroom door opened and a man walked in carrying a satchel full of papers. His coat barely hung on at the shoulders and his tie was off to the side, exposing strained buttons trying to hold in a mammoth belly. His hair looked as though it hadn't been combed in a week and there were gravy stains on his shirt.

The man walked over to Sherman and shook his hand. Then Sherman motioned me to come over and told me what I had already surmised. "Joe, this is Phil Canter, the Assistant Attorney General handling this case."

I could feel Sherman start to work his magic. He moved a little closer to Canter and put a collegial hand on Phil's shoulder. His smile was so warm you'd have thought it was genuine. "What are we going to do with this case?"

Canter didn't look up as he rooted through his satchel of papers. He'd evidently dealt with Sherman often enough to know to avoid the magic. "Missus Fisk claims your client kicked in her door and knocked her and her grandchildren up against the wall and chased her son down and beat him up. We don't put up with that in this county. No, sir."

Ah, now I had it. A little self-righteous indignation to counter Sherman's magic.

The faintly amused expression on Sherman's face told me this wasn't the first time he'd kicked Canter's ass in court, and it wasn't going to be the last. In fact, Sherman was looking forward to it.

I wasn't as amused by the exchange. Between Joey's deployment, Peach's death, and the wasted day, I was in no mood to watch attorneys play power games.

It must have shown in my face. Sherman grabbed my arm and pulled back a little. While there was no way he could make me move if I didn't want to, it was his turf, not mine. I headed back to a corner of the courtroom and sat down and shut up.

In a few minutes Sherman sauntered over to me, his confidence evident in the way he moved. "Canter agreed to my motion to waive a grand jury and try the case right now. We let this judge decide, here and now." Sherman's voice was smug so I knew something was up. He confirmed my suspicion when he said, "I haven't told him yet that I have copies of the 911 tape of the call from the Fisk house the day of the arrest. It completely backs up your story."

Good old Sherm. I kept my poker face as I looked at him. "You're the man. I can't wait to see that lying bitch squirm on the stand when you cross-examine her."

The court was called into session and we sat through the calling of the docket. Quick pleas and announcements were followed by a ten-minute recess.

Sherman informed me we were next up. We took our place at the defense table. Canter and Fisk sat on the prosecution side.

Everyone in the courtroom stood as the judge entered, then took a seat on the bailiff's command. The judge settled into his tall chair behind the elevated bench and said, "Okay, people, let's hear it."

Sherman stood. "Your Honor, the State has agreed to try the case today."

"Is that right?" The judge seemed amused as he surveyed Canter and Betty sitting at the other table. I don't know if he couldn't believe the prosecution had agreed to the motion or was looking at the contrast between the two tables. Betty was not a stranger to this court.

"Yes, Your Honor," Canter answered. "We're ready to proceed."

"Your Honor, I think I can save the court some time, if you'll allow me." Sherman held up a cassette tape. "This is a tape of the 911 call originally made by the complainant that day. If I could have a moment to set up my tape player, I think we can resolve this matter quickly."

The judge nodded, the amused expression on his face growing more pronounced. Betty might not be a stranger in his courtroom, but neither was Sherman.

It took Canter a little longer to catch on, but then he lumbered to his feet. "Your Honor, I object! We're not aware of any tape."

"If it please the court, we've got no objection to a short recess to allow the prosecution to hear the tape. Since counsel has already agreed to try the matter today..." Sherman just couldn't resist rubbing it in just a bit more.

I was impressed. If Sherman had disclosed the tape earlier, Canter might not have agreed to try the case today. Then this would have just been a preliminary hearing. All Canter would have to have proved was probable cause, a much lighter burden of proof, your basic legal slam dunk. Then the matter would have been bound over to a grand jury. As it was, Canter had screwed himself.

The judge granted a recess and Sherman and Canter took the tape over to the 911 dispatch office next door to listen to it. Betty and I waited and I tried to avoid giving the bitch the look of death.

Half an hour later, the door to the dispatch office opened. Sherman had lost none of his bouncy confidence while Canter looked even more disheveled than before. Canter motioned abruptly to his client, the much-aggrieved and cruelly assaulted Missus Fisk, and she followed him into a vacant office. A few minutes later they came out and Canter spoke briefly to Sherman, who then motioned me to join them.

Canter looked on as Sherman spoke. "The State has agreed to drop charges. Betty Fisk has decided not to proceed with the complaint if you are willing to agree that you won't sue her."

I stiffened. That wasn't winning, not in my book. "Agree not to sue? I want to prosecute the bitch for perjury. I want her on the stand!"

Sherman interrupted me. "You want to get this over with today or you want to keep coming up here for more court dates? The court will dismiss charges today and the State has no objections to an expungement order."

I knew he was right and was a little embarrassed that even Canter seemed to be impatiently waiting for me to accept the obvious. It was a win, even if it wasn't the win I wanted. "Okay, let's get it over with. Anything to get the hell out of here."

The court was called back into session and all charges were dismissed. The judge signed an expungement order, which basically meant that the day never happened.

Of course, making a whole day disappear doesn't come cheap. The fact that it never happened didn't keep Sherman from sending Frank a hefty bill.

# five

With Betty Fisk and her progeny off my calendar and out of my life, I went back to my routine. What goes around, comes around. If there was any justice in the world, Missus Fisk herself would someday show up on my chase board. I doubted she was any smarter than her son was.

I started off the week catching up on paperwork and updating the chase board to reflect the current status of my runners. A couple of names were removed because the law caught them. With the last of the photos scanned, my final entry into the database brought my arrest total to nine hundred seventeen.

One recent skip had a really good reason for missing court: he died. I'll take that as a valid excuse.

I confirmed the death with the funeral home and then made a note to check with the health department in about a month and get a copy of the death certificate. It doesn't matter what shape I find them. Once I give the court the death certificate, we're off the bond and I turn in the receipt to get paid. Compared to a live body, hauling paper is easy. It also beats bringing a skip in tied facedown across the back of a horse like in the old days.

Just as I was about to forward all incoming chase calls to my cell phone, my office phone rang. It was Homer, my Barney Fife buddy in Morristown.

"Joe. Homer here. Is the line secure?" he whispered.

I sighed and shook my head. Did he really think Red and Wiley knew a lot about wiretapping? "Yeah, Homer, it's cool. What's up?"

Evidently Homer was not convinced. Either that or he thought that whispering would keep his identity a secret. I could barely hear him as he continued. "Wiley was seen with Red yesterday. They were picking up old car batteries—had a whole pickup-truck load. I was also told they had containers of denatured alcohol."

Interesting. That was a partial list of ingredients for making methamphetamine. "Who saw Wiley?" I asked.

"I can't tell you. Those people would kill me or whoever gets in the way of them making that shit. I tell you, Red is hiding Wiley and they're making the stuff."

"You think they're making it at Red's place?" I asked. "The place behind the church you showed me?"

Homer was slow to answer. "Yeah, that's the place, behind the church, right next to my daughter's house. You could sneak up behind the church and look down on his whole place. The only other way is to drive up the one road into the holler. They would see you coming that way, though."

I figured I already knew the answer to my next question, but as a decent, law-abiding citizen, I had to ask. "Why haven't you told the law, Homer? You're a part-time deputy. Why not make some points?"

Homer's voice cracked. "Shit, who do you think's protecting him? There's too much money involved. As soon as I told anybody, my daughter's house would be burned down and no telling what else."

Now that sounded a whole lot more likely than my phone line being tapped. As much as Homer was a pain the ass, he had provided some useful information and I didn't want him spooked. "Settle down, Homer," I said. "This will stay between me and you. I'll get back to you in a day or two. I need to check out some things." I wasn't about to tell Homer that I intended to do a little recon at Red's place.

I decided to drive an older-model white van to check out Red's, one that wouldn't draw attention if I left it parked unattended behind the church. The van looked like the sort that would belong to someone in the area. It even had a rack on the front for holding those orange cones that workers put in the street for barriers. A hard hat sat perched on the dash and the top of the van sported a ladder rack.

I had used this particular vehicular disguise many times and found that realistic work vans didn't arouse suspicion in most neighborhoods.

People see them, think they look familiar, and vaguely remember hearing that some sort of work was going to be going on. Even so, this would be the only time I would drive it up there, in case people started watching for it later.

Having the right vehicular disguise gives me a lot more flexibility, too. With a work van parked right under me and the right work clothes, I can get out and stare at telephone or electrical poles—or anything else handy—and pretend to jot down a few notes. The same technique works really well for getting a close look at license plate numbers. Once I even had the skip I was watching mosey right on up and ask me what I was doing. I love the easy ones.

I pulled around to the back of the church and parked the van. My fashionably soiled work coveralls were zipped up to cover the Glock in my belly holster. A Caterpillar cap, sunglasses, and work boots completed the wardrobe. Every disguise requires just the right accessories, too. I had a pair of compact binoculars hanging around my neck as an accessory. The finishing touch was the set of handcuffs in my hip pocket.

Red's property started along the top of a ridgeline behind the church. The one-hundred-yard steep climb to the top was complicated by slick mud, the result of a recent rain.

A well-maintained fence running along the ridgeline marked Red's property line. The five strands of barbed wire were pulled tight and there were no gaps in the fence. The thick cedar posts, some with bark still on them, were planted deep. Large orange and black "No Trespassing" signs were posted every fifty feet.

There was a large oak tree near the top of the slope, and I stayed low behind it while I looked and listened for several minutes. A rough dirt road ran the entire perimeter of the property along the fence line. Thick woods on the other side of the road provided good cover for me once I crossed onto Red's property.

I placed my hands between the barbs and pressed the tightly stretched top wire of the fence down as far as I could. I threw one leg over the fence. My feet barely touched the ground on the other side. Standing on my tiptoes with a wire pulled tight as a banjo string between my legs was not a position I wanted to stay in long. I hiked my other leg over the fence and turned the wire loose. The wire snapped back into position when I released it.

I quickly got off the exposed road and went a few yards into the woods. The trees were thick but not so dense that I couldn't move through them. I walked parallel to the road, just inside the cover of the trees.

Stealth was the order of the day. I made slow progress, stopping often to crouch down nearer to the road and look and listen. Being detected would mean spooking Wiley—or, even worse, getting shot.

Ahead of me, I saw a wide clearing in the woods. A large hole had been dug in the middle of it, on this side of the road. As I got closer to the hole, I could see what looked like the top of several truck passenger compartments. It turned out to be five new pickup trucks of various models. They were all up on blocks and their tires had been removed.

Somebody had gone to a lot of trouble, digging a hole big enough to hide five trucks. I wondered why.

I scanned the area for several minutes to make sure no one else was around, then ventured out of the safety of the woods. The ground was rippled with bulldozer tracks, which made the footing uneven. A narrow driveway led into the man-made crater.

None of the trucks had tags and the identification numbers on the dashboards had all been removed. In fact, the entire dashboard had been removed from some while others just had various parts and pieces stripped from them. It looked like Red, ever an enterprising soul, had gone into the auto parts business.

Another thing that caught my eye were the empty Copenhagen tobacco and Natural Ice beer cans littering the beds of some of the trucks—Wiley's trademarks.

Moving on, I climbed out the opposite side of the hole and continued to make my way through the woods, paralleling the road. The terrain started to slope as the road wound its way down the ridge into a hollow. I was looking down into a clearing. Two houses and a trailer sat at the end of a long dirt drive. There was also a barn with a large pond next to it and what looked like a garage on the other side of the barn. The garage's two tall doors were open. I could hear faint voices but couldn't tell from which building they were coming. A gate barred access from the main road.

I sat down behind some thick cover and pulled out my binoculars to get a closer look at the buildings. Just then the wind shifted, bringing with it an all-too-familiar putrid odor. Once you smell a meth lab, you never forget the stench.

Making methamphetamine is a dangerous business. Some of the individual ingredients that make up meth are highly explosive. Many meth labs have gone up in flames along with their self-appointed pharmacists. When drug agents raid meth labs, HazMat crews go in right behind law enforcement officers.

The stolen vehicles, the meth lab, and no telling what else—it was all adding up to a high-dollar operation. Red was also known to make moonshine and grow pot. Because of the kind of money involved, I had to be careful who I told about this. There are many good officers in this area of the state, but an operation this size most likely had a lot of people on the take, including a couple of police officers. Hell, everybody around here was related by blood or marriage, anyway. As much as I wanted to see the place busted, there was nothing to be gained by spooking Wiley or letting Red find out they were being watched.

The sounds of leaves rustling on the ground, faint but getting louder, got my attention. The terrain made it difficult to tell which direction the sounds were coming from, but the noise seemed to be heading up the hill toward me.

I stayed low and froze, scanning the area, looking for any sign of movement. The sounds got louder.

Then I spotted them: two blue tick hounds were wandering aimlessly toward me, sniffing the ground in a desultory fashion. Suddenly, one of them stopped abruptly and stuck his nose in the air.

I love dogs, but sometimes they're a pain in the ass. There's nothing like sneaking over a fence and finding yourself face to face with a pit bull or having a yard full of yapping mutts wake up my skip.

The one who'd scented me started moving again, slowly and purposefully now. The short bursts of air sounded like air pistons as they rushed through his nostrils while he scanned the light wind. The other dog picked up on what his buddy was doing and started scenting the air as well.

Suddenly they both froze. In unison, they both let out a loud and continuous bellow that bounced off the trees and echoed back down the hollow.

I didn't wait to see if the racket brought any reaction from the homestead. I stayed low and darted deeper into the woods, heading back toward the road and the fence line. I was covering ground quickly, but not running, which allowed me to listen for any approaching sounds. The dogs were more mouth than bite as they showed no inclination to follow me.

In short order I was back across the road and over the barbed wire fence. The terrain was steep going down to the van. I kept my feet planted sideways on the slope, allowing them to dig in and control my descent as I hurled myself down the hill.

There was no way anyone from the hollow could make it up the ridge before I would be long gone. For all they knew, the dogs might have jumped a rabbit.

Once I was on level ground, I broke into a run, clicking the remote control to the van to unlock the doors while I was in full stride. I was in the van and driving down the road within minutes.

While I hadn't caught Wiley, the trip had been well worthwhile. Knowledge is power, and now I knew a lot more about what I was facing. No, I didn't know for sure that Wiley was there, but things were starting to add up. There was a lot of illegal money being made in that hollow and nobody could be trusted. The job now was to figure out a way to smoke Wiley out, or at least to find out for sure if he was there. If he was there, he would be holed up a while. He would feel well hidden and secure in his illicit occupation. Despite my visit from the blue tick hounds, I was pretty certain he didn't know he was being watched.

Many of the spur-of-the-moment lessons I teach in the dojo are inspired by the events of the day. Sometimes I'm teaching a technique that worked well—sometimes one that didn't. Other times, the lesson is on awareness or on using the environment, both of which are important parts of any basic self-defense class.

It's hard to beat field testing as a way of proving the effectiveness of a technique, even though I'm getting too old for trial and error. New ideas are good, but it's hard to abandon the tried and true. The interesting parallel is that I teach techniques, tactics, and awareness from the perspective of the stalker. After all, that's my job.

The terrain surrounding Red's place was still on my mind as I drove to the dojo and pulled into the parking lot. In our system of karate we have an empty-hands form, or kata, known as *Chinto,* not to be confused with the religion *Shinto.* Chinto kata teaches maneuvering and fighting on hillsides and other uneven surfaces. On the street, the lessons taught in Chinto can be applied to curbs, stairs, and other urban obstacles.

Legend has it that the kata is named after a Chinese sailor who was shipwrecked on Okinawa. He lived in the caves that dotted a bluff overlooking a village and would sneak down at night and steal food from the villagers. Complaints to the authorities resulted in some of the best martial artists on Okinawa being sent to confront the thief. Each confrontation occurred on the side of the hill and, one by one, the Chinese sailor defeated some of the best fighters on the island. The situation was settled when the authorities wisely decided to hire the renegade sailor to teach them his hillside techniques. Chinto kata was the result and is one of our eight empty-hand katas.

At the dojo, everybody was working Chinto kata on the flat surface of the floor, and a few were finding it difficult to maintain the correct angles. It's impossible to get the real feel of this kata without running it on the side of a hill. We were in luck because right next door was a fairly steep little hill on the property of a church.

I led my students across the parking to the church's hill and formed them up on the steepest part. The sun was low and the western sky was a bright orange. A slight breeze blew leaves around our feet. Cars whizzed by on the busy four-lane highway to our left as we looked down the hill. We were already getting stares from some of the travelers and a few slowed down to look. I proceeded to demonstrate the correct way to run Chinto kata and ignored the gawkers.

Anybody who has grown up in the mountains or done a lot of hiking already knows many of the principles found in Chinto. The sides of the feet should dig into the ground as you move laterally up the hill instead of trying to walk straight up or down the slope heel to toe.

Running Chinto on a hill, the way it is intended to be practiced, is like playing a sophisticated form of "king of the hill." Climbing up a hill, a person uses much more energy than going down the same hill. Conversely, slowing down when heading downhill can be a problem. The object is to catch the opponent on a lateral plane while he is in the process of either climbing or descending.

Another main principle in Chinto is maintaining an awareness of the *sweet spot*, a place where the footing is more secure than the surrounding area. A sweet spot can be a flat area on the slope or a place where the ground is not as loose or slick as it is elsewhere. Chinto teaches you to keep your adversaries on the slippery slope while you are standing firm.

Practicing kata and fighting in the dojo can be too restrictive for practical application. It makes you tough but the surrounding area is controlled. An important difference in an actual street-fighting environment is the word *variables*. If you can use the environment to your advantage, your adversary is fighting both you and his surroundings. On the street, this means first being aware of the presence of slick surfaces, debris, and other obstacles, and then using them against your opponent.

One of my younger students was performing the kata when a car honked and somebody yelled something inaudible out the window as the car drove by us. She turned her head away from the direction it should have been facing and looked around to see the car. I yelled at her to freeze her position and walked up the hill to her. She knew what she had done and her eyes looked down to the ground as I spoke to her.

"Do not allow yourself to be distracted. You are practicing to defend yourself on a hill and that's where your concentration should be, not on the cars. If you were really fighting on this hill, I guarantee your opponent would have your undivided attention. Everybody get ready for some sparring."

I paired up individuals to spar each other on the side of the hill. No boundaries were defined and you knew who lost by who went flying down the hill with the winner still standing: the king. The monarch was disposed of that evening on several occasions, and nobody felt much like royalty when we bowed out for the night.

Most instructors in many martial arts schools have never been in an actual street fight. They train in a controlled environment like a ring or matted area, the boundaries carefully marked and the surface level.

Don't get me wrong, that type of work is invaluable. Nobody could hold up long being slammed onto concrete day in and day out. But then again, that's the point.

Learning how to survive the *variables* of real world conflicts takes a great deal longer and requires the mind to be flexible. Training exclusively in structured conditions restricts the mind and dulls the senses. Learning to recognize that sweet spot or reflexively see a potential weapon in a natural environment takes realistic training.

On the way home from the dojo, I thought about how I'd had to handle the terrain at Red's place and how it applied to that night's workout. We'd covered some of the physical aspects of using your surroundings in a fight, but not all of them. I hoped they'd gotten another lesson out of the workout as well: to gain a substantial advantage, one needs to know as much about the enemy as possible.

That's what today's recon had been all about. Now I knew at least as much about the environment at Wiley's farm as he did, which meant I could confront Wiley at a time and place of my choosing. I was stalking him; he was my prey.

*Know the other, know yourself,*
*And the victory will not be at risk;*
*Know the ground, know the natural conditions,*
*And the victory can be total.*

Sun Tzu

Natural terrain isn't the only sort of environment you have to consider in this business. Man-made structures pose challenges all their own. The next morning Frank called me on the cell phone as I drove around in the courthouse's underground parking lot looking for a parking space. I had gotten a late start that day and it was already close to 11:00. The dockets must have been full, because there were no vacant parking places until I got all the way down to the fifth level. The reception on the cell phone was not good and the transmission kept breaking up as Frank spoke.

"You need to go to Thadeus Cordeal's momma's house. A snitch we bonded out said he was there right now," I heard him say.

The signal on the phone kept coming and going as I parked and talked loudly into the mouthpiece. "I don't have his warrants on me but I can get certified copies while I'm here at the courthouse. Did you hear me, Frank?"

The reception was too bad to continue, so I hung up. There was no point in calling Frank back. Each of us knew what to expect from the other and there was no need for polite chitchat.

I made my way to the elevators and the main floor, then up the stairs to the criminal court clerk. It was a lot quicker to pick up a certified copy of the warrant while I was here rather than drive to the office to get our paperwork. The court-certified copy was the legal instrument I needed to make an arrest.

I didn't need a picture or the rest of my chase file. Thadeus Cordeal was a repeat customer. His forte was burglary and he'd been a client of the bonding company for well over ten years. He had always taken care of his court dates, even when he knew he was facing jail time.

Thad was a bit different from most of our regulars because he didn't drink or use drugs. He had no habit to feed. He just couldn't see himself doing the normal nine-to-five job and he enjoyed being a thief. Thad's momma was also a familiar face at the office since she came in every week to make payments on any of Thad's outstanding bond fees.

Frank would often extend credit to regular customers. After all, if they're in jail, they're not likely to get into more trouble, or at least not the sort of trouble that would require our services. If they don't get in trouble, they won't get arrested. If they don't get arrested, they won't need another bond. We had some people out on three or four bonds at a time, and that included Thadeus. Like I said, Frank was a good businessman—most of the time.

Although Thad had always taken care of his court obligations, he was not always prompt. One time, several years ago, he knew he was looking at pulling a couple of years in the penitentiary and had exhausted all his legal delays. He knew that his last taste of freedom for a while would be the day he walked into criminal court for his guilty plea and sentencing. This was one of a few times that a runner called in ahead to let us know he was going to skip.

Frank called me over to his desk and handed me Thad's file. "Thadeus Cordeal called in and said he wasn't going to show up for criminal court tomorrow. He asked me to give him thirty days to get his affairs in order and gave his word he would turn himself in."

"Whatever," I said. "I'll pick up the warrants and hang on to them."

According to Frank, that was good business. He made a reputation for himself by helping our clients whenever he could. Thad knew he wasn't going to get any more time for missing this court date and just wanted to delay going to jail. I can't say that I blamed him.

Frank couldn't lose because if Thad did turn himself in, Frank wouldn't have to pay me to catch him and he would have an appreciative client. If Thad didn't surrender, Frank knew I would catch him anyway. Frank also knew that when Thad eventually got out of jail, he would be calling on our services again. Besides, Thad's mother had put up her house as collateral on the bond.

Sure enough, the next month Thad came into the office and surrendered. He had packed extra socks and underwear and had some money for the commissary. My job was basically just to give him a ride to jail. If he was going to resist he wouldn't have turned himself in, so there was no need to handcuff him. I let him smoke in the back seat of the van all the way to jail and then we walked right in the front door. After turning in his paperwork, we shook hands and the jailers took him back, another satisfied customer.

A couple of years later I was sitting in my office and saw Momma Cordeal (as she was commonly known) come in the front door, bracing her large frame on a cane as she made her way to Frank's desk. Her body swayed as her weight shifted back and forth from her good leg to the cane as she approached Frank. She maintained a prominent role in the black community and was considered a fierce churchgoing woman. Her presence in church and community activities resulted in her having access to local politicians as well as the media. Momma Cordeal had a reputation for telling it like it is, and she was not afraid of the devil himself.

Her blue dress, which could've served as a small mess tent, hung down to her ankles. She was wearing a red cowboy hat slanted to one side with a matching plume feather protruding predominately on one side. The shuffling steps of the snakeskin cowboy boots were intermittently interrupted by the thud of the rubber tip of her cane on the floor.

The chair in front of Frank's desk hardly looked large enough to accommodate her as it disappeared under her girth. The long dress draped down around her seat completely, covering it. She was here to get her boy out of jail again, and it had been less than a year since his release from the penitentiary.

Frank called the jail to inquire about the charges against Thad, and I could tell by the look on his face that a high bond had been set. It appeared that Thadeus had really messed up this time. Thad preferred breaking into houses when nobody was home and carting off all he could carry, and we'd never known him to be violent.

This time, things hadn't worked out that way. Apparently, old Thad got a shock when, after climbing in a jimmied window, he came face to face with an elderly gentleman coming out of the bathroom. Nobody was supposed to be home and it's hard to say who was more startled. The old man had a heart condition and the excitement was too much for him. He collapsed on the floor and activated his medical alert device, which summoned the authorities.

Thad hastily burst out the front door and drew the attention of neighbors standing in the yard next door. It just wasn't Thad's day. One neighbor dialed 911 on the cordless phone he just happened to have in hand.

The emergency dispatch informed the neighbor that the authorities were close and asked for a description of the perpetrator. Things still weren't going Thad's way. At six feet four inches, one hundred forty-five pounds, a black man with a shaved head and wearing a red jersey running through a predominantly white neighborhood was not hard to spot.

Thad was arrested in short order. This time the charge wasn't just burglary, but aggravated burglary, home invasion, and aggravated assault. Luckily, the old gentleman was all right or Thad could have been charged with murder. I was surprised that the total bond for all charges was only $100,000.

Momma Cordeal brought in $5,000 in cash and the deed to her house. The problem was not that she only had half the bond fee, because Frank knew that she would pay off the debt, but her house that she wanted to use as collateral was only worth about a third of the bond. It was a small well-kept house, but it bordered some housing projects. Most of the other properties in the area were either run down or abandoned, and her yard was like an oasis in the destitution. She had wisely installed steel bars over her windows and there was no back door. The front door was solid steel with heavy-duty locks and deadbolts.

Despite the improvements she'd made to it, the house would be hard to sell for even its appraised value. Frank was hesitant but went ahead and made the bond after Momma Cordeal cried and carried on about how the devil had taken her son.

That was a year ago, and Thad showed up for his preliminary hearing and the grand jury indicted him and a criminal court date was set. He had miraculously managed to stay out of more trouble during this time, and Momma Cordeal paid off the other $5,000 she owed on the bond fee. I think it was just a matter of Thadeus not getting caught versus changing his ways, because there would be no other way for his mother to come up with that kind of cash.

We knew Thad had not shown up for criminal court before I actually picked up the paperwork. One of our bondsman was in the courtroom and when they called the docket, there was no Thadeus. As a courtesy, Frank called Momma Cordeal who said her son was just scared and would turn himself in, just like before.

But there was a big difference this time, since Thadeus was looking at doing some serious time and his Momma's house was not even close to being adequate collateral. Frank was over a barrel and he damn sure didn't want to pay me the $10,000 fee for catching Thad. Frank agreed to give Thadeus a month to get his affairs in order. That was four months ago.

Frank begrudgingly turned Thad's file over to me and I searched Momma Cordeal's house on several occasions. She offered to swear on the Bible that she had not seen Thad for months and carried on about how this was killing her. At first, she tried to prevent me from looking through her house and even called the police to have me removed. The officers explained to her that Thad listed this as his residence and I had the right to search any time without notice. Momma Cordeal threw up her hands, ranted and raved about being harassed, and said she was a good churchgoing woman but was going to sue all us goddamn sons-of-bitches.

Frank got lucky when one of our bondsmen got a business associate of Thad's out of jail on a receiving-stolen-property charge. Lucky us—we bonded out Thad's fence. The fence only had a small portion of the required bond fee. Having the ability to get somebody out of jail is a powerful negotiating tool. The fence was quite willing to work out payment in the form of ratting on Thadeus. He dropped a dime on Thadeus so fast he was out of jail in record time. We were holding his bond fee and in return he would call us when he was supposed to meet Thadeus to buy his stolen loot.

We only had two months to catch him before the court would order Frank to ante up a hundred grand. As soon as Frank hung up from talking with the snitch, he speed-dialed me; luckily I could hear him well enough, even given the lousy reception in the parking garage, to know what had happened.

It took me about thirty minutes to have the warrants in hand and to drive to Momma Cordeal's house. I could only hope Thad was still there but there was no need to be covert about my approach. If he was in the house, he couldn't get out without my seeing him. Additionally, I had the right to enter the house any time I wanted to.

Around noon, I pulled the van right in front of the house. I walked up and started pounding on the locked wrought iron barrier that provided extra security for the front door. I knocked and pounded for a good five minutes without a response. A quick look around the house assured me that there was still no way out of the house except through the front door.

Now I was starting to get pissed. I went to the van and retrieved a heavy crowbar. I returned to the front door and started yelling.

"Miz Cordeal, I know you're in there. Open the door now or I'm taking it off the hinges. Call the law if you want, but I'm coming in." Just then I could hear the door being unlocked and there stood Momma Cordeal dressed like she was going to church.

"Lord have mercy," she said. "There's no need for all this commotion. I was in the bathroom and got here as fast as I could. Please, come on in. You folks have been so nice to us and I want to show you that I'm not hiding my son."

Her abrupt change in attitude did not go unnoticed. I let her continue uninterrupted. "What he did was wrong and he must pay for his sin. I've been praying every night he would give himself up, and if I knew where he was, I would turn him in myself. Oh Lord, Oh Lord, how could my boy do this to his momma? Come on in, child, look all you want. I wouldn't hide him out."

I wasn't exactly expecting this cordial a reception and looked behind the door as it swung to the inside before I walked into the house. Momma Cordeal didn't have her cane with her. She picked up a Bible off the coffee table as she shuffled over to a sofa and sat down.

The house was very neat and clean and the carpet looked new. Little porcelain figurines were arranged on the coffee table and on shelves around the living room. They were mostly religious statuettes and included a Christmas manger scene and lots of shepherds and sheep. There was not a speck of dust anywhere.

"Who else lives here with you?" I asked.

She looked up over her Bible. "Just me, I live alone. I have another son and daughter who gave me beautiful grandbabies and they come to visit sometimes."

As I scanned the room, I tried to make pleasant conversation. "That must be nice. You see them often?"

She smiled and nodded. "I see them every weekend. They live across town."

I didn't know for sure whether Thad was in his Momma's house, but it seemed like a good idea to lock the deadbolts on the front door to at least slow him down if he made a break for it while I was searching the rest of the house. Momma Cordeal seemed unconcerned about my being there.

I stepped about halfway into the kitchen as I kept an eye on the door. It was a small kitchen with a dining table in the center with a plate of food steaming and a glass of tea filled with large cubes of ice. Another plate with food scraps and an empty glass were in the sink. A clothes hamper in the laundry room contained several pairs of men's pants and the washer and dryer were cycling. I looked in the dryer and saw men's shirts and more pants. The pants were Thad's flavor, thirty-eight inseam, thirty-inch waist.

I didn't bother asking Momma Cordeal about it because either Thad was in the house or he wasn't. There was nothing to say, but I was watching her to see if she got nervous. I checked out the kitchen cabinets, especially under the sink. Momma C was as cool as a cucumber, which told me I was cold. She sat there reading her Bible as if I wasn't there. The hall leading to the two bedrooms and bathroom was back through the living room. It was a very small bathroom, and a quick look around the door sufficed as a search as the shower curtain in the tub was pulled open to one side. In between room searches I looked for changes in Momma C's demeanor. I watched her face as I went into her bedroom to search it.

Most people check all the usual places—like under the beds and in closets. A few would think to search the slightly unusual places—like behind dressers, in drawers, or under piles of clothes. I've found skips hiding in all those places and in some even odder ones as well. Some of these people can fold themselves up and hide in places that would get Houdini stuck. They hide between the mattress and box spring, in cribs, in heating and air vents, clothes dryers, refrigerators, and tiny crawl spaces. There's no end to the ingenuity of some of these people when it comes to concealing themselves. It's a grown-up version of hide and seek.

I cleared Momma Cordeal's room and watched her face as I went into the other bedroom. She still sat there and appeared unconcerned. The last room was full of toys and kids' coloring books. It was a playroom for the grandkids, and I just lifted up the small single bed and looked under it. There was nobody in the room.

I had noticed the attic entrance in the ceiling before and had searched up there in the past. It was late August and I was willing to bet you could bake potatoes in that attic. Access to the attic was provided by one of those pull-down and fold-up collapsible sets of hinged stair steps. I looked down and saw a small piece of insulation lying on the floor. It was directly beneath the attic door.

The heavy springs of the door creaked as I pulled on the cord that hung down from the panel. The stairs folded down and led up to the dark attic. I quickly looked around at Momma Cordeal. She'd quit reading and was staring straight ahead. Her breathing appeared shallow and her posture was stiff. She was either praying real hard or was very nervous, or both. I drew my 9mm, flicked on my flashlight, and pointed it and the gun up the stairs into the attic.

About halfway up the stairs the heat started to cook my face. As soon as my head got to the top, my lungs started complaining about the searing air they were breathing. The insulation was thick and there was no way I was going to crawl around in it, especially in this heat. My shirt was drenched in just the brief time it took me to scan the small attic with my flashlight. It was too hot to stay up there long and if Thad was up there hiding in the insulation, he had to be about well-done.

Adding a little basting to the recipe for "Thad well-done" seemed to be in order. It was in good taste to yell a warning first, but it achieved nothing. I unsnapped a pouch on my belt and pulled out my can of pepper spray. Spraying in large sweeps, I saturated the entire attic, hurried back down the steps to avoid being overwhelmed by it myself, and slammed the attic door shut. Time to let the recipe simmer. A watched attic never boils, they say.

Momma Cordeal was now rocking back and forth. Her hands were folded together tight on her lap. Her voice was broken.

"If you're through searching, you can leave now. This is harassment. I told you I haven't seen Thadeus."

Just then, the ceiling bumped. I turned to Momma. "You got rats? Sounds like a big one."

She didn't answer me and her face drew tighter. Just then another bump, then another. Loud, heavy steps were now jarring the drywall ceiling and I could hear coughing. The stomps were bouncing the overhead light fixtures as the commotion passed right over our heads. He had nowhere to go and must have been delirious from the heat.

Momma C threw her head back and raised both her hands as her voice cracked. "Oh, Lord, Oh God, please help my boy. Please, sir, don't hurt my boy."

Pieces of drywall fell around the figurines on the coffee table, making them look as if they were standing in snow. It was a particularly nice touch for the manger scene. I kept my gaze glued upward as the loud thumping turned into a crash.

A foot smashed through the ceiling. Thad had missed a rafter and stepped directly onto the Sheetrock ceiling, which was not about to support him.

He moaned and cursed as he attempted to pull his leg back up through the hole he'd made. The leg of his jogging pants were riding up, exposing his calf. Sweat was running down his leg into his Reebok and soaking the soiled sock drooping below the ankle.

I jumped up and grabbed the dangling leg, pinned his ankle under my armpit, and squeezed his calf in a bear hug with both my arms. My two hundred-plus pounds stretched his leg out like a bungee cord. Thad's yell was followed by another loud thud as my weight on his limb was attempting to pull him through the ceiling. His trapped leg was between two rafters that supported his other leg on one side and his torso on the other. The effect of his predicament was the same as a cheerleader doing the Chinese splits. Somehow, I didn't think Thad was naturally that flexible.

My assumptions must have been right because Thad started to scream. "Man, please let me go. Oh God, you're tearing my leg off."

Momma C was howling just as loud. She bent over as if to touch her toes then threw her arms up and leaned back as far as she could, over and over as she bellowed, "Oh Lordy, Oh Lord, please don't hurt my boy."

I started swinging on the leg like Tarzan on a vine. This caused Thad to sink down lower. My feet raked the rest of the figurines and everything else off the coffee table. Finally, Thad had to give it up as the combination of the heat, pepper spray, and screaming groin muscles was more than he could bear.

The relatively small hole in the ceiling exploded into a crater as his entire body fell through the attic drywall. I landed butt-first on the coffee table, flattening it. It was a good thing the figurines were no longer standing. Extracting the wise man with the curve-handled staff from any part of my body would have been a painful procedure.

Thad's body slammed the floor like a limp rag and he lay sprawled out and motionless. He was covered with insulation and drywall fallout, and the speckled white in his hair made him look like an old man. Basting him in the pepper spray hadn't done much for enhancing a youthful appearance either.

The room looked like a small bomb had exploded. The dust-filled air was thick and smashed furniture and figurines were scattered about. Momma C had collapsed on the sofa and was—for once—speechless.

Thad groaned and moved his legs as I cuffed him. His skin was hot to the touch and the chemical spray on his skin stung my hands every time I touched him. His eyes were red and stinging and his mucous membranes were starting to drain. He was unable to speak but there was no doubt what he needed. The game was over.

I knew better than to touch myself anywhere until after washing the chemical from my hands. Thad stumbled to his feet as I helped him up and into the bathroom. He knelt on his knees and leaned into the tub as I let cold water run over his face from the faucet. I had to rinse off the pepper spray without letting the runoff touch him because that would only spread the chemical.

Finally, I was finished. I told Momma C to get him something to drink as I washed my hands in the sink. She was quiet and her eyes were filled with tears as she observed the condition of her son. The solemn fact that Thad was going away for a long time was also starting to settle in. Her steps were labored as she brought him some ice water, as though something vital had seeped out of her.

My concern at that point was whether or not he needed medical attention. The effects of the spray would wear off but injuries from the fall and heat exhaustion were possible. I decided not to take any chances and told Momma C we were going to the ER and that she could follow us if she wanted.

Thad was shackled as I led him in the front door and into the waiting room. He complained about his shoulder and elbow from the fall and trouble breathing from the spray.

After about a two-hour wait in the ER, we went back to the examination area. Thad had been hydrating with cold liquids the entire time and my concerns of problems from the heat had subsided somewhat. Even though it had been his choice to hide in the attic and attempt to escape, I felt no joy in seeing him suffer. Even after all the lies that spewed from Momma C, I felt sympathy for her. She was only trying to help her son, although she now realized the consequences. It could have been a lot worse and she knew it.

Thad was X-rayed, probed, and prodded. His vitals checked out and there were no broken bones. He was released from the ER and I was careful to hold on to the medical clearance slip from the nurse, knowing full well that the jail would not accept him without it. It's a matter of economics. If the county has to take him to the hospital, it comes out of the jail's budget. This way, the bill would go to Momma C.

She still got off cheap. Although Frank could legally charge her a lot of money for the fees he has to pay me, he only collects actual expenses. She could have lost her house.

Momma C gave Thad a long hug in the parking lot as she wept. He was crying, too, as he looked at her. "I'm going to be gone a long time, Momma."

She wept harder and held him tighter, unable to speak through the tears. I didn't rush them.

When they seemed about spent, Thad slipped into the back of the van. Momma C stood looking at him as the door slid closed, then glanced over at me. "I'm sorry," she said. "I'm so sorry. God, please forgive me."

I didn't say a word and got in the van and drove off. She stood in the middle of the parking lot and grew smaller in my rearview mirror as we headed for the jail.

# six

Thad was just the beginning of a long run of arrests. They say that luck is when preparation meets opportunity, and I'd have to agree. All at once, all my groundwork on every case was starting to pay off. I was closing case after case and the surrounding jails were getting tired of seeing me pull up to the sally port. One jailer even asked me to take a few days off. A hot-rod show in town had resulted in a bumper crop of assaults, drunk and disorderlies, and just general criminal asshole behavior. There's nothing like a hot rod to make some guys think that they are one.

But even success has a price: too many meals from drive-up windows, too many cups of coffee, too many weird smells in the van (some of them mine). I'd been catching quick naps in the van for more than a week, and by now I had to check my watch if I wanted to know what day of the week it was. Three hours of sleep in bed was starting to sound like heaven. I was on a roll but the fatigue was winning. It was time for a break before I got stupid.

Finally, the time came. There were no more telephone messages about the Freddies or Thads or other miscreants of the world. No e-mails from their loved ones, families, or victims, all who wanted to help me for their own reasons. No more calls from snitches. So I did what had seemed completely impossible just a few hours before—I went home and crashed.

The sheets were fresh and my pillow the softest thing I'd touched in days. REM sleep was screaming my name and within seconds of turning off the light, I was headed for the sheer luxury of eight straight hours of sleep.

I was just spiraling down when my cell phone rang. A female voice asked "This the bounty hunter?"

I was tempted. "No. Wrong number. Sorry." I could hang up, give in to the paralyzing fatigue—just this once.

Not likely, but my patience was short along with my answer. "Yeah, who's this?"

Her voice was a low, rough whisper. "I'm Tamara Fields, Wiley's cousin. He raped my little girl. I hear you're looking for me."

I shoved the covers back, flashing on the adrenaline surging through me, sweeping out the cobwebs.

Tamara Fields! People with kids are usually easy to find, but she'd gone underground and disappeared without a trace. There are lots of ways to do that—not only did I want to talk to her about Wiley, but also I wanted to figure out how she'd managed it.

The most important thing about talking to sources of information is to make them believe you're on their side. If I'm dealing with the loved ones of a skip, I talk about how much safer it'll be for me to find them instead of the cops. With folks who stand to lose bail money or assets they've posted, there's the financial angle. With victims of a crime, it's even easier. It doesn't take a rocket scientist to figure out we're usually on the same side.

Usually—but not always. The second she'd said her name, I'd headed to the home office and plugged the telephone number on my caller ID into a tracing program. With a helpless child involved and a mother with information, I had no problem hiding my excitement behind sympathy. "Yeah, sweetie, I've been trying to find you. I need to talk to you. There might be something you can tell me that will help me find Wiley. You *do* want the son of a bitch that did that to your little girl to pay, don't you?"

"DAMN STRAIGHT, MISTER!" Then Tamara reverted to her earlier quiet voice. "But I have to be careful. You don't know these people like I do. He threatened to kill me and my little girl."

Now I was pissed. I've got a special place in my heart for children, and my desire to kick Wiley's ass swept away the last traces of fatigue. The anger in my voice was genuine. "Tamara, after I catch him, he won't hurt anybody ever again." Just then, the tracing program on my laptop coughed up an address. Still, I wanted to see if she would lie to me. "I need to meet you. Where are you now?"

"I'm in Bristol," she said. Bristol matched the location my phone trace gave me, so at least she was telling me that much truth. "Me and my old man are headed down to Morristown in a little bit. We can meet you somewhere."

It's one thing to read a bonding company file on somebody, another matter entirely to talk to someone who knows his hangouts and habits. I had to talk to Tamara—had to. Sleep would have to wait, just like it had so many times before. It was time to take a ride to Morristown.

Tamara and I agreed to meet at an isolated location by the lake. She and her current "old man" would take a ride with me in my van and show me some of Wiley's haunts. I reassured her that the van had dark tinted windows in the back and nobody would be able to see her.

It's always my practice to show up early at a rendezvous to avoid any surprises. Prudence dictates recon to plan a couple of escape routes. Getting there first also lets me check the area for ambushes. You'd be surprised how lazy bad guys can be, showing up at the last moment to get set up. More than once I'd avoided serious trouble just by practicing the virtue of being early.

My gut told me Tamara was telling me the truth, but you don't last long in this business by being naïve. Although the phone trace had told me she was telling the truth about her location, she wasn't exactly a pillar of society.

On the way to Morristown, another personal safety precaution occurred to me, this one more a matter of personal hygiene than bullets. For the last several months, I'd been tracking Tamara through the school system. One of the elementary school principals I'd interviewed told me Tamara's daughter had been sent home on numerous occasions for what he called "hygiene issues." When I pressed him for specifics, he told me it was because of body lice. He'd called the parents into his office to discuss the problem and found out to his dismay they'd had the same problem. The trail ended at the next school, as there were no more requests for a transcript transfer.

Now, getting shot at or otherwise placed at risk of bodily harm is all part of the chase. But I draw the line at body lice. Halfway up to

Morristown, I stopped at a pharmacy and picked up some disinfectants and air fresheners. I was sure Frank would appreciate my thoughtfulness and reimburse the expense—after all, it was his van.

I was supposed to meet Tamara and company under a highway overpass on the banks of a lake. Before I pulled off the main road, I drove up and down the highway around the exit a few times. There were no cars parked anywhere along the road. Even if there had been, the rough terrain would have made for a long, arduous hike. If there was an ambush in the making, it would be staged from somewhere other than the highway.

I pulled off the highway and headed for the rendezvous, noting possible avenues of escape as I drove. Judging by the bait containers and beer cans on the ground, this was a popular fishing spot.

Finally satisfied that I knew the area well enough, I backed under the bridge so I could see anyone approaching before they could see me. I pulled my Glock out of the holster and rested it on my lap, then rolled down all the windows so I could hear vehicles or people approaching.

It was a warm day with just a hint of fall in the air, and the days were growing noticeably shorter. Dusk was settling on the lake and the crickets began to chirp as darkness fell. My eyelids started to feel heavy. I fought off the fatigue with swigs of coffee from a travel mug, but I was getting past the point where that helped much.

A car missing a muffler, approaching from the opposite direction, drowned out the night insects. It slowed as it crossed over the bridge. Its headlights swept the trees on either side of my hiding spot. I heard it turn and start down the short dirt road that led underneath the bridge.

My eyes were already adjusting to the twilight. I knew I would be blinded when the headlights hit me and I wouldn't be able to see the occupants. Well, no point in playing fair: I turned on my own headlights to put us on an even footing.

The other vehicle turned off its lights as it approached. As I said, I don't play fair—I kept mine on, giving me the tactical advantage.

An old rusted-out brown Belair clattered as it pulled up next to me and parked. Our vehicles were facing opposite directions. Three people were sitting in the front seat.

Their next move confirmed my suspicions about their failure to adequately maintain their vehicle. Evidently the passenger side door didn't work; something worth noting in case they later wanted to leave the area quickly.

The person next to the passenger door crawled out through the window. He was followed by a female, who exited in the same manner. The female approached. She leaned in my passenger window. "Are you Joe?"

My gaze remained fixed on the guy standing by the van as I answered. "Yeah, are you Tamara?"

She nodded. "That's is my old man, Snake," she said, pointing at the man who'd crawled out of the car with her. "That's Junior in the car, my ex. We all live together."

Somehow that didn't surprise me.

I opened the back sliding door and told them to get in. Snake got in first and Tamara slid in next to him. It only took me a second to realize that picking up the air freshener had been a good call.

Snake's long brown stringy hair was matted to his forehead and hung down to his shoulders in the back. Large teardrops were tattooed at the corners of his eyes. Bare bony arms covered with body art hung out of a leather vest open at the chest. It looked as if I could place my hands around his waist.

Tamara was significantly more well-nourished than Snake. Not fat, but not hungry, either. Her black greasy hair almost shined. A long, dirty T-shirt hung outside equally soiled blue jeans, which had holes in both knees. Air freshener wasn't enough—I kept the sliding door open.

The guy who'd stayed in the Belair was staring at us. I couldn't see much of him and that made me uneasy. "Why doesn't he come over?" I asked.

Tamara leaned forward and answered, "Junior don't like me meeting you. He's my little girl's daddy and wants to get Wiley himself."

"I can understand that," I said. "Tell you what, when I catch Wiley, I'll bring him to you so you can kick the shit out of him before I take him to jail." I had no intention of doing it but figured it would break the ice. "One thing I can tell you is that Wiley will be a very old man when and if he ever gets out of jail."

Tamara leaned even closer to me, evidently reassured by my good manners in offering to let them take a first shot at Wiley. "Junior is all talk. He's scared of Wiley and his friends. You don't know what kind of crazy people they are. They'll kill you. I know of people they buried up the woods. They're mean as hell."

I told Tamara to sit back and relax, mainly because her breath smelled like day-old road kill. She and Snake agreed to take a ride and show me where Wiley was known to hang out. I didn't relish the prospect of driving around with them with the door closed, but there was no way around it. Junior stayed parked under the bridge as we drove all over the county.

I drew maps to the various places they showed me and wrote down names and their connection to Wiley. It was close to midnight before we concluded the tour and they were reunited with Junior. Tamara was tasked with contacting her relatives in the area and telling them to keep their ears open. I promised to keep her posted on any developments and I'd make sure no one knew where she was.

The drive back to Knoxville was torture. I felt like I'd run into a brick wall. My eyes were refusing to stay open and the van reeked of Tamara and Snake. I pulled over at a roadside market to fumigate the van. The market's coffee was fresh and it was probably the only reason that I was able to make it back. It's dangerous to drive when that tired but I just wanted to get home.

I push the limits, but even I know when to quit. I promised myself that the next day I'd sleep in and work at home. It was time to back off.

The next morning, I woke up when one of my dogs started barking. Debbie had slipped out quietly to work and let me sleep. I propped myself up on one elbow and cracked one eye open to see that the cable box displayed 8:00 A.M. On the off chance that the dog was barking a warning, I sat up. A few more seconds were all it took for me to realize it wasn't a warning bark, it was more like a pay-attention-to-me bark.

A difficult decision presented itself. Should I stare at my feet for a few hours or go ahead and get up? What I really wanted to do was fall back and curl up in the warm sheets, but the incessant barking of my loyal companion had woken me up just a hair too much. Of course, the moment I swung open the back door to yell "Shut up!" he did just that. Damn dog.

I was up, if not completely awake. Habit carried me through the next few minutes as I found the coffee, still hot enough to steam in my oversized cup. I tossed a bagel on a plastic dish and punched in the seconds on the microwave, then walked a bit more steadily to my office. The computer whirled and booted up in harmony with the microwave's humming and turntable-moving noises. The house was coming alive, but without me.

A distinct ding from the kitchen told me the bagel was ready. Still foggy and numb, I got to my feet and lumbered through the dining room. Sparkling rays of morning light streamed in through the windows, adding a surreal feeling to my slow trek to the kitchen. I downed my bagel and orange juice and waited for the carbs to kick in. After two more cups of coffee, I was as good as I was going to get without more sleep.

I had a backlog of case files that needed to be entered into my database. Fortunately, that didn't require too much concentration, so I turned on the TV for background noise.

My brain was still operating on just a couple of cylinders—maybe a shower would wake me up. Shuddering, I remembered Tamara and Snake and their stench in the van the night before. Yeah, definitely a shower—a long, hot one, hot enough to kill both the smell and the memory of it.

I headed back into the kitchen through the living room, intending to put my coffee cup up before heading for the shower.

Usually I cue on sudden interrupts in morning news programs, so I was surprised to see the "Breaking News" graphic on the TV. The picture on the screen stopped me dead in my tracks and I plopped down on the sofa.

Smoke billowed out of one of the buildings of the World Trade Center. The commentators sounded as confused as I was. Nobody knew exactly what happened except that it was some kind of plane accident.

Like millions of other people, I watched as the second plane hit the towers. Time stopped. It was too much to comprehend.

The phone rang. It was Debbie.

"You watching the news?" Her voice was shaking.

"Yeah," I answered.

"All those people. It's so awful. You know Joey's unit will be the first one out to get whoever did this. I think I'm going to throw up."

I tried to sound reassuring, but she was right. His MEU had already deployed and they were going through their final work-up training in Australia. They were the closest battle-ready unit. "We don't know what's happened yet," I said. "It'll be okay." We both knew it would be anything but okay for a long, long time, but what was happening was too big to take in all at once.

Not long after we hung up, the news reported the other two plane crashes—one into the Pentagon, and one into a field. Even as the earliest reports came in, the sequence of events had a feeling of inevitability to them. Someone had dared attack us on our soil and America was about to do some serious ass kicking.

Of course, I was worried about my son and the danger he would be heading into, but I also knew there would be nowhere he would rather be. Damn, where did he get that?

I called Frank at the office. "I won't be in for a couple days." There was no need to say anything else. Frank was watching the news like everybody else.

"Take all the time you need," he said.

Even if I hadn't been worn out, I still wouldn't have had the energy or the desire to do anything but just sit in front of the TV. The phone rang and I started to ignore it. But the last time, it had been Tamara.

After I picked it up, I was glad I had. It was Joey. "Hey, old man. What's up?"

My answer was short. "Everything's going to hell. Where are you?"

"Darwin, Australia. We just finished two weeks of training in the field with Australian forces. I was just sitting down to a steak and a cold beer when the MPs and Shore Patrol rushed in and told us to get back to the ship. They're rounding everybody up."

I hesitated a minute. "Have you heard what happened?"

"Just what I heard in the bar. Rumor is we're heading to the Arabian Sea."

I filled him in on what I knew from the news reports, which wasn't much. I could hear someone yelling at him in the background. "I have to go now, Dad. They're making me get off the phone and head for the ship."

There was no telling when we would hear from him again. "I love you Joey. E-mail as much as you can."

The yelling in the background got louder. "I will, Dad. I love you, too." The line went dead. One touch on the speed dial and I had Debbie on the line.

"Joey just called," I said. "They're rounding everybody back on the ship. He thinks they're headed to the Arabian Sea."

Having her fears confirmed was more than she could take. "I'm coming home," she said.

Like everyone else in the country, we spent the rest of the night glued in front of TV, our emotions fluctuating from dread of the unexpected to raw anger. The country was under siege, thousands were dead, and our only child was headed into harm's way. Everything else was trivial, and minor annoyances evaporated. How could anything else matter? The only problem was that we didn't know who to hate.

The news showed scenes of family and friends hoping to hear of survivors out of the wreckage. We pulled out old family photo albums. People were holding up their own pictures of missing loved ones, begging anyone in the television audience who'd seen them to call. They were desperate. We looked back in time, at pictures of Joey growing up.

In the days that followed, everyone's priorities got realigned. The realization that we, along with the rest of the nation, had let trivial things eat up time we could have spent with those no longer with us gripped us like a vice. People called each other more often and sat a little closer to loved ones as we watched the full horror of 9/11 unfold.

Everyone seemed to be feeling the same way. Our neighbor was standing at the end of our driveway with her kids waiting on the school bus. I hadn't seen her in months. She stood and watched the bus drive out of sight.

I tried to talk Debbie into staying home the next day but she had a project deadline. Frank already knew I wasn't coming in, so I spent the day in front of the TV, reflecting on what was happening to us and to the nation. You ask yourself, why didn't I spend more time or pay more attention to the important things? Then you see how they turned out and decide everything worked out well.

It's a circle that took me back to my own childhood. My father had been focused on making a living while I was growing up, just as I had been when Joey was younger. We had good, quality times, but there are never enough of them.

By late Wednesday afternoon, I was getting restless. There was not a lot of new information coming out in the news reports, but each time I saw the atrocities replayed, I felt more and more frustrated. Like the rest of the nation, I couldn't *not* watch it. But the self-imposed imprisonment was just that. This wasn't like chasing a skip—there was nothing I could do except get back to my daily routine.

Fortunately, Wednesday was dojo night. Good thing, too, because that was the only thing that could have made me leave the house.

That night, my senior black belt and two beginners were the only ones who showed up to train—no middle-ranking belts, just the most senior and the most junior. It was a shame because all of my students could have used the break—yes, getting pounded on can be an escape from the rest of the world, believe it or not. The moment you bow in, the rest of the world disappears. It has to—there's no room for distractions. During a crisis like 9/11, it's a relief to have a threat you can touch, see and smell, understand, train against—and sometimes beat. It's concrete, right in front of you, in contrast to the overwhelming helplessness and impotent rage watching the World Trade Center die.

My senior black belt had been with me for many years. Early on he'd relied heavily on his previous boxing skills, and those techniques worked well when he faced equally inexperienced opponents. People who went toe-to-toe with him quickly realized the error of their ways.

But that was when he faced other beginners—I know how to fight boxers and I know how to turn them into martial artists. Even more important, my job in the ring wasn't to win—it was to keep his warrior spirit alive while teaching him the skills to back it up.

Time after time, I took him in the ring and showed him what worked—not through words as much as by example. I kept my distance, out of range of his boxing techniques, taking away his strengths. At the same time, I used techniques against him that showed him in a rather forceful way the flaws in his strategy.

He was dedicated and the training took. Now, years later, not many folks looked forward to stepping into the ring with him. He didn't even look like the same person who started as a white belt with me so long ago. Those who train hard and earn a black belt from me—and they are few and far between—all show the same sort of transformation.

My other two students who showed up that night were Larry and his step-daughter Elsie. Larry weighed in at well over three hundred pounds and had done a stint as a professional wrestler. Elsie was eleven years old.

Larry had a reputation for frequenting the local adult beverage establishments and, after considerable consumption of certain products, proceeding to clean them out of any and all patrons he found objectionable. Most of the time, that meant everyone else in the bar. After a certain point, Larry preferred his own company. Needless to say, Larry wasn't interested in studying martial arts because he felt intimidated by others.

Larry's fist was the size of a side of beef. His technique of choice was a haymaker that came from the back forty. He drew it behind his head as he wound it up, dropped it halfway to the floor, and turned it loose like a Mack truck hitting fifth gear.

That haymaker was devastating in barroom fights. Like me, he'd come to rely on what worked. The problem was that a trained martial artist could see that punch coming the moment Larry started thinking about it. There was plenty of time to either move in hard on Larry and beat him to the punch or—if you were slower—to get out of the way. The only sure thing was that you didn't want to get hit by that punch.

The other problem with Larry's haymaker was what happened afterwards. Once he unleashed it, he had no control and would lose his balance. If you could avoid the fist, all you had to do was swarm his back or take his feet out from under him.

But that punch had worked so well for him for so long that it took quite a lot of pounding on him over time before he realized it wouldn't always pay off.

While that lesson was sinking in, Larry started developing counters to my attacks. He developed a high back kick that he could land underneath the chin of an opponent who was trying to rush his back. He learned to plan follow-ups and improved his balance and control.

As he progressed, his punches lost none of their power, but he learned to throw them without telegraphing. Watching a brawler turn into a real fighter who could generate so much power with a strategic, well-executed technique was awesome. I must be crazy.

Based on input from her schoolteachers, Elsie had been diagnosed by doctors as suffering from attention deficit disorder. Over the years, I've had numerous young people come in with the same diagnosis, so I knew what to expect. Sure enough, her mind wandered, she forgot what she was doing during drills, and, on top of all that, she lacked the level of respect for elders that I require of everyone in the dojo.

Society's answer: a trip to the pharmacy.

I use a different prescription, one I call the triangular approach. It's made up of push-ups, grass drills, and leg raises. Whenever she forgot her *sirs* or *ma'ams* or her mind wandered, she found herself in the triangle. First came push-ups, then grass drills—running in place, hitting the floor on command, then jumping back up again—followed by laying on her back and holding her feet six inches off the carpet.

Sometimes Elsie would have to go round and round the triangle without stopping, especially if she tried to quit. I have found that many kids today have been allowed to quit. It becomes a habit; it's the easy way out. Elsie was quickly finding out that it didn't work in the dojo.

After a few weeks, her attention span improved and she became quite the well-mannered young lady. She was able to stay focused on tasks, and her physical conditioning was markedly improved. Not long after being introduced to the triangle, she was competing against others her age and doing well. Her grades in school came up and her level of medication went down until she was taken off drugs entirely. She radiated self-confidence. It's not an instant cure, but it's a long-lasting one.

While I watched my students work out, my thoughts drifted to my senior-most student, Nick, a senior in college who runs his own school in the middle of the state. Like Elsie, he started with me at age eleven.

When Nick first came to the dojo, he clung tightly to his mother and didn't want to leave her side. I had serious doubts about whether he would make it through even a month of training. Nick was an extremely sensitive child. Even a cross look would start the tears flowing.

But Nick was very intelligent and learned quickly. As his self-confidence grew, so did his assertiveness, and I had the distinct pleasure of watching him grow up. He was always polite, but soon bullies at school were no longer taking advantage of his gentle nature. He turned out to be an intelligent, sensitive, and thoughtful man with a side kick from hell. I am so very proud of Nick.

A dojo workout had been just what I needed to get the juices flowing again. I woke the next morning with a strong desire to get back to the chase. The dread of the unexpected was replaced by an attitude of "bring it on."

I powered up my sleeping cell phone, its beeping and chiming audible throughout the house. A miniature envelope appeared on the display. I felt a surge of anticipation as I called my voice mail. It was indeed time to get back to living.

There were surprisingly few voice mail messages, given that I'd been on a two-day hiatus. The majority of the messages pertained to a nineteen-year-old subject named Jimmy. The messages were from Judy, his new bride. She was worried about him and had finally decided to come clean.

Jimmy was out on a $10,000 bond for theft. In addition, his own mother had taken out a warrant against him for vehicular assault and theft. A nice wholesome family—evidently he'd gotten a bit upset with dear old Mom after she found his crack stash and decided to smoke it herself. I could understand his position. After all, he was the one risking life and limb robbing and stealing from local Mexican gang members so he could feed his own habit. Under those circumstances, who wouldn't be angry with Mom for helping herself to his stash?

I'd been looking for Jimmy for about a month before he tried turning his mother into a hood ornament, and I knew she'd been lying to me about knowing his whereabouts. She hadn't been particularly cooperative until young Jimmy tried to run her down.

Jimmy's mom went by the name of "Skag," a street term used to describe a particularly ugly woman. She didn't seem offended by the nickname and answered to it readily. Like I said, a nice, wholesome family. She was living in an apartment at the back of her brother's house.

A few weeks ago, I had driven up the narrow trash-littered alley that led to her residence. The maze of side streets would make it easy for a person on foot to disappear in a matter of seconds. The short driveway was boxed in by a tall wooden fence that was missing several of its weathered planks.

Turned-over trash cans and car parts formed an obstacle course to her apartment door. When I knocked on her door, loose paint flaked off. I guess not a lot of her visitors knocked. The door itself was loose in the frame and threatened to fall off its less-than-secure mounting with each rap of my knuckles.

Skag opened the door, which exposed its hollow inner core. She left it open and walked back into her living room. I followed her in, assuming correctly that this passed for "Please come in," in her society. Skag parked herself on a ragged sofa next to a younger female who turned out to be Jimmy's wife, Judy.

Judging by the shiners Judy was sporting, her experience thus far with matrimony was less than blissful. Black bruising surrounded her bright blue eyes and made her look like she was wearing a mask. Her blonde curly hair fell to her shoulders and tight shorts and a tank top covered a petite frame. With just a little effort, she could have been a very pretty girl.

Skag was a different story. The scars on her shaved head showed she was no stranger to altercations. A couple of scabs were coming off the older scalp wounds. One of her bony arms was in a sling and the other was reaching for a cigarette. My fingers would have gone around her biceps easily. It was impossible to decipher any of the many tattoos that were distorted by her loosely-hanging skin.

Skag placed the nonfiltered cigarette between her lips, showing a mouthful of rotting teeth. Judy lit it for her. Skag drew on it so hard her gaunt face looked like a skull.

"Tell me about him trying to run you down," I said.

Skag's eyes protruded from their orbs as she took another draw before she answered. "I been clean for two months. If I ain't drunk all my Old Granddad, I wouldn't of smoked his stash. Can't remember much."

Judging from her barely intelligible slurred words, she had apparently restocked on the Old Granddad. I turned to Judy. "Were you here when this happened?"

She nodded her head. "Yeah. He took her keys and when I tried to stop him, he hit me. Skag tried to stand in front of the car and he hit her with it. Somebody said he sold the car for a hundred dollars across town. He broke into his uncle's house last week and stole a TV, and his grandmother's the week before and took some money. He's got it bad. The crack, I mean. Ain't nobody he won't steal from. He robbed some Mexicans with a baseball bat and stole their lawnmower. You got to stop him before somebody kills him."

"You know where I can find him?" I asked.

Judy shook her head. "He don't stay in one place. I see him walking the streets. He sleeps at different crack houses but he calls me sometimes."

Running back and forth trying to catch him every time they caught a glimpse of him would be a waste of time. By the time I got to where he'd been seen, he'd be gone. Catching him would have to be a setup. One of these two was going to have to delay him for me.

"He's been back here, hasn't he?" I asked.

They looked at each other, then Judy answered. "Yeah, he drops by, but he don't stay."

I shook my head in acknowledgment that I knew what she was going to say. "Well, I know you don't want him to know you ratted him out, but there's no other way. The next time he comes here, you have to keep him here, any way you can, and call me. Otherwise, I'll just let the Mexicans handle it."

Judy was genuinely worried about Jimmy. So was Skag, or at least as worried as much as her closer friendship with Old Granddad would permit. "I swear, Mister, I'll call you and keep him here any way I can, I swear," Judy said.

It had been a couple of weeks since I'd interviewed Skag and Judy. Since I'd heard nothing from them, it was time to reestablish contact with them. My voice mail had several messages from Judy and one inaudible tirade from Skag, which had something to do with wondering what the hell I was doing. The messages were spread over three days and I was in no hurry to answer them. Given the attack on the World Trade Center, Jimmy's well-being was the last thing on my mind. I had rather hoped the Mexicans had caught up with him.

Just as I finished reviewing the messages, the cell phone rang. Caller ID told me it was Skag.

It was only mid-morning but Skag had obviously been visiting with Old Granddad again. Her words were garbled but I could translate them well enough to understand that Jimmy was at her house and Judy was upstairs with him. It was time to go back to work.

Other than the Wednesday night workout at the dojo, this was my first time out of the house in days, and the transformation in the landscape told me that I wasn't the only one deeply affected by the events. There were American flags everywhere—on houses and cars, even in the projects. Cars had flags flapping from their windows and the stars and stripes were hanging from the porches of houses and apartments on some of the meanest streets in town. The back streets seemed to be vacant of the usual parade of prostitutes, and I heard on the radio that arrests were down. People were pulling together, becoming a community.

Not good for the bonding business. But I wasn't worried. I knew it wouldn't last.

A trash can blocked the alley leading to Skag's apartment. I got out of the van and silently moved it out of the way. Not only did I want to make a quiet approach, but also I don't like anything blocking my egress routes. With the alley clear, I eased a little closer to Skag's apartment. I parked two houses down and walked the rest of the way.

The door was open and Skag was slouched to one side of the sofa. She didn't or couldn't speak and just pointed upstairs.

The stairs creaked under my feet, so a quiet approach was out of the question. I ran up the stairs in long leaps, touching down on every third or fourth step. Without breaking stride, I pulled my gun and kicked open the door at the top of the landing.

The first thing I saw was Jimmy's bare ass. He was on top of Judy with her legs wrapped around him. I must say that she was indeed doing her duty to make this a more law-abiding community.

When the door crashed open, Jimmy leaped out of bed. Judy grabbed the bed sheets to cover herself up. Jimmy stood in front of me at full attention. He didn't hesitate to raise his hands when I ordered him to.

His hands were not the only things raised in the air. "Damn, boy," I said. "Turn around before it goes off. You could put somebody's eye out with that thing." Jimmy turned around. I told him to put his hands behind his back and he complied immediately. I cuffed him.

Meanwhile, Judy disappeared under the covers. She emerged fully dressed and gaped at Jimmy. I took her expression to mean he was not yet at half-mast. I reached down and grabbed the chain on the handcuffs to prevent him from turning around to face me while he was still locked and loaded.

"Judy, when he settles down, put his pants on for him," I said. She just smirked and sat there staring in admiration.

I would have thought that having your bedroom door kicked in during an intimate moment and then looking down the barrel of a gun would dampen one's romantic mood. Not so in Jimmy's case—or in Judy's, for that matter. I don't know if it was because Jimmy was nineteen, on crack, or a combination of the two, but it took several minutes before the danger of an accidental misfire passed.

Finally, Judy reached for his jeans and he stepped into them. After she zipped them up, I spun him around and sat him on the bed. She laced up his shoes, her hands trembling slightly.

I led him downstairs. His thin, shirtless frame turned so he could glare at his mother as we walked past her. Skag was only semiconscious. Neither of them said a word. Judy walked out to the van with us and I let her give him a hug before we drove off.

"I love you Jimmy," she said. "I had to do it. You had to be stopped."

Jimmy remained silent until we were almost to the jail. Then he began to squirm and had a sour look on his face. "You could have at least let me finish."

My eyes made contact with his in the rearview mirror. "I felt a duty to help preserve the gene pool."

His face looked puzzled as he muttered, "Huh?"

"Never mind," I said.

# seven

A cell phone is one of my most valuable tools and I'm rarely without mine. The folks I hunt aren't known for their reliability. When they turn up, you have to be ready to react immediately, and usually the first sign that it's time to chase is a blinking red light on a cell phone. My cell phone is mounted on my dashboard so that I don't have to take my attention off the road to use it, and because my radio at full volume drowns it out if I keep it in my pocket or on my belt.

I was on my way back from the jail when the blinking red light caught my attention. The caller ID told me one of my favorite members of the shallow end of the gene pool was calling: Homer, my very own Barney Fife.

I switched to the radio channel that corresponded to the earpiece transmitter on the cell phone. Homer's voice came through loud and clear over the van speakers.

"HELLO, HELLO," he said.

My ears screamed for relief. Even if it had been someone I liked, it was way too loud.

"I'm here Homer, what's up?" It was hard to sound pleasant with my teeth still clenched and a grimace on my face, but I tried.

There was a long pause before he answered. "They found out I'm helping you look for Wiley. Sons of bitches shot my daughter's dog and left it lying on her front porch with a book of matches. It means they'll burn her house down. I started getting calls in the middle of the night. Death threats."

"How did they know you were helping me?" I asked.

Homer's voice sounded shaky. "I been snooping around, asking questions. It must've gotten back to Wiley—or Red."

My head shook as I let out a sigh. "Homer, I told you to just keep your eyes open. You weren't supposed to be going around looking for Wiley. The…"

Homer interrupted me. "Well I ain't looking no more. Ain't helping no more either. Done quit working part-time at the sheriff's department. Won't be calling you no more." When a man like Homer gets scared, the first thing to go is his pronouns.

Without waiting for me to answer, Homer hung up. I knew there was no need to call him back. So much for his dream of working a big case—he was finding out what it was really like.

I pulled into a shopping center parking lot to document my discussion with Homer and had no sooner started to leave when the phone rang again. This time it was Ken Philips. There was a hushed excitement in his voice. "Joe, can you talk?"

"Yeah, Ken," I answered. "What's up?"

He sounded like his hand was over the phone as he spoke. "My man has a meeting set up with you and Red tonight. Can you make it?"

I rifled through my memory, trying to figure out who he was talking about. Then it hit me and I groaned. Why, oh why, did all the wannabes in the world seemed determined to help me out? "My man—you mean that so-called bounty hunter I met at your place? What's his name, Bob? Is that who set this up?"

Ken hesitated before he answered. He was pretty pleased with himself for setting up this meeting but somehow he caught some subtle tone in my voice that told him I thought he was an idiot. "Yeah. Can't nobody know about this. Some of Wiley's buddies who work for me have been acting funny. I think something's up. Is it okay if I give Bob your number so you can set it up?"

"Why not?"

"There's something else," Ken said. "Tamara, that little girl's mother, just called me. She wanted some money. Said I owed her since I got Wiley out of jail and now she's scared. I had Bob meet her at the same place where you met her and give her some money. She said you knew how to get in touch with her."

My tone turned harsh. "Ken, you're getting taken for a ride by both of them. Now, it's your business if you want to throw your money away, but one thing you have to keep in mind: if I don't catch Wiley, you are going to be out of a LOT of money. You cosigned his bond and telling anybody *anything* about this case is not helpful. I guarantee it's going to cost you in the long run."

Ken was not pleased, but he didn't have much choice about it, not as long as we held the bond he'd cosigned. I couldn't get a clear read on what his agenda really was. Was he just another Homer, getting off on being part of a "big case"? Or was he like a lot of self-made men, who figured nothing would get done right if they didn't do it themselves?

There was only one way to find out what was really going on. Finally, I agreed to talk to "my man," Bob the Bounty Hunter.

As I hung up the phone, the van's engine RPM decreased markedly as the air-conditioner's compressor kicked in. I sympathized—I felt the same way myself. The results of 9/11 were still reverberating around the country, and like a lot of other people, I was conscious of how much our lives had changed overnight and how much our priorities had changed.

No other vehicles were parked around me in the isolated corner of the parking lot. My mind drifted as I watched cars pull in and out of the shopping center. Almost all of them had an American flag displayed. Flags were mounted on windows, flapping from antennas, stuck magnetically to doors, or decaled on the glass. So many flags all over—why hadn't they been there before? Why did it take tragedy to bring out the fundamentally patriotic nature of our people? A more cynical part of my mind wondered how long it would last.

My musing was abruptly interrupted by yet another cell phone call. It seemed almost rude to interrupt thinking about things important to our country to answer the phone. Once I found out who was calling, it seemed even profane.

A deep voice on the other end barked, "Hey, brother, it's Bob."

I bit my tongue before answering. The cell phone came close to becoming airborne. I wasn't his brother—we had nothing in common. Instead, I took a deep breath and gave my template response for the day. "What's up?"

Bob had what I call a long-distance confidence. After our last encounter, when he'd practically rolled over and exposed his belly to me, he would not have dreamed of using that tone of voice if he'd been within arm's reach of me. We both knew what had happened back at Red's office that day. But the fact that he didn't have to face me physically at the moment let him pretend that we had some different understanding.

"I got something for you, brother," he continued. "You owe me on this one." *Yeah, right. The day I owed Bob a favor would be the day I quit for good.* "Red Crawford wants a meeting and it's set up for tonight."

"Interesting," I said. "Why does Red want a meeting and why is he setting it up with you?"

The image of him stumbling over the carpet in Ken Philip's office flashed across my mind as he spoke. "I'm the man to talk to around here. I've been checking it out. Red's been feeling some heat and wants to set things straight."

The man to talk to. A familiar throbbing in my temples told me my blood pressure was rising. I countered the autonomic response by concentrating on my breathing, but there wasn't much I could do about the burn smoldering in my stomach.

Stress is like that. You can counter the immediate effects, but there's always a price to pay. If it's not released, it's corked up, but only temporarily. Sooner or later, it's coming out.

Tamara's little girl—Wiley had to pay for that. If it meant putting up with Bob for a few minutes, I'd do it to catch the scumbag. I tried to echo his tone of voice, feeling like puking. "Set it up, Bob. Tell me where and when we need to meet. Good job!" My guts were clenched so tight I was surprised I could speak so calmly.

There was a pronounced swagger in his voice. "No problem, bro. Red wants it private and close. How about that place you met Tamara?"

I didn't like the idea of his knowing so much about my business. There was one advantage, though—since I'd scouted the area out before, it wouldn't be unknown territory, and the risk level appeared acceptable.

On the other hand, the hairs on the back of my neck were stiff. Paying attention to my neck hair status has saved my ass too many times to be ignored.

Bob said he knew that area well and the meeting was set for 6:00 P.M. that evening. "Sounds good, bro," Bob said. One more "bro" or "brother" out of him and he was looking at months in a wheelchair. "You going to be in the black van?"

My neck hairs bristled even more as I answered. "Yeah, tell him to look for the black Windstar. What's Red driving?"

"He'll probably be in one of his trucks," Bob said. "You can't miss him. He's got a head full of red hair."

"Go figure," I said.

As soon as I hung up, I used a subscription information service to trace his cell phone number to a billing address. Billing addresses aren't always physical addresses, but a quick check of utility records told me this one was. If the first call had told me his bills were going to a P.O. box, then I could make another call to give me a physical address for that, too.

These services aren't cheap, but Frank never questioned my decision to use them. My instincts—not to mention my neck hairs—have been right many more times than not.

It would take me about an hour to drive to the rendezvous point, so I had plenty of time to go by the house and pick up my *white* van and still be up there early. It was an E-350, a one-ton Econoline, not a Windstar. In other words, a small bus with a gross vehicle weight of 9,600 pounds.

I pulled up next to the Econoline and tossed my equipment bags into it. The nylon carrier clanked as it landed on the floorboard. It was packed with just about every type of human restraint known to man: handcuffs, thumbcuffs, shackles, and belly chains—you name it, I've got it. My leather bag contained canisters of pepper spray, ammo, holsters, belts, cameras, and binoculars. It also held special tools like tire deflators, lock picks, knives, and other entry devices. A first-aid kit, latex gloves, various types of disinfectants, a change of clothes, and toilet paper completed the inventory. All of those things have come in mighty handy at one time or another.

At the last minute, I decided to add the shotgun to my armory. The meeting place was fairly secluded, and seeing the 12 gauge mounted between my seats gave me a warm and fuzzy feeling. An ammo belt loaded with thirty rounds of 00 magnum buckshot topped off the accessories.

I arrived a good hour before the appointed time. A lake was on the east side of the highway. A series of overpasses bridged the road where the lake passed under it to form watery coves. A junkyard full of old cars was on a hill just about a hundred yards across from the cove where we were supposed to meet.

I made several passes up and down the highway and then decided to park under the next bridge up from the rendezvous point and wait. From there, I'd have a clear view of the scheduled rendezvous point under the other bridge, and I could also see up and down the highway. Other vehicles were pulled over in spots and people were fishing from the banks. There was nothing about me that looked out of place, and Red and Bob were looking for a black Windstar, not a white Econoline.

There was just a hint of fall in the air. The change from daylight savings time was only a couple of weeks away and dusk was arriving earlier. It had been a dry year and the leaves had forgone a bright color change. Many of the trees were bare early this year, and the ground was covered with a crunchy, dead brown carpet. The sun had disappeared behind the wooded hills surrounding the coves, and the indirect light made the calm lake look like a sheet of glass.

The radio played as I watched the light traffic up and down the highway. A carload of people pulled over to fish, taking a spot just recently vacated by another group. I watched and thought about the flags in the parking lot again.

It was still thirty minutes before the meeting time when a brown Chevy pickup slowed as it passed over the bridge I was parked underneath. It turned onto a road that looked like it led up to the junkyard. The hairs on my neck were demanding my attention.

Surprise, surprise. Oddly enough, the brown Chevy bore a strong resemblance to the one parked in the dug-out hole in the woods overlooking Red's place. New, but the tires were mismatched, with different brands on the front and rear wheels. No hubcaps. Just amazing what coincidences there are in the world; that same truck turning up while I was waiting for Red. The truck disappeared as it followed the dirt road that wound around behind the hill, instead of heading for the agreed-upon meeting place.

The song blaring on the radio faded as the station went to a commercial break. I waited.

The Chevy pickup reached the top of the hill and pulled forward so that it had a clear view of the rendezvous point. Then the driver backed it up a bit until it was slightly hidden by a junked-out car.

The cab of the truck was visible from my vantage point. My curiosity got the better of me. I reached for the binoculars.

A big, burley, mountain man type with a long thick beard was sitting in the front seat. This guy certainly didn't match Red's description.

Mountain Man looked at his watch, then lit a cigarette. He got out of the truck to take a look around, leaving the driver's side door hanging open. He looked at his watch again and walked back to the open door. He reached inside the cab and pulled out a long case, which he then laid on the ground.

Thanks to my keen powers of observation, years of study, and prior experience in law enforcement, I was able to deduce the nature of said case. I was willing to bet that it didn't contain a telescope, and a few minutes later Mountain Man proved me right.

Mountain Man opened the case and pulled out a rifle with a scope already mounted on it. He laid it across the hood of the truck and took aim on the spot I'd met Tamara, the next bridge up from my current location. I saw his hands fiddling with the focus rings on the scope. The rifle looked to be a 30-06, and he was definitely sighting it in.

It wasn't gun season in this area yet and something told me he wasn't hunting deer anyway. Since big game isn't known for hanging out in parking areas, I was fairly certain he wasn't a poacher.

Okay, I'll admit that my occupation tends to make me overly cautious sometimes, and I never hesitate to do a reality check if I think it's warranted. Coincidences do happen. But what were the odds of somebody sighting in a high-powered rifle at the time and place where I was supposed to be parked? This was not delusional paranoia. I made a mental note to thank my barber for not trimming too close. My neck hairs had been right again.

So what was I going to do now? Did Bob know about this setup or was Red using him? No point in confronting the sniper directly—he'd simply deny everything. Not to mention the little complication that he had the vantage point and long-range firepower.

Bob's cell number was still on my caller ID. Bob answered on the second ring.

"Hey Bob, this is Joe," I said.

There was a long pause. "Uh, hey, bro, where are you?"

"Hey, buddy." I tried to make my voice friendly and good old boy. Just two bounty hunters working a case—except one of them just set the other up. "I'm sorry, but I can't make it to the meeting. I'm still in Knoxville. Something's come up and I can't get up there. I would have called sooner but my cell wouldn't get out for some damn reason."

Bob's voice was a few notes higher and I took some pleasure in the anxiety I heard. "Man!"

Wow, I was no longer a brother. Funny how that worked. And here I'd been thinking we were starting to bond—just like Cain and Abel.

"You sure you can't make it?" Bob asked. "Red wants to meet you. He's there now."

"No, I'll be tied up here all night," I said. "Set it up for tomorrow. Tell Red I'm sorry."

Unless Red had dyed his hair, that wasn't him on the hill. My guess was that he was surrounded by upstanding citizens at this very moment, or at least by people that a court might find credible alibi witnesses.

"Yeah, whatever," Bob said. The connection went dead. So much for brotherhood.

Just then the great white hunter on the hill walked back to the cab of his truck. He was holding a cell phone to his ear. In short order, the rifle was back in the case and the truck was leaving the junkyard. It came down around the curve and stopped before pulling out onto the highway.

The truck passed right back over the bridge that I was parked under. My phone rang while I followed the truck at a distance. It was Tamara.

"This Joe?" she asked. "I couldn't make it either. My car broke down on the way. I called Bob and told him and he said you didn't show either. He sounded pissed."

"Tamara, does Bob know where you live?"

"No," she answered.

"Keep it that way," I said. "In fact, don't call him anymore. This meeting was a setup. We can't trust anybody."

Her voice was frantic. "Oh, shit."

"Listen, Tamara, I'm busy now. Don't talk to anybody. Just wait for me to contact you. I have to go. Bye."

It looked like Bob and Red had planned on killing two birds with one stone. If I were out of the way, the hunt for Wiley would be over. With Tamara gone, the case might go away altogether.

I tried to think while I concentrated on following the truck. There were a couple of vehicles between us, and perhaps a quarter of a mile. Besides, he was looking for a black Windstar, not a white Econoline. I had to do something now, while I had the advantage of surprise—but what?

We turned off the highway and drove through town. The cars between us turned off the road. I stayed about fifty yards behind him. The surroundings got real familiar as we drove up the road leading to Red's property.

It was one of those spur-of-the-moment things. I had closed in and was right behind him. Mountain Man slowed down and was about to make a right turn into Red's driveway. He had the front end of the Chevy cut hard in that direction. Somehow, at the moment his brake lights went out, as he was starting to turn, my foot slipped off the Econoline's brake.

It was like banking a billiards shot. The impact shoved the truck into a ditch with its front end resting on a tree stump. The rear bumper of the truck was damaged on the left side. The tank I was driving had only minor scratches and they blended in with past altercations.

I was concerned that Mountain Man might be injured. I quickly pulled over and rushed to offer assistance.

The driver's side door of the Chevy cab opened just as I approached. Mountain Man's expression, general demeanor, and size caused me quite a bit of concern. He appeared agitated and angry. There are so many terrible stories of road rage on the news these days. Just terrible. Every motorist should learn to recognize the danger signs.

I was especially concerned because there was a rifle case visible on the front seat of the truck. Mountain Man leaned over to crawl out of the cab, and it seemed to me as if he might be reaching for the case. This, of course, put me in fear of serious bodily injury or death, so adequate defensive measures seemed prudent.

Just as Mountain Man's foot hit the ground, I delivered a side kick to the door. His leg was smashed between it and the frame of the truck. This straightened him up and caused him to yell loudly—actually, it was more like a howl.

I opened the door and grabbed his beard up and over his face, which jerked him out backwards. The door slammed again, trapping his neck and leg. He was looking up at the sky, exposing a bushy cluster of nasal hair. The long beard stuck straight up like a mountain of steel wool, and he was twisted in a way that the human body was not designed to bend. I sensed that this might be an opportune time to begin negotiations.

"Stick your goddamn hands out the window or I'm going to break your fucking neck," I said.

Red faced, he struggled to speak. The truck door still had his neck pinned. "Ugh, I... I can't."

Keeping pressure on the door, I looked inside the window. Sure enough, his left arm was trapped between the door and the seat. He was trying as hard as he could to stick his right hand out the window, but it wouldn't reach. His free arm flopped back and forth from his chest to the seat as he tried. My request must have been persuasive.

To help him out, I planted my foot on top of his foot and opened the door just enough to grab the hair on the right side of his head. My hand tightened on his hair and a robust pull brought him out with a slight spin to his right. His left foot was on the ground and his right leg was still in the car. My foot was planted next to his left foot, which prevented his foot from following the rotation of his body.

Under normal situations, a person's knees point in the same direction as his toes. When the knees don't follow the toes, something has to give. In this case, it was his left knee. I heard his knee crack loudly as he landed on his right side—I hate it when that happens.

He let out a muffled scream when his knee popped. Now, although my first-aid skills were a bit rusty, it appeared to me that he needed some assistance in moving. To make him more comfortable, I helped him to roll over on his stomach—with my foot.

My CPR certification had long since expired, but the general principles of how to perform the life-saving maneuver were still clear in my mind. In fact, it seemed to make perfectly good sense to administer the chest compression without rolling him off his stomach, as that would have wasted vital seconds.

My knee dropped on his back between the shoulder blades. He threw his head back and a rush of air was expelled from his mouth and nose. Reassured that his airway was clear, I decided that no more resuscitation was necessary.

He didn't appear able to get to his feet on his own. His left arm was under the truck, so I crawled around from the front and stretched it out in order to cuff him to the spring close to the axle, thus ensuring that he would not try to move about and complicate any other injuries he might have suffered. It's important to keep any victim of a traffic accident from moving around too much.

Only then did I take the time to examine his armory. The rifle was a Remington 30-06. It was a shame to have to bend its barrel with the truck frame but I couldn't take it with me, and I sure didn't want to leave it with Grizzly Adams. Owning a firearm requires a certain degree of personal responsibility, and as he didn't have any identification on him and the truck was without a tag or V.I.N. numbers, I doubted that he was caring for the gun properly.

Even though his accident occurred on private property, the proper thing to due was to notify the authorities. Oops, dang it, wouldn't you know it? If it's not one thing, it's another. For some reason, my cell phone wasn't working.

There was nothing else to do but mosey up the hollow to Red's house and use his home phone. Funny how things worked out.

My tires threw up gravel as I peeled off up the driveway. "Rooster," by Alice in Chains, blasted out my speakers.

Do you know what "the zone" is? It's living on the edge, moving in concert with things when the future is uncertain, events are unfolding, and all you can do is react. Music sounds a little better, food is tastier, and everything is just more real. That's where I was right then. What started out as an ordinary meeting was anything but. Things were happening on the fly, demanding immediate reaction. No planning, no plotting—events were in motion, the situation was still fluid, and it was time to adapt and overcome. The zone—I love it.

I pulled up into Red's front yard with the headlights on high beam and parked just a few feet from the house. The house was neat and well kept, the paint faded but not yet peeling. The oak trees around the house had already shed their leaves, carpeting the grass, and a light breeze swirled them around a bit.

I left the headlights on, lighting up Red's front porch like a stage. The leaves crunched under my feet. I chambered a round in the 12-gauge shotgun and approached the house.

The screen door opened and an angelic figure appeared. The spotlights from the van illuminated strands of wispy salt-and-pepper hair blowing in the slight breeze. The woman wiped her hands on the apron that covered the bottom half of her knee-length polka-dot dress. The petite woman turned her head slightly and squinted, blinded by the headlights, as she tried to make out my silhouette. Her eyes widened when I stepped up on the porch and she spotted my shotgun and badge.

"I've got warrants for the arrest of Wiley Smith," I said.

The woman cupped her hands over her eyes and tried to look past me to see if any more vehicles were in the yard. The noise from my van's engine and the headlights masked any other sounds or sights.

"He's not here," she said, still trying to survey the yard. "He packed up and left a few days ago. I didn't know anything about him being in any trouble."

"Well, I have to make sure he's not here. Where's Red and who are you?"

"Come in and look all you want. Wiley's not here now. Even when he was, there was no way he was coming in the house. He stayed in the barn, in the loft. Red's at the VFW, watching wrestling with his brothers. I'm his wife, Kate."

Like I'd figured—Red was in a very public place and surrounded by a crowd of people. Still, it sure was nice of her to invite me in. This wasn't Wiley's last known residence and there'd been no positive sighting of him here—therefore, I had no legal grounds to forcibly enter her house. An invitation, now—that's a different matter.

Kate walked inside then held the door open for me. A sweet apple fragrance hit me just inside the door. The air was thick, but not smoky with the aroma of freshly baked pie. Lace doilies were carefully positioned on the arms of every piece of furniture. Kate took a seat on the sofa and clasped her hands in her lap on top of her flour-covered apron.

I believed her. There was no way Wiley Smith ever set foot in this house.

There was one other little matter to attend to. "Oh yeah," I said. "There was a little traffic accident in your driveway. The driver was a big burly guy with a beard in a brown Chevy. He was turning up your driveway. You know him?"

She raised one eyebrow in recognition but didn't answer the question. "Was anybody hurt?" she asked curtly.

I smiled. "Nobody was hurt in the accident. Didn't catch the guy's name but he's still hanging around. You might want to call the police and report it since it's on your property. You know, for insurance reasons," I added sarcastically.

Her face changed at that and she looked me straight in the eyes. "You're not the law? Just who are you?"

A direct question. It was very important that I answer it accurately. "I'm a bondsman. Never said I was the police, just that I had warrants for Wiley. When is Red going to be home?"

"You do what you have to do and leave," she said. "I don't have anything else to say."

Well, that sounded to me like her permission to keep searching the premises. I reached in my pocket and retrieved my cell phone. "Would you believe it? This stupid thing seems to be working now. Want me to call the police for you?" She stared straight ahead and pursed her lips. I took that for a no.

After I'd finished searching her house, I backed the van out of her front yard and drove down to the barn. The double doors on a large garage next to the barn gaped open and deep ruts from truck tires gouged a path into it. The putrid smell of meth got stronger as I got closer.

The garage was completely empty. The dirt floor had even been raked. It looked like Red was expecting trouble and had cleaned out his operation.

In contrast, the barn looked more like a Wiley habitat. It was littered with junk and used car parts. Garbage bags filled with Natural Ice and Copenhagen cans filled the loft. An old bedroll lying on a filthy floor completed the decor. Wiley had definitely left tracks here, but if Red was expecting trouble, I doubted he would be back.

On my way out, I stopped to check on my bearded buddy. He was partially upright, sitting with his head and upper back resting against the driver's side tire. His left arm was under the truck with his wrist still handcuffed to the frame.

I tossed one of my cards in his lap. "Here's my information in case you want to turn this in to your insurance. You can keep the cuffs. It's a cheap set anyway."

He didn't say a word. I left him chained to the truck. I doubted he'd be calling his insurance company to report the accident. Stolen vehicles usually aren't covered, at least not on behalf of the thief.

I felt like I'd just pumped out a septic system. Sometimes you have to just stir shit up and see what floats to the top. Although I hadn't caught Wiley, I'd eliminated a potential hiding place. No way Red would hide him out at his place after what had just happened.

Adrenaline fade—it always comes after living in the zone for a while. Anger had replaced adrenaline and this was a time to be careful. My mind strained to overcome emotion because it would be really easy to stray into a perilous, and legally dangerous, situation.

I was no longer in the zone. Things were forced rather than being allowed to flow. My teeth were clenched and both hands had a death grip on the steering column. The radio was off. I raced toward Bob's house.

I had one last little piece of housecleaning to take care of.

A truck with its hood up was parked just outside Bob's trailer. Good old brother Bob was leaning over the fender, tinkering with the engine. The long scabbard was still hanging from his camouflage pants. A can of beer sat on the fender and a Confederate flag was draped across the back window of the cab. He didn't seem concerned about who had just pulled up and didn't rise up out of the hood until I was standing next to the truck.

It was like having my foot on the brake and accelerator at the same time. There was no flow. My mind was stopping my body from taking the actions my emotions were screaming for.

Bob finally looked up. His eyes bulged and his mouth dropped open. He stood there, speechless.

*Move, damn you. Make one move.* The slightest flinch on his part would be all I needed.

Bob reached for the scabbard.

The web of my hand, just between the thumb and the forefinger, struck him right below the trachea. I had just enough presence of mind not to place it any higher, as that might have been fatal. Then I slammed my right knee into his testicles, lifting his 250-plus-pound frame off the ground. I tightened my grip around his throat and set my right foot down behind his left foot, hooking his leg low. Then I extended my left arm, throwing him backwards off his feet.

The back of Bob's head smacked the ground. Rolls of belly fat flopped up to his chest and back down again like a tidal wave. Bob rolled over onto his left side and attempted to gag and puke at the same time.

I leaned over him and unsheathed the long bowie knife from his scabbard and stood over him. The outside lights caught the blade just right and it glistened. The reflected light shone in my eyes as I stared down at him. Bob curled up in a fetal position.

He was right to be terrified. At that moment, I knew I was capable of almost anything.

Chills ran down my spine. I tossed the knife away and let Bob live. He stayed curled up in a fetal position while I left.

Before I pulled out of the driveway, I called Ken Philips. It was a one-way conversation and my own voice sounded unnatural to me. "I just fired Bob. If you like, he can fill you in. He's home if you want to call, but a bit indisposed at the moment, so give him a bit. I'll talk to you tomorrow." I terminated the call before he had time to say anything.

I don't know how it happened, but somehow Mountain Man's cell phone wound up in my pocket. Must have happened during the rescue attempt. The only proper thing to do, of course, would be to mail it back to him. It might take scrolling through all the stored numbers in the phone's address book to make sure I got his address right. It was the right thing to do. I wouldn't have it any other way.

The trip home was boring. The music sucked.

Paperwork ate up most of the next day. Just in case any of the incidents resulted in a lawsuit, I wanted to have a fresh account of everything down on paper. A lot of people put that off and their later accounts are often filled with inconsistencies. It's vital to get one's story—I mean facts—organized. I got everything written down, my database updated, and the whole thing backed up on disk just in time to make it to the dojo.

The usual crowd was at the dojo, including all my black belts. Everyone seemed restless, like they needed to let off some steam. We'd been concentrating primarily on kata work for the last few weeks, so a little extra time in the ring was in order.

There are two things you learn in the ring: technique and flow. The first is a matter of repetition, and it's usually best learned from sparring with someone more experienced. The latter, a form of being in the zone, comes later.

I took my black belts in the ring first, sparring with each one in turn. For them, being in the ring with me was a tune-up, a calibration. My job was to help them recognize their own flaws and vulnerabilities.

I was having a blast sparring with them. It's a real thrill to watch each one develop his own style. But anything more than pointing out one or two things they needed to work on wasn't helping them as much as it was fun for me.

They all hold back just a little when in the ring with me. They're tapping the brakes on their techniques, in a way. They stop the flow.

Part of the reason is that most of the time I know what they're going to do before they actually do it. Either that or they tell me what they are about to do with slight movements or gestures. After all, I started them from day one and knew them in this way better than they knew themselves. Because of this, they can't flow with me. It's just not there. I can cut them off before they can get rolling, and even if I don't, they know I can.

My job was to show them what was stopping them from getting into the zone, to show them where their technical weaknesses held them back from being in the zone. It's like cutting your steering wheel when starting to skid. If you think about it, it's too late. Most of them were just getting to the stage where they could fully understand the lesson.

It's different when they spar each other. Then, they turn it lose. They're not trying to hurt each other—well, not much—but it does get rough. Instead of the forced strategies with me, the techniques are more spontaneous.

After I finished with them, each of the black belts had a round with each of the under belts. Again, the under belts were stifled the same way with my black belts as the black belts were with me. The difference was that the under belts weren't at the stage yet where they could understand what was being taught. It was just a matter of not enough repetition.

Everybody was dripping with sweat and the only two under belts who hadn't yet been matched up were Larry, my big fellow, and Brent, his cousin. Both were anxious to get in the ring. Larry's much bigger, but

Brent is younger, still in college, and has been an athlete all his life. Brent is lean, but big-boned and strong as an ox.

I nodded at each of them. They hopped up, bowed into the ring, and then bowed to each other.

From the very first second, the fight was on. They went at each other with abandon and threw caution to the wind. Bare knuckles thumped on ribs, kicks on elbows or legs, and the only pause in the action was when they stopped to allow one or the other to catch his breath.

Then Larry threw a hard roundhouse kick, one he'd been working on for a while. Brent brought his elbow down hard, blocking it. *Crack!* Larry collapsed on the floor, wrapping his massive hands around his foot.

I stepped into the ring to take a look at Larry's foot. His smallest toe was crooked and already swelling. Probably broken—best not to try to straighten it out.

I scolded him profusely. "How many times do I have to tell you to curl your toes back when you kick?"

He bowed to me as he hobbled back to the starting line. "Sorry sir, I know, sorry."

They bowed to each other again, touched fists and the fight was on. Their techniques were crude and without finesse but they were unrestrained. Brent threw a wild spinning back kick that missed by a mile and Larry stepped in hard as it went past him. He didn't mean to, but one of his big forearms caught Brent square in the back. It knocked Brent across the ring. More important, from my point of view, getting nailed hard made Brent mad.

Brent started to load up his techniques and was trying to force the issue. All of his spontaneity was gone and the only thing on his mind was getting even. Larry was catching him right and left and started to dominate the match. The madder Brent got, the worse his techniques became. After a few more minutes, I stopped it. My black belts smiled and nodded. They recognized what had happened.

I looked at Brent. "This started good and you were equally matched. It was about even until you lost your cool, until you lost the flow. Larry's reading you like a book."

Brent hung his head. "Yes, sir. I'm sorry sir. You're right." There were no hard feelings and the two combatants bowed to each other then hugged before leaving the ring.

The night ended with my black belts having a go at each other. It was a study in magnificence, poetry in motion. The techniques were precise and fluid without any of the stilted movements they had with me. Watching them spar was like watching a violent chess game. These guys took home lessons from each workout and studied how to improve. They exchanged hard blows but never lost their tempers. One might get disgusted with his own mistakes but still appreciated a good technique even if it was at his own expense. That's how one learns, that's how one flows. There's no place for anger. It's all the same.

I hydrated with about a gallon of water after the workout and wasn't that hungry. Debbie had dinner ready and put it in the microwave for me to heat up later. We had just sat down to watch some news when I heard the instant message alert on my computer.

Debbie looked over at me. "Is it time to get perverted again?"

"Very funny," I said, on my way back to the office.

The pop-up from the internet instant messenger dinged again. His real name was Jack but he went by the screen name of "Studly." He was looking for me, or whomever he thought was using the screen name of "Sweetcakes."

Jack's weaknesses were stealing and women's underwear—not necessarily in that order. It seemed he preferred his ex-wife's undergarments when she was not in them—and, in fact, not even present. For some odd reason, she found this objectionable and wanted out of the marriage. It wasn't a complicated divorce since this type of intimacy isn't conducive to producing offspring. A dejected Jack complied with her wishes but maintained an amiable relationship with his ex–in-laws.

Jack had a steady job as a tow truck driver but was not very fiscally responsible and was always broke. He would often augment his income by stealing the contents out from the vehicles he towed and had built up quite a criminal record of petty thefts. The bonds, court costs, and restitution only added to his financial woes.

For someone in Jack's financial straights, his friendship with his ex–in-laws turned out to be very convenient. His ex–in-laws were truck drivers and went on long hauls together, sometimes for weeks at a time. They needed a house sitter. Jack was always broke and couldn't afford to pay rent anywhere. The deal was that Jack would watch the house for them while they were gone and in return got his own room. It was free lodging and all he had to pay for were his own groceries and his part of the telephone bill. They even let him drive one of their cars.

At first, it was a match made in heaven. Then the ex–in-laws started to notice things missing, little bits at a time. First it was power tools and pieces of jewelry. Then ex–momma-in-law's panty drawer started coming up short.

They shrugged it off at first. You know, sometimes people forget who they let borrow things, and for a while ex–momma-in-law just figured her washer and drier were eating her underwear.

But one night, things went a little too far. The ex–in-laws were almost home from a two-week haul when Jack called them on their cell phone. He explained that while he was at work, a burglar had broken into the house and stolen almost everything. Not to worry, he assured them, because he'd already filed a police report and their insurance would cover everything.

When the ex–in-laws got home they were shocked. Everything except the heavy furniture was gone. The TV, stereo, computer, microwave, can opener, and anything else that was worth more than a couple of bucks.

My clients have never been known for their mental prowess, but Jack was a standout in the dense department. As her husband listened to Jack explain what had transpired, ex–momma-in-law snuck out to the car they were letting Jack borrow.

Lo and behold, the glove compartment was stuffed with pawn receipts. By some remarkable coincidence, the items listed on the receipts matched the list of items missing from her house. (Except for her underwear.) Jack was meticulous about keeping records. There were pawn tickets in the glove compartment for items that had been missing since he'd moved in.

Jack was also a pack rat. He never threw anything away. Never. Digging through a rather large cardboard box containing dozens of pairs of women's underwear of various shapes, sizes, and colors, ex–momma-in-law discovered her missing underwear.

Ex–momma-in-law immediately called the police and Jack was arrested on the spot. The good news was that the couple got their possessions back immediately. The bad news was that about a month later Jack never showed up for court, and the ex–in-laws received a $1,200 telephone bill.

It seems Jack was fond of meeting women in internet chat rooms. If they hit it off, they would arrange for a more meaningful relationship via instant messaging. If they *really* hit it off, Jack would get the woman's telephone number. Hence the large phone bill. The ex–in-laws were more than happy to provide me with a copy of it so I could trace the numbers in hopes of finding Jack.

I spoke to four women who actually paid their own ways and flew to Knoxville to meet Jack. They came from all over and as far away as St. Louis and Chicago. Each stayed at the house while the ex–in-laws were out of town, and the women often treated Jack to dinners and bought him gifts. Jack's story was that the house was his but all his money was tied up in a trust. He assured each woman that any day now he would be getting a large inheritance.

Most of the women hadn't heard from him in a while but a few still got instant messages from him intermittently. None of them was pleased to hear the truth about Jack. The fact that the "nasty little bastard" stole their underwear didn't bother them as long as they thought he had money.

One of the last women I talked to was from Nashville. She had been planning to drive to Knoxville to see Jack when her husband stumbled upon the messages between the two stored on the computer.

The husband answered the phone when I called. He and his wife had reconciled and he was more than willing to help me catch Jack. He was so enthused that he pressured his wife into helping me set a trap. She gave me her username and password for her instant messenger account. In the blink of an eye, I became "Sweetcakes."

My computer dinged again.

Studly (Jack): u there sweetcakes? . . . :)
Sweetcakes (me): Hi baby. I'm here. Been so worried. Missed you bad. Where you been? xoxoxo
Studly: Missed u 2. Bad family stuff now. xoxoxo
Sweetcakes: When can I see u. I miss u soooooo much. :(
Studly: Soon sweety, soon. So whatcha doing now? :)
Sweetcakes: Nothing . . . sitting here . . . missin u . . . :(
Studly: Can I ask u something?

Sweetcakes: Sure.
Studly: What kind of panties r u wearing?

I didn't even need to look before I answered.

Sweetcakes: I'm not.
Studly: u not wearing any panties?
Sweetcakes: Nope.
Studly: y not? . . . :) :) :)
Sweetcakes: I never do.
Studly: mmmmmmmmmm. Wanna know what I'm doing right now? . . . :)

That was all I could take. Bond or no bond, if it meant going down that road, Frank was going to pay this one off.

Sweetcakes: Oh shit. Gotta go. Hubby just got home . . . im me tomorrow . . . bye . . . :(

It went on like this for about a month. I heard from him every two or three days but couldn't wiggle his location or even a phone number out of him.

It wasn't like I was hanging out by the computer all the time waiting for him, so several times we missed hooking up. This type of game could go on forever, so some kind of twist had to be introduced to the plan.

Finally, I had an idea that I thought was worth a shot. The opportunity presented itself the next time the instant messenger paged me.

Studly: u there sweety?
Sweetcakes: I been trying to im u.
Studly: Sorry baby . . . just got your im's . . . been missing u . . . xoxoxoxo
Sweetcakes: I come into some money. Leaving hubby and going to Florida. Wanna go? :)
Studly: Really? When u leaving?
Sweetcakes: ASAP. Was waiting for u . . . :) . . . xoxoxox
Studly: No shit? R u sure? . . . :)

Sweetcakes: Oohhhhhhhhh yes . . . :) :) :). Pleaseeeeeeeeeeeeeee cum with me . . . xoxoxox
Studly: Where can we meet?

He was taking the bait. He knew Sweetcakes lived in Nashville, although he'd never actually met her and they'd spoken on the phone only once. I didn't want to spook him, but at the same time I hated the idea of traveling that far to catch this fool.

Sweetcakes: I got to see my sister before I go. I'll stop by on my way down. u know where Athens, Tennessee is?
Studly: Yea. It's about 4 hours for me to get there . . . tell me when . . . xoxoxox

That told me he probably wasn't in Knoxville. Athens was only about fifty miles to the south. He probably wasn't south of Athens, either, or he would've offered to meet farther from Knoxville.

Sweetcakes: I'm sooooooooooo happy :) :) :). Day after tomorrow. Gotta get out of here. I'll give u my sister's cell phone number but don't call till u are there . . . . her husband isn't cool. I'll get us a room somewhere . . . xoxoxoxo
Studly: ohhhhhhhhhh baby. I'm soooooooo there.

I gave him directions to a motel right off the interstate and the cell number of one of the company's bondswomen. She was happy to help—for a small fee, of course.

I IM'd Jack that I'd register under a false name in case "Sweetcakes's" husband was looking for her, and told him to call me on my cell phone when he got off the interstate exit. I also told him I'd just bought a new black Ford Windstar van. There was no telling whether he would show up, but I've taken much longer trips on thinner leads.

My bondswoman called on the cell phone just as I switched channels on the motel room TV. "Your boy just called. I gave him the room number and told him I was getting in the shower and would leave the door open. Just like you said."

I chuckled. "Thanks, honey. I'll let you know what happens."

I hurried into the bathroom and turned the hot water on in the shower. My suitcase was lying on one of the double beds and I'd turned the other bed down. A couple of towels strategically strewn about the room completed the decor of our love nest. I left the door to the room slightly ajar, held open only by the safety latch turned outward.

I positioned myself to be behind the outside door when it opened. My foot was placed so that if he flung open the door, it wouldn't break my nose.

Steam poured out of the bathroom, fogging up the mirror in the main part of the room. The sound of a vehicle pulling up seeped through the crack in the door.

The car's engine gurgled and rattled before it finally quit. My ears strained to pick up any sounds and the wait seemed like eternity.

The door twitched ever so slightly, a tiny deliberate movement. Not the wind—Jack, testing the waters before he made his move. I felt like an angler in a bass boat who'd just felt a nibble, waiting for exactly the right time to set the hook.

Suddenly the door swung open, stopping just short of hitting my foot. Jack wasted no time heading for the bathroom. He had his shirt off and his belt undone before he was halfway across the room.

I slammed the door behind him. He jumped like he'd been shot. When he turned around, he was staring down the barrel of my gun.

I was grinning from ear to ear. "Hi, Studly. I got your Sweetcakes right here."

He just stood there in shock with his mouth gaping. It didn't sink in until I screamed at him to get the fuck on the floor before I blew his brains out. He complied, not even taking the time to ask me what sort of panties I was wearing. I had a feeling a lot of other folks might be asking him that same question in the coming days.

# eight

Something about the Wiley Smith case had been bugging me for days. I could understand Red hiding Wiley out, but Wiley's neck was hardly worth the risk of having me shot.

Red must know that I'd scouted his place and uncovered the stolen vehicles and meth lab. That was the only explanation that made sense, and it was one I could understand. That kind of meth operation brought in a lot of money and people have been killed for a lot less. Which brought me to the next problem: how to keep that from happening.

Only two people knew about my little hike up at Red's place: Homer and Ken Philips. The only person who knew Homer was helping me was Ken. Ken had to be the leak and the reason that Red's people decided to scare Homer off.

Frank wanted to keep Ken in the loop and didn't want to piss him off. Although Ken swore he would stand by his obligation to the bonding company for cosigning Wiley's bond, people have been known to change their minds. If Frank had to sue Ken for the bond amount it could take years to actually collect on a judgment, which meant the company would have long since forked all the money over to the court.

Frank didn't like that possibility and wanted to keep Ken reasonably happy. No doubt Frank would win the case, but since property was not pledged as collateral, collecting would require execution of assets. I hate politics and have always found the direct approach more to my liking.

This was my first full day back in the office since September 11. The neglect showed, and it took all morning and most of the afternoon to catch up on filing and updating the chase board. Our boxes at the courthouse were crammed full of forfeitures, which didn't make Frank very happy. Many of the skips had already taken care of themselves either because they turned themselves in or the cops caught them. Still, Frank didn't like seeing skip paper.

Through the one-way mirror in my office, I watched Frank at work. He was short when answering the phone and cross with others in the office. Every now and then he would glare at my one-way mirror. There was more to his disgruntled disposition than too much skip paper.

Frank couldn't see me through the mirror and it bothered him not to be able to tell if I was looking at him. I knew it was just a matter of time before he couldn't stand it anymore and came back into my office.

Sure enough, Frank rolled his chair away from the desk and placed both hands on his knees. He pushed off and stood up. There was a pained expression on his face as he grabbed a file off his desk and lumbered toward the back of the office.

I was on the phone when Frank appeared in my doorway. He just stood there and looked over the chase board until I hung up the phone. "What happened between you and that bounty hunter from Morristown? Ken Philips said you kicked his ass." I let my irritation show. "What's Ken Philips doing hiring a bounty hunter and why is he calling you?"

Frank's voice got gruffer. "What he does is his business. You —"

I cut him off. "Wait a minute. What he was doing was *my* business. His bounty hunter tried to set me up. The guy went for his knife and I plastered him. Philips has been running his mouth and fucking this up from the beginning."

"You finished?" Frank asked. "He's the cosigner on this bond. I'll deal with him from now on. You just do what you have to do and catch the son of a bitch. But, right now, I got something else I need you to do."

Frank tossed the file on my desk. It belonged to a Ray Shanks and Frank had been hanging on to it. The $50,000 forfeiture came from a neighboring county and was issued some two months prior. I knew this meant Frank thought he could get him caught without having to use me—guess it turned out he was wrong. Can't say that I really blamed him, except most of the time it meant jumping into a case cold.

"He's at the Fifth Avenue Hotel right now," he said.

"Just how the hell do you know that?" I asked.

"I've got my sources, too," he snapped back. "I was going to get him myself, but you were here anyway."

I knew what that meant. Frank figured that he'd found this guy, was just passing on an "easy" pickup, and he'd be taking a cut of my fee. Frank caught a lot of people in his day but now he has leg problems, diabetes, and a heart condition. The odds of him catching anything but a cold were slim to none.

Frank stood in the doorway staring at me. "Well, you going, or not?"

I wasn't all that pleased with Frank at the moment. His insistence on keeping Ken in the loop led to the leak that had almost got me shot.

In his day, Frank was damned fine at bringing skips in. But that was two hundred pounds and three heart attacks ago. Either he's in denial about what he is now or he's got too much ego to admit he can't do what he once did. Sure, he's still got a network of snitches and contacts feeding him information, but he can't do what I do. Sometimes I have to remind him of that.

"Well?" he said again, leaning against the doorframe for support.

I stood up abruptly. The chair I'd been sitting in slammed back against the bookcase behind me. Frank knows I move pretty fast, but it still startled him enough that he moved back.

Enough of this bullshit. I held the file out to him. "Every time I jump into something somebody else has started, it turns into trouble. I don't know anything about this guy or the case. Hell, I don't even know what he looks like. Either I study this file a while or you go get him yourself."

Frank turned around and walked out without taking the file. I waited until he was back at his desk before I returned to perusing the file. I could still see him—he couldn't see me. I don't necessarily like making my point with Frank through physical intimidation, but sometimes that's what it takes. It was his company—if he didn't like it, he could try to find someone else who could do what I do. Good luck.

According to his file, Ray Shanks was a bad boy. The manila folder was stuffed with arrest records and computer-generated mug shots. He'd done time in multiple states for assault, robbery, home invasion, and attempted murder. Yeah, Frank, an easy pickup. And there was one other little tidbit Frank evidently hadn't seen. Ray collected resisting-arrest and assault-on-an-officer charges like Studly collected women's underwear.

Ray's bond application showed he was married to Kate Shanks—there was a note from Frank saying they were traveling together. Kate was no stranger to a jail cell and she'd beaten up a cop or two herself. Soulmates, a match made in heaven. Or, more likely, in the local lockup.

After flipping through the paperwork, I knew why Frank had handed the file over to me. He needed Ray caught quickly. Ray was also wanted for federal parole violation, which meant the Feds were looking for him, too.

I've mentioned before that most bail jumpers aren't noted for their intellectual prowess. Most of the time, this works in Frank's favor. He'll hold off handing over files to me, hoping that the skip will do something stupid and get himself arrested before Frank has to pay the bond. This gamble usually pays off and that always makes Frank happy—he doesn't have to pay the court and he doesn't have to pay me.

But sometimes it doesn't. You guess wrong too many times and you'll be out of business pretty fast. They call a bond in, the courts expect the bonding company to pay up pronto.

If a skip's in custody in another jurisdiction, usually a letter from his current landlord—a.k.a. the warden—stating that they've got him will satisfy a judge and the bond won't be called in. Theoretically, a federal facility is suppose to hold the skip until the state can come get him, once his federal time is served.

That's the theory. In practice, it doesn't always work out that way. Sometimes the Feds snafu the paperwork and let the skips just walk out the front gate. We eventually find out, but by then we're chasing a cold trail again.

Frank didn't want to take that chance. He wanted me to arrest Ray before the Feds found him and take him to the jail of our choice. Then the Feds would have to wait in line to get him and we would be off the bond.

Both Ray's and Kate's families lived in the county that had issued the warrant. One of Frank's snitches had told him that the couple was sneaking into that county at night to visit relatives, and Frank had been counting on the local cops catching them during one of their late-night forays. Usually, that would have been the winning bet, and under other circumstances Frank might have been willing to play the odds of stupidity winning out for a while longer. But the federal warrant threw a wildcard in the mix, and Frank wasn't willing to rely on the Feds' reputation for efficiency to turn Ray over to the state when they were done with him. There was too much money at stake.

I watched Frank rock back and forth in his chair, glancing at his watch every couple of minutes. We'd had our showdown for the day—and my one-way mirror still worked just fine. I took my time sifting through the file.

Reading the Shanks file was like leafing through a family album. Despite the care that the jail photographers had no doubt taken with the photos, none of the pictures would qualify as glamour shots.

There were decades of photos of the two, taken from a variety of official angles. No problem telling when or where they were taken—the states involved had been kind enough to label each portrait. Not unexpectedly, there were no pictures of the two of them together. Mug shots aren't done that way.

Ray and Kate were both tall, with Ray pushing six foot two and Kate just under six feet. Over the years, they'd sported different hairstyles with varying combinations of facial hair. Kate probably didn't appreciate how the booking room light accented her five o'clock shadow. Noses went from straight to crooked and front teeth migrated, becoming spaced further apart. New scars appeared, faded, and were covered up by beards. You flip through the mug shots fast enough, it was like a bad movie.

Several of the pictures showed them smiling, almost snarling, at the camera. These two liked it.

The Shanks obviously didn't believe in aging gracefully. Neither of them would have ever been described as petite, and the booking records showed they'd both gotten larger over the years. Their faces grew wider as the hair got shorter and scars got thicker. The effects of age and gravity are never kind, especially when combined with the lifestyle these faces were forced to endure. Thick jowls hung down in layers and swollen ears protruded from too many nightstick encounters. The most recent intake records showed Ray dressing out at about two hundred eighty pounds, with Kate a distant second at two-twenty.

I love that one-way mirror. The longer I took studying the file, the more Frank fidgeted.

There was no way Frank had even looked through this file. He knew nothing about Ray or his tendencies. If he did, he would never have considered going down to pick up Ray himself. All Frank had done was jot down notes from snitches, playing the odds that the Shanks would fall back into state hands before the bond was called in. All in the hope that he could keep from having to pay me.

And *he* was irritated at *me* for taking time to read the file before going out on this alleged "easy" pickup? He was clueless about Ray Shanks and if I'd just taken him at his word, I'd have regretted it.

The more I thought about it, the more pissed off I got. I felt like telling Frank to go ahead and catch Ray by himself, but I couldn't do it. Even though Frank was willing to chisel me on my fee, I wouldn't set him up like he'd almost set me up. Ray liked to fight—this is something I understand—especially with cops, and odds were this was not going to be the "easy" pickup Frank thought.

I walked past Frank's desk on the way out the door and tossed some paperwork on his desk. He looked down at his watch again and told me to be careful.

"Always," I answered. Yeah, right, careful like you were before you handed me a cold file and told me it was "easy."

The Fifth Avenue Hotel sits on the corner of Broadway and Fifth Avenue in downtown Knoxville. Decades ago it was an upscale, elegant hotel, but time hasn't treated it any better than the Shanks. It's absorbed the character of the surrounding urban decay, and now it's flanked by homeless shelters and soup kitchens.

In warm weather, interstate overpasses house the overflow from the shelters. When it's colder, many of the homeless sneak into the halls of the Fifth Avenue Hotel for a few hours sleep. Lodging rates were what you would expect for an establishment of this prominence, and several of my skips have used it for temporary lodging.

The hotel's management and I were on good terms. If I were there any more often, they'd probably start charging Frank rent. I understand they have hourly rates.

By the time I reached the Fifth Avenue Hotel, it was midday. The usually invisible homeless were congregating and the lines at the food kitchens were forming for lunch. The people came from every direction: alone, in pairs, and sometimes in groups. It wasn't unusual to see whole families waiting in line and women pushing strollers.

Hookers and cops played their cat-and-mouse games, too. The hookers trolled the streets, skimpily clad and favoring sequins and spandex, brazen until one of them spotted an approaching police car. Then they disappeared into the alleys and dark places the homeless had just vacated, laying low until the car passed.

Not that the cops were really there to arrest them—not really, not unless there's a sting operation targeting that part of town. (Prostitutes are generally territorial, and our bondsmen can usually anticipate who's going to be calling according to what sections of town the police have set for sting operations.)

But mostly, the cops wanted the hookers off the main streets. So they cruise by, the girls do their disappearing act, and then reappear when the coast is clear.

Two alleys flank the hotel. The one that opens onto Broadway leads to a parking lot that is hidden from the main street. I waited for a group of people on a food pilgrimage to move out of the way and then eased the van down the narrow alley.

The lot was littered with broken bottles, trash, and the remains of some activities I'd rather not describe in detail. There were no spry valets waiting to take my keys, but good old-fashioned American capitalism was at work. The local inhabitants had reclaimed the right to regulate the parking.

A guy in a black wooly cap and old army jacket approached me and I gave him five dollars to "watch the van." A wise investment, as anyone who'd parked in the area before could tell you. There were only two other cars in the lot, both without windshields.

The other alley led out to Fifth Avenue and was partially blocked by overturned garbage cans. Side entrances to the hotel gave easy access to the hallways and rooms and provided a little shelter from the street. Many a brief transaction of one kind or another took place in these doorways as the participants ducked out of sight. I walked down the alley to Broadway and went in the main entrance.

Inside the hotel, the smell of urine was overwhelming. The fresh excrement couldn't entirely mask the odor of aged piss that had soaked into the floors and walls over the years. Large chunks of ancient acoustic tiles were barely attached to the ceiling, and several of the light fixtures dangled precariously from electrical wiring. Paint peeled off the walls, speckling old linoleum with lead-based snow.

The small entrance foyer led to a single hallway, which was lit only by light from the open door of the office at the end. Plumes of tobacco smoke billowed out, twisting in the block of light from the open door. I walked in the office and fanned the air, trying to clear out a breathable swatch through the thick smoke.

Mavis looked up and smiled. "Hi, honey. Who you looking for?" Mavis was a tiny woman. Her arms were folded on the desk in front of her, level with her chin. She had a cigarette in one hand smoldering dangerously close to her left eye. She was the hotel manager and had probably been there since before I was born.

"How you doing, Mavis?" I asked. "When are you finally going to get a booster chair so you can see the top of your desk?"

Mavis just laughed, as did the three other women sitting in overstuffed chairs surrounding a TV next to her desk. Each one had a lit cigarette and all but Mavis were still in their robes and bedroom slippers. The gray-haired quartet was huddled around watching Jerry Springer. I guess I was flattered that they found my arrival more entertaining than the show. I gave Mavis a picture of Ray. She flicked her cigarette, but the ash just rolled off the mound of butts piled up in the ashtray and fell on her desk. "He's here," she said.

Mavis passed the picture around to the other old gals, as it probably seemed rude to her not to do so. Each one in turn took a puff, looked at the picture, nodded, and exhaled a plume of smoke. There was no doubt about it. The consensus was in.

Mavis took another drag on her cigarette. "I'll get the maintenance man to let you into his room." *Maintenance* is a term that has a different meaning at the Fifth Avenue Hotel. It's not like he actually maintained anything—he wasn't even an employee per se, just a guy she let stay there for free in exchange for occasionally shoveling trash out the door.

Mavis gave me the room number and told me to go on up and wait for the maintenance guy. "Just be patient, sweetie. It might take a bit to wake him up."

Walking down any hallway in the Fifth Avenue Hotel is like negotiating an obstacle course. Bodies slouched against the walls and others just lay in the middle of the hall, all sleeping off whatever had seemed like a really good idea the night before. I stepped over legs, arms, and torsos, carefully sweeping wine bottles and syringes out of the way as necessary. The urine smell got stronger and was combined with the fragrance of months-old body odor and vomit. The hall was filled with the sounds of various types of bodily functions, making it impossible to hear anything inside the rooms. Once I got to Ray's room the only thing to do was to wait.

"Maintenance" finally arrived. Once you see him, you know where the expression "something three cats dragged in" came from. His hair was matted on one side and a straggly mustache looked as if he tried to blow his nose without the benefit of a tissue. "I'm Eddie. Mavis told me to let you in," he said. "I used to work security. I got your back if it gets rough."

I didn't know if Ray had any weapons inside, but things would go a lot easier if I could get him to come to the door. I'd retain the element of surprise, and I'd be on him faster than if I had to rush him from the doorway. "Does Ray know you?" I asked.

Eddie nodded. "Yeah. They stop their toilet up all the time and call me to fix it."

"Good," I said. "How about you knock on the door and see if he answers? Say you have to fix a leak or something."

There was a sudden gleam in Eddie's eye. I recognized the signs of another wannabe, just like Homer.

Eddie straightened up, pulled back his shoulders, and stuck out his chin. He clenched his fist and knocked on the door, rattling it in its loose frame. "Maintenance!" he shouted. The authority in his voice caused a stir in some of the squatters in the hallway.

We stood and waited. No response.

I nodded at Eddie. Eddie knocked again, louder this time. "Maintenance! I need to check for a leak." Still no answer and, as far as I could tell, no sounds coming from Ray's room. Okay, so we didn't get to do this the easy way. "Open it," I said. I drew my gun.

Eddie turned the key in the lock and stepped out of the way. I eased the door open, kept my Glock in the low ready position, and scanned the room.

A shirtless man was sitting up but passed out on an old brown couch that was leaning to one side. The man, who matched Ray's mug shots, had his head thrown back and arms spread at his sides like a giant bird. His head and chest rose in time with a ripping snore that filled the room as he inhaled. The exhalation came in the form of a gurgling sound from the gaping mouth and the cycle started again. There was no sign of Kate.

There looked to be about a case of empty beer cans scattered about on a cheap coffee table in front of the couch. Several of the cans had rolled off onto the patched linoleum floor. Drunk, passed out, no Kate around—hey, maybe this would be an easy one after all.

There was a bathroom just to the other side of Ray. Through the open door I could see a sink stained yellow and brown, a toilet, and a dripping shower faucet. Still no sign of Kate. A doorway just to the left of the couch led into a tiny bedroom. I glanced over it quickly, then returned my attention to Ray. Kate was nowhere to be seen. She was either hiding, or, hopefully, not at home. Not wishing to lose the advantage of Ray's comatose state, I holstered my gun and quietly slipped over to the couch.

I moved slowly, stepping around the beer cans, taking my handcuffs from their case. Ray's snores hadn't missed a beat, and it was pretty clear he had no idea he was no longer alone. Even being cuffed in front would be sufficient restraint to prevent any problems. I reached over the table and cuffed his left hand, gently lifted it up and laid it on his stomach. No reaction. At that point, I was pretty sure he would have slept through an earthquake.

I had my back to the bedroom and was bending over him to get the other hand into the cuffs. Just as I touched Ray's right hand, a loud scream erupted behind me. Kate had emerged from her hiding place with her mouth wide open and her lungs in good working order. Her bloodshot eyes bulged as she screeched.

Kate's scream must have set off all his internal alarms. His mouth snapped shut and his eyes opened. Slightly disoriented, he glared at me with a crazed look and then snarled.

In a split second he was on his feet, trying to shove me away. I sidestepped him and swept his left foot out from under him. He reeled to the side, lost his balance, and collapsed onto the coffee table. It shattered, flattening under him and fragging the room with bits of wood debris. I bent over to cuff his hands behind him.

Suddenly, my knees buckled. Two-hundred-plus pounds of enraged Kate landed on my back, clawing and scratching, screaming like a wildcat as she peeled off chunks of skin and flesh from my neck and face with her nails. Her hands stabbed at my eyes, trying to get a grip.

I grabbed one of her hands, turned, and threw her against the wall. I pulled the pepper spray canister from my belt and nailed her with a direct stream of the potent stuff into her face. Without waiting to see her reaction, I turned back to Ray.

I had a split second to note that Ray had picked up a leg from the shattered table and was swinging it like a baseball bat. Then the piece of wood nailed me low on the forehead and right between the eyes. There was no pain, at first.

My training took over. I delivered a hard kick with my right shin to the side and slightly to the back of his left knee. The blow to the tendon of the femoris muscle and illiotibial tract produced the expected result of bringing his head down and turning it slightly. I closed the distance between us with a short half step and smashed my forearm into his jaw just below his left ear. That spun him around to his right and he fell to the floor on his knees, his face down on the couch. His feet were positioned with the toes down and heels pointed straight up toward the ceiling. I brought a cross kick down hard on the Achilles tendon he'd so graciously presented. It snapped, twanging like a guitar string breaking.

Rupturing an Achilles tendon causes excruciating pain, but Ray didn't react. He was out cold again—if he'd just stayed that way from the beginning, things would have been a lot easier.

Blood from my forehead was getting in my eyes. I wiped it away just in time to see Kate sticking her head in the shower. She howled as the water washed the pepper spray down her chest and lit up the lower parts of her body. If I'd been in a better mood, I would have warned her about that. Kate was busy dealing with the pepper spray, so I gave Ray my full attention.

Blood streamed down my face and dripped on Ray's back while I struggled to put restraints on him. He was almost too big for me to position his hands close enough together to cuff him behind the back. He didn't move as the handcuffs clicked shut. I took off my shirt and wrapped it like a headband around my forehead to keep the blood from blinding me.

I grabbed one of his feet with both my hands and dragged him out of the room facedown. The ankle with the ruptured Achilles tendon was already discolored and swollen to about the size of a grapefruit. This made it too big to hold with one hand, so I placed his feet under my armpits and clung to his shins. His limp body was still facedown as I dragged him into the hall.

A short flight of stairs led down to the sidewalk at the Fifth Avenue. A steady thump, thump, thump as his face bounced down the concrete steps accompanied us all the way down.

Just as we got to the sidewalk, two police cars came to a screeching halt at the curb. My intrepid maintenance man, Eddie, must have "had my back" and enough sense to call 911. Both officers recognized me immediately.

As they approached, Ray woke up. He tried to stand but his inability to break forward momentum due to the ruptured tendon caused him to fall right back down on his face. Ray still wasn't feeling pain, and he kept trying to get up and kept falling down, over and over. One of the officers opened the back door of his cruiser and we heaved Ray onto the backseat. The car door slammed behind him as he flew in headfirst and hit the door on the other side.

A police sergeant arrived on the scene and made a report. I sat on the steps and kept pressure applied to my forehead as they verified my warrants. Perspiration was running into the scratch wounds on my neck and they started to sting. The sergeant called me over to the car and handed back my warrants. Ray sat up, leaned over in the backseat, and tried to spit on me. He was too gone to realize that the window was rolled up and his bloody saliva just ran down the glass.

The officers took the unprecedented step of offering to transport Ray to the county line and transfer him to their custody for me. They were afraid we would have trouble the whole way and were probably right. I jumped at the idea because there was no doubt he needed medical attention, and waiting with him at the ER was not on my list of preferred activities.

Kate charged down the stairs like a mad bull. She had a wet towel draped around her neck and was screaming profanities. She swung her fists wildly at the officers. They wrestled her to the ground, cuffed her, and loaded her into another car.

The bleeding from my forehead wound had slowed to a seeping weep. I drove straight to the office to fill Frank in. Any time there are injuries and the police are involved, he needs to know about it as soon as possible.

The first person to see me when I walked in was Frank's wife. She covered her mouth with her hands and ran back to one of the bathrooms to get sick. Frank sat there with his mouth open as he looked at me.

"Had a little bit of trouble," I said. "I'll write up a report and give you a copy."

I went into a bathroom to check out the damage. A flap of meat and skin hung down from my forehead onto the bridge of my nose. The blood was clotting but a small steady stream of a light-colored discharge flowed down the side of my nose. Long scratch marks peeled layers of skin off my face and neck. There seemed to be something sticking in my forehead wound. I poked at it a bit and found it was wood splinters. The gash was numb, but the scratches stung like hell when I cleaned them up with hydrogen peroxide.

Frank was standing outside the bathroom door when I came out. "Get your ass to the hospital and get sewn up. Bring me the bill." He handed me a check for the full amount of the fee for catching Ray. "I'm damn glad I didn't go after that son of a bitch myself."

I guess Frank figured it wasn't a good time to negotiate. He was always fair and his business dealings had never been an issue.

Making that kind of money for two hours work ain't too shabby. I've actually made more than that in less time and without the fight, but there have also been times that chasing a hooker skipping on a $500 bond took up the better part of a week. You have to take the good with the bad. It's like anything else.

The doctor in the ER plucked out all the splinters and sewed up the wound with ten stitches. "It's going to leave a scar," he told me. "Watch out for infection in the scratches."

I went back to the office and filled out my reports while the incident was still fresh in my mind. The police report wouldn't be available until tomorrow.

By the time I was finished, the forehead wound had started to swell and discolor. Both of my eyes were turning black, and the shot at the hospital to deaden the feeling was starting to wear off. Still, I'd left some work undone to go catch Ray and I wanted to finish up. I filed the rest of the files and made a few phone calls relating to other cases. Everyone else had gone home, leaving me to lock up the office and turn on the alarm.

Debbie was in another part of the house when I got home. "Hi, Sweetie," I called out. "I'm home." My somewhat warped sense of humor caused me to carry on as if there was nothing out of the ordinary and wait for her to come into the kitchen. My back was turned when she walked in. I suddenly spun around. "Hi, baby."

Her eyes flew wide and mouth dropped as she gasped, "Oh my God! What happened?"

I laughed.

She wasn't amused.

Her shock turned to anger as I told her the story. "That bitch," she said, examining the scratches. Debbie was good fighter back in her days at the dojo. The look in her eyes reminded me of when she was in the ring. It was a look most people regretted seeing.

This was a karate workout night and her tone was stern. "You're not getting in the ring tonight. Right?"

"I might be crazy," I said. "But I'm not stupid." Debbie raised one eyebrow, making it pretty clear she thought I might be both.

You want to get your students' attention in the dojo? Walk in looking like you've been hit by a truck. I did, and the reactions were predictable, if a bit more varied than the one at home. My senior students just nodded knowingly and gathered around to hear another good story. They pay attention and they learn from my experiences. Some of the junior belts and beginners looked confused. Understandable, and definitely a teaching opportunity.

All martial arts students at one time or another wonder if what they are learning will actually work. They're right to be concerned. Most of what is being taught today is crap.

While there are many excellent martial artists in the world, the percentage of good versus bad is being tilted to the negative at an ever-quickening pace.

The meaning of being a black belt has more often than not been watered down. The vast majority of instructors have never been in an actual street fight, at least not a life-or-death one. This may, in fact, be a testimony to their intelligence—but not to their ability to teach practical, situational combat techniques.

You can't teach what you don't know. Anybody who teaches students to use a jumping, spinning back kick followed by a triple gainer in a street fight has never been in one. The fancy stuff doesn't work when you're facing big bad Bubba who just loves to kick the crap out of people. Most karate schools these days are costume baby-sitting services. They dress the kids up in cute karate uniforms and keep them busy while their parents work late or go shopping at the mall. These places make a lot of money, but any resemblance to a true martial arts regimen is a facade. The large commercial schools pander to a child's worst instincts. Some of them have installed their own video arcades and offer incentives and prizes. Given a choice between the hard work and discipline required in real martial arts training and the scripted violence and quick gratification of videogames, guess which ones the kids choose? Then tell me which choice is better for the child.

Martial arts training is supposed to be hard. True training is *exclusive*, not *inclusive*. Students should be tested and tested hard. They must step up to the plate and prove they have what it takes. It is this that promotes inner growth. Facing and overcoming one's fears is what creates confidence, not have something given to them.

Most schools have sold out. Is it any surprise that many people doubt the benefit of martial arts training? It's bound to raise questions when they see a twelve-year-old black belt who gets his butt kicked after school. Even worse is when the black belt gets into trouble and is a bully himself. In my school, that's what gets them thrown out for good.

I have a handful of techniques that I've found reliable. They're founded on the premise that if a person can't see, breath, or stand up, he's whipped.

But there's more to becoming an effective fighter than learning the techniques I use on the street. Continuous kata practice gives my students the physical ability to execute the moves. Hard sparring puts bark on them and makes them tough. It also improves timing, distance awareness, and mental toughness. All that comes together to provide the tools necessary to perform.

We trained that night on the old reliable techniques that we've worked on so often, the ones that I use every day and the ones I will continue to rely on. When something has saved your ass time and again, you become reluctant to experiment. A good martial artist trains to be well-rounded, but a life and death situation is not the time for trial and error.

In the end, though, you fight like you train. Sparring in a ring in the dojo is just a means to an end. It's not actual fighting, not the way it is on the street.

The vast majority of karate schools teach point kumite, or sparring, for the purpose of going to tournaments and winning trophies. If one's training is primarily geared for competition, call it what it is: a sport, not martial arts. I've seen more than one point fighter get his ass handed to him on the street.

I have been fortunate to train with some very tough guys and learned a lot from them. Some of them are crazy enough to be into full-contact and no-holds-barred cage fighting. No doubt about the toughness of these guys. Would I crawl into a cage with an experienced cage fighter? Hell no! I'm not that nuts. (Not now, anyway...maybe.) Can I take a cage fighter down in a street fight in order to make an arrest? You betcha. The cage is their world; the street is mine.

Anytime one trains for a specific form of competition, it means training to rules. There aren't any on the street. For example, sparring rings in the dojo or cages all have a level, consistent surface. They both have fixed dimensions, time limits, and, probably most important, one can always "throw in the towel" or quit if things go badly.

Not so on the street. The terrain is uneven. Curbs, slick spots, trash, and traffic all have to be taken into account—or, even better, used to your advantage. The number of opponents can vary and so can their weaponry. If you train to fight by a specific set of rules, your mind will not be flexible enough to deal with the variables of the street. That's why many so-called black belts have been whipped by a big, flat-nosed, bar-smashing, street fighter.

Most, if not all, of my students are merely interested in saving their skin in case big bad Bubba comes after them. That's why most people start martial arts training in the first place, and it's exactly the reason one should begin training. But unless you train with somebody who deals with Bubba on a consistent basis, how do you know if what you're learning actually works?

The other big weakness in commercial martial arts training is that it doesn't teach students to deal with stress. You get attacked, you're going to experience an adrenaline dump. No doubt about it. If the training doesn't include that, it's seriously deficient. The concept of turning one's body into a weapon is mostly ignored today. Training has become softer and less effective. Avid proponents of pressure point, or dim mak, insist that light pinpoint strikes can yield devastating results. I know this to be true and I use it and study it myself as part of being a well-rounded martial artist.

But can a person be expected to place pinpoint strikes on a spot smaller than a dime and in a certain direction when Bubba is swinging a machete at him? I think not. But again, my judgment might be clouded by experiences—by Bubba.

My students train to be able to defend themselves against any threat: Bubba, a boxer, or another trained martial artist. I take the responsibility seriously. I teach them to execute a devastating attack when threatened and then to run like hell. Unfortunately, some of my students have been assaulted over the years, but they were equipped with the tools to survive. Hearing how their training saved their ass is a gratification that defies description.

We worked without a break on street techniques that night. One of them was exactly the same series of moves I used earlier that day against Ray. "Nobody says you won't get skinned up," I said. "I'm training you to be able to walk away."

We bowed out at the end of class and everybody left. The day's events played through my head and the process of analysis began. I worked on my shin kicks on the heavy bag and followed them up with the forearm smash. A quick study of the acupressure chart sent me back to the bag to further refine my angle of attack. My focus then turned to examining better distance coverage between impacts.

God, I love it! There's never a plateau, never an end to the work.

I looked at the clock and knew that dinner would be cold and Debbie would be pissed. There was just enough time to get in some makiwara work to improve my tension.

On the way home, my cell phone rang. It was Tamara Fields.

"You've scared the shit out of them," she said. "Snake's been snooping around. Red moved Wiley and his meth operation because of you. He thinks Wiley might be hiding in the woods somewhere and cooking the stuff. Snake's going back down there in a few days."

"Snake needs to be careful and just keep his ears open," I said. "Tell him to call me next week. At least we got those assholes jumping." Sometimes it pays to just stir up shit and see what floats to the top.

I hung up the phone just as I pulled into the driveway. My head was throbbing and my stomach growling. The phone chimed as it powered down. No more calls tonight.

# nine

Nobody wants to be in jail during the holidays. As the weather turned cooler and the leaves started changing, more and more of our clients skipped their court dates and hit the road. It's a noticeable change from the summer, when I'm often not too busy. Then, most lightweight offenders figure they can do their time and be out by Thanksgiving or Christmas, and they turn themselves in. So they miss getting a tan—not an important item on most of their lists.

But Thanksgiving and Christmas are different. Even scumbags have mommas, and skips want to see their families over the holidays. That's where I know they'll be, so that's where I go looking for them. You drop your hook where you know fish are biting. (Funerals, while not as predictable as the holidays, are also excellent places to trip the snare. Some might think that's in poor taste, but it's not like the dearly departed are going to miss them. The way I look at it, by arresting the type of people I'm looking for, I'm preventing assaults and murders that might result in funerals for more innocent folks.)

What was true for my skips was true for us as well—the holiday season wasn't the same without Joey. While this wasn't the first Christmas he'd been deployed, it seemed like the bleakest. We didn't know for sure where he was at the moment, but we had a good idea where his unit was headed. He did e-mail us from the ship to say he was fine, but he couldn't reveal his location or destination. Staying busy arresting holiday skips wasn't a problem; it helped to ease the anxiety.

The fall season had really slipped up on me. The weather was past the point of cool and getting downright cold, especially at night. It suddenly occurred to me that I'd missed one of my favorite roundup times: Halloween. When else is it normal to knock on a door wearing a mask? Admittedly, I did derive a certain ghoulish pleasure from knocking on a door dressed like the Grim Reaper and saying, "Trick or treat—you're under arrest."

Between tracking down leads and following up on snitch reports, I hardly had time to check for new warrants at the courthouse. I racked up thousands of miles on the van, crisscrossing county lines, sometimes transporting several busted skips at once. I was starting to feel like the Staten Island Ferry as one prisoner after another found himself housed courtesy of various and sundry sheriffs' departments.

On my way back from dropping off a prisoner in Anderson County, my cell phone rang. An informant told me a skip by the name of Jose had cruised into town to see his family. His rather large group of kinfolk shared a house in a rural part of the county.

My records indicated Jose was driving a white 1986 Chevrolet Monte Carlo and gave me his family's address. With the exception of a few family squabbles and mild altercations with drinking buddies, Jose was not known to be a violent man.

Jose had his own prescription drug plan, one offering a couple of options. Most of the time, he'd simply break into a pharmacy at night and fill his own prescriptions. No deductible, no co-pay, no worrying about substituting generics.

Occasionally Jose would be brave enough to jump over the counter during business hours, help himself, and run out. His escape was usually well planned and the cops hadn't had any luck catching him.

Jose got away with both methods until he had bad luck on one of his over-the-counter stunts. As he left, he ran right into the arms of a cop who'd stopped by to have a prescription filled.

As soon as he bailed out, Jose took his show on the road and left the area. The local drugstores were all on the lookout for him anyway, making it difficult for an honest drug thief to make a decent living, and his short stint in the local jail had taught him that confined spaces weren't to his liking.

I had a few hours to spare, so I headed out for Jose's family's location and found it easily. The house was located on a one-lane asphalt road that dead-ended on the other side of the highway. Alongside the short road were four houses evenly spaced. The small brick structures were carbon copies of each other and there were enough vehicles parked in the combined yards to form a respectable used car lot. Weathered sofas sat on the front stoops, guarding the children's toys scattered about. My skip's car was parked in the yard of the second house down on the right.

I backed the van in beside an old country store and gas station that had evidently been out of business for quite some time. My binoculars afforded me a view down the only approach to the house and the highway. I took some time to check out the surrounding area.

A sea of fields surrounded the houses. The dozens of acres to the left of the road were dotted with stubbed corn stalks. A large barn with several tractors and their various attachments strewn about was in the distance. Behind the houses to the right were long rows of plastic sheets that covered tobacco plots. Vast tracts of hay fields surrounded the plots, and the grass flowed around the bales to the foot of a hill and stopped at a barbed wire barrier. Like a medieval castle on a mountain, a huge residence overlooked the valley.

The house on the hill undoubtedly belonged to the property owner. A long concrete driveway passed through a brick-columned entrance and wound its way up to the house. White-planked fencing flanked the driveway and bordered the citadel like a moat. Cattle grazed on the hillside at the hay that had been ferried up from the fields below. A towering pole marked the crest of the driveway and the flag flapped lazily in the shifting breeze. A picnic table sat under a majestic oak that looked down on the land below. I envisioned iced glasses of lemonade providing relief under the shaded perch as the land barons looked down to survey their holdings and the work going on.

I went back to watching Jose's family's house, keeping both my binoculars and attention focused on them. Not a creature was stirring—well, except for a dog taking a nice long stretch in a patch of sunlight. At least half a dozen people lived in my skip's house, so a frontal approach wouldn't be prudent.

This job involves a lot of sitting and watching and waiting, just like fishing or hunting. Since the van was also my mobile office, it seemed like a good time to catch up on paperwork. I tilted the seat back, slid a Dave Matthews Band CD into the player, and laid out my protein bars and bottled water. The volume was low on the stereo. The laptop whirred as it booted up. The hard-copy files were arranged in my briefcase according to the order of capture. I pulled the first one out and started entering information into my database. I could get quite a lot done in my van, although I'd have to wait until I got back to the office to scan the pictures in.

An hour and a half later, I was done with my paperwork and there was still no sign of activity at the house. The bottled water was taking its toll so I opened the car door and stepped around to the back of the building. I left the van door open and key in the ignition, letting the warning chime keep me company as I improvised some plumbing. The sun felt good on my face and washing down the back wall of the store felt even better. The irritating chiming noise ceased when I got back in the van and closed the door. I settled in to wait some more.

Two more hours passed when my cell phone rang. It was Tamara Fields.

"Snake's been snooping around and thinks he's getting closer to finding out where Wiley's hiding," she said. "It's the cave where Wiley hid after he shot his brother-in-law years ago."

"Why would he hide there?" I asked. "They found him there before."

"Yeah, I know. But they had to use bloodhounds and that was years ago. Besides, the local law there ain't looking for him. If Red Crawford turned him out, Wiley wouldn't have nowhere to go. His own kin hate him."

"Does Snake know where this cave is?" I asked.

"No, but he can find out. He's on it."

Just then, something moved inside my skip's house. "Hey, Tamara, I got to go. Call me when Snake finds out something." I flipped down the cover to my phone and picked up my binoculars. Jose and another male walked out of the house and were getting into the Monte Carlo. Jose was driving and his buddy was riding shotgun. I slouched down low in the seat as the car drove out and turned right onto the highway, heading away from me.

I started the van and eased out onto the road, staying about a quarter of a mile behind them. They slowed down when a car in front of them stopped to wait for oncoming traffic before making a left-hand turn. This forced me to drive right up behind them and stop. They didn't appear to notice me or act differently and we both continued after the car turned.

I wasn't very far behind them when Jose stuck his arm out the window and signaled a right-hand turn. He pulled into the parking lot of a roadside convenience store and continued around to the back of the store. I pulled into the parking lot and waited, with the engine running, next to a pay phone.

The passenger got out of the car and walked around to the front of the store. Jose was left sitting in the driver's seat and didn't appear nervous or as if he was looking around.

Once Jose was alone, I drove around to the rear of the store and parked next to the Monte Carlo, on the driver's side. I got out, my jacket concealing my gun and cuffs. The electric side door on Jose's side and was opening as I walked around the front of the van. Jose returned my friendly wave and nod before turning his head and glancing away.

As soon as he broke eye contact, I drew my gun and opened his door. I grabbed his coat, jerked him out of his vehicle, and slammed a wide-eyed Jose to the pavement between the two vehicles.

Jose offered no resistance, so I quickly cuffed him from behind and heaved him facedown onto the floor in the back of my van. The leg shackles were pre-positioned by the door and I clicked them on his ankles as soon as he hit the floor.

Then I reached inside the Monte Carlo, removed the keys, and stuck them in my pocket. Jose's buddy was going to have to run really fast if he was going to catch us.

The electric side door was closed by the time I got back in the van. Jose was quiet as a mouse as we backed out and drove around to the front of the store. His friend was still in line at the counter as we pulled out onto the highway and headed for the jail.

Nobody had seen anything. It was a textbook snatch: now you see him, now you don't. His buddy must've walked out and wondered what the hell happened to Jose. It must have blown his mind when he found both Jose and the car keys gone. I hoped he had some good friends he could call—otherwise, he was looking at a long walk home.

I knew that the booking process at Jose's new residence was exceptionally slow. It would be eight hours or more before he could make a phone call and let anybody know where he was.

I handed his car keys to the intake officer at the jail along with my paperwork. Jose never said a word the whole time.

Days, miles, and arrests bled into one another. Once on the trail, there's no telling where it will lead or how long it will last.

For the past several weeks, I'd had to delegate much of the teaching at the dojo to my black belts. I took a great deal of comfort in knowing things were in good hands with them. In fact, having an opportunity to be in charge without me being there was good for them, too. They were excellent instructors in their own right but had a tendency to be a little inhibited when I was present. I've always encouraged them to find their own styles and grow. Some of my instructors have gone on to open their own schools, with my blessings and support.

Finally, tonight, I was able to get to the dojo myself. They'd been busy in my absence. After we bowed in, the black belts showed me what they'd had people working on.

You know how it is when your children are young? When you're with them every day, you don't even notice how fast they're growing up. But stay away for a few days and all at once you can see how rapid their progress is.

That's the way it was in the dojo that night. Everyone had improved on their kata performance and showed a new focus in their movements. They had developed new strategies and techniques in sparring, and I saw the increased confidence in the way they moved.

Most of all, I was proud of my black belts. It was one thing for them to tell me what they'd been doing—another to see the hard evidence of it in the junior belts.

Whenever I'm shaking off dust from the road, my classes tend to be even more street-oriented than usual. In addition to taking skips to jail, I bring what I've learned on the road into the dojo.

Sometimes when people ask me what I do, I tell them I'm a professional kidnapper. After all, I find, stalk, capture, and abscond people, just like kidnappers, stalkers, serial killers, and rapists do. The difference is, of course, my hunt is legal and in service of the court. Nevertheless, the speed and stealth of some of my captures would make even Hannibal Lecter envious.

My job is not to enforce the law or to serve the public—even though my efforts sometimes have that result. It's to bring a specific fugitive into the court so I can get paid. The most cost-effective way to do this is with as little fuss and muss as possible. It doesn't always work out that way, but my objective is to steal away with my skip like a thief in the night. This gives me the rare opportunity to train my students from the perspective of a predator.

The best way to not be a victim is to stay out of harm's way in the first place. Sharp eyes and fast feet have saved more butts than any fighting technique or weapon. Avoiding trouble helps ensure longevity and, at the very least, maintaining situational awareness about your surroundings can provide a strategic advantage if you are forced to fight. The environment can be used to equalize differences in size and strength. This is all part of learning martial arts, as opposed to just "taking karate."

Basic self-defense classes and the like are helpful, but most instructors don't know how a predatory human thinks, acts, or plans. Nor do they emphasize either the individual's capabilities or using the environment. In their minds, one size fits all, one plan works for every scenario.

This is foolish, and the consequences can be severe. Unless you learn to understand your own capabilities, the role the environment plays in any engagement, and how your attacker is likely to plan his approach, you aren't learning martial arts. Effective training encompasses all those things—and more.

I told the students how easy it had been to snap up Jose. Then, with that real-world application in mind, we worked on awareness and situational drills, discussing antisurveillance measures and how to spot stalkers. "You got to know one to be one," I told them. "I *are* one, and this is what I would do to sneak up on you."

We moved on to trying out different tactics, learning what would work for different sizes and strengths in various scenarios. The women and kids concentrated on kicking and screaming, the men on pounding the opponent and leaving. I had a strong, big-boned brown belt pick up a young female student and hold her off the ground in a tight bear hug. She reacted immediately, grabbing the hair on top of his head and jerking his head back, exposing his throat. She opened her mouth wide and mimicked chomping down deep and hard on the exposed windpipe, simultaneously drawing her knee back, and then slamming it into his groin.

It sounds vicious—and it is. If an adult assaults a child, the retaliation should be nothing short of a lioness going for the throat of a water buffalo. A full-fledged bite to the throat is obviously effective. The knee to the groin is just for good measure, to erase any indecent desires the attacker has. If he survives, that is.

Real fighting is raw, violent, and potentially deadly. That's why it's vital to avoid it at all cost. Even if you win, you lose, but it's still a whole lot better to win.

Our training encompasses three primary phases. First, avoid the situation altogether by practicing the perception drills and being aware of your surroundings. Second, learn how to be part of the environment and how to use it to your advantage. Third, if you do have to fight, unleash hell. We're talking about life and death situations. The news is full of abductions, missing persons, and murder. There are a lot of sick people out there.

There are also a lot of good people, and not all self-defense situations justify such brutal responses. Suppose you're trying to rescue someone from drowning or to get a disoriented person out of a burning building. You have to be able to control people without hurting them. A true martial artist trains to have a full spectrum of responses ranging from definitely fatal through damaging and incapacitating to physically controlling a person without inflicting permanent damage. True mastery is when you're able to control a person or a situation without your opponent even knowing there was a conflict. Developing that range of responses is like building a house. The foundation is the kata, developing the mental focus and physical skills to perform the techniques. The walls are the kumite, to toughen the spirit and improve timing and distance abilities. The roof is the *bunkai*, or street-fighting techniques, that shield us from harm. The inside of the house is not empty, but made up of makiwara, heavy bag, and other conditioning to fill in the core. It's all training to be a warrior.

The night ended with the men working on shin kicks and forearm smashes and the women polishing their foot stomps and eye gouges. There's nothing like good clean fun. We bowed out and everybody left a little tougher, a little wiser, and a lot safer.

In the aftermath of 9/11, I was far more conscious of how fast time moves, and of my family. Debbie and I were used to a hectic lifestyle, but we were seriously in need of some personal time together. Between my preholiday chasing schedule and her trips to Atlanta to visit her ailing father, we had no time to ourselves. Even worse, when we were together, my preoccupation with my caseload always weighed on one part of my mind.

I've developed a system of mentally "cubbyholing" cases I'm pondering and putting them aside. It works well for me. The break from hard concentration allows my brain to work subconsciously. The beauty of it is that I can think hard about a case and then put it away. Often a solution, feasible or not, occurs to me later. The downside is that sometimes the solutions pop out of their cubbyholes during personal, family times. Sometimes I find myself staring off into space, evaluating the new solution, and then hear Debbie, understandably irritated, repeating a question or statement. Damn the timing.

Debbie left right after work that Friday for Atlanta. She would be back sometime late Sunday afternoon, leaving me alone for the weekend. As much as I hated to see her go, it did give me a chance to spend some time with the other two members of our household. Ben and Lindo, my two German Shepherd Dogs, were restless from the neglect. (And please note that "Dog" is part of the official name of the breed, the only breed so described. Not that I'm a GSD chauvinist or anything like that.)

I loaded my two canines into the travel crates in the back of the truck and drove the twenty miles or so to our seemingly forgotten training field. Lindo, my older dog, was imported from the Buesecker Schloss kennel in Germany and has a black sable coat. In his younger days we competed in several national championships. He achieved the working dog title of Schutzhund III twelve times and holds several advanced tracking titles. Most of his days now are spent sleeping in front of the fireplace or crumb-cruising through the kitchen.

Ben, who has a close black and tan coat, hails from Holland and was sent to me as a young dog. I trained him up to the title of Schutzhund II, and he possesses the drive to do just as well and probably better than Lindo on the national stage.

But training for that level of competition takes an enormous amount of time, and time was a scarce commodity in our lives. Just finding the time to take him out to exercise was taxing.

Schutzhund is similar to police dog training but much more stringent and time-consuming. It's a competition involving obedience, tracking, and protection. The sport itself was originally intended as a selection process for breeding. All the obedience portions of the training are off-leash for Schutzhund III and parts of it are performed with blank gunshots being fired. The course obstacles include scaling a wall and negotiating a brush hurdle on the retrieval exercises. Tracking involves the dog scenting down a path taken by someone at least an hour before, and the dog must locate articles that are dropped along the track by the individual. The protection phase includes searching for a bad guy. When the dog finds the bad guy, the canine must "bark and hold" without biting him. The biting exercises test the courage of the dog and are executed with strict control.

Besides being an investigator, my duties with the sheriff's department included being its canine trainer and handler. After leaving law enforcement as a sergeant, my interest in working dogs continued and I trained them for other departments and competed in the sport.

Watching a competent Schutzhund team perform is a thing of beauty. The magnificence of the animals and the skill of the handlers is something to behold. Preparing to compete at a national level is tantamount to having a full-time job.

I've used both of my dogs on chases, with excellent results. I would put one in a "down" at the backdoor and he would stay there while I approached from the front. Not surprisingly, nobody has ever tested my dogs by trying to get past them.

The dogs are also handy to have when a fleet-footed skip has had a head start on me. Most of the runners give up before the dog reaches them, and I have enough control over the dogs to stop them from biting if the skip surrenders. I can't, however, prevent the runners from wetting themselves.

I'm far too tenderhearted these days, so my dogs don't go with me on chases anymore. I couldn't stand it if something happened to Ben or Lindo.

Ben and Lindo are also my primary security measure at home. Oddly enough, there's a sizable group of folks who wouldn't mind seeing misfortune fall my way. Some of them have been vocal about what they'd like to do to me and my family—downright vindictive, even. All that over a few little arrests. It's not like they weren't used to it.

As a result, I always take home security seriously and have precautions in place to keep my address confidential. But nobody knows better than I do that anybody can be found if somebody looks hard and long enough. I'm not concerned about them trying anything when I'm at home myself. That's what body bags are for.

Debbie is a damn good shot herself. We had a small arsenal that was strategically concealed about the home and she was proficient with each weapon. I knew from past experience with a couple of scumbags bent on retaliation that she wouldn't hesitate to draw her weapon and shoot.

That is, if an intruder survived long enough for her to shoot him. Anybody breaking into my house would have to get past two well-trained and pissed-off German Shepherd Dogs. My mind was at ease with the dogs guarding the home front, so that's where they stayed.

As the truck turned onto the road that led to the training field, the dogs started whining in their crates.

By the time I got to the field, Donald, my helper, had already set up the blinds. Blinds are barriers constructed of fabric and metal poles, around six feet tall, and used to give the helper/assailant somewhere to hide.

Neither Donald nor I had worked the dogs seriously in a while. Today, we primarily wanted to give them some exercise and relax ourselves.

Donald slipped the heavy protection overalls over his cleats (you'll see why he wore cleats in just a bit), pulled them up, and fastened the shoulder straps. He pulled the thick jute-covered leather bite sleeve over his left arm and armed himself with a padded stick. Then Donald hid in one of the blinds.

I brought Lindo onto the field. My hand pointed to an empty blind and the old dog lumbered to it and looked in as he rounded back toward me. I directed him next to Donald's hiding place. Lindo was almost out of gas when he finally found Donald and couldn't muster more than a couple of barks.

Then Donald raised the stick and moved, Lindo's cue to attack. Despite his obvious exhaustion, Lindo swallowed the sleeve like an alligator with a full-mouth grip. His eyes rolled back into his head in sheer pleasure over a job well done. The foreplay of the search climaxed with the reward of the bite.

That was enough of a workout for the old boy. Donald slipped the bite sleeve off his arm. Lindo pranced back to the truck with it in his mouth and jumped into his crate. He was still panting as I gave him some water.

Lindo's spirit was willing but he just couldn't do as much as he used to. By the time he'd run the two blinds, he had covered a couple hundred yards at his top speed. Lindo was still more than capable of running the length of the house and taking out an intruder if necessary. I left Lindo to a well-deserved rest and turned to Ben's crate.

Ben exploded out of the crate as soon as I opened the door, almost unable to contain himself, a striking contrast to Lindo's performance. Time and time again Ben repeated the same blind search that had worn out Lindo, never losing any of his energy and focus.

Ben was a strong, big-boned dog and the ground thundered under him as he streaked across the field. It took a while to use up his energy, and we finished with a courage test.

Donald has developed his helper work into an art form. He stood at one end of the football-sized field and Ben and I at the other. Donald yelled and charged us at a full-bore sprint. I released Ben and they met at about midfield with a loud *whack*. The dog hit him like a linebacker and took the sleeve all the way back to his molars. It takes a great deal of skill and athletic ability for a helper to run all out yet pivot and turn in time to prevent injury to the dog or to himself. The momentum almost took Donald off his feet, and he rewarded Ben by slipping the sleeve.

After watering Ben, I did the helper work for Donald's dog. He has a nice little black sable female that he got from me. She was a lot like her mother and liked to push the helper around in the blind. The dogs needed the workout and the owners needed the break. It was a fun day. As soon as we got home I fed both dogs and they settled in for a long nap. Lindo sighed as he stretched out in front of the fireplace, content, with a full stomach.

Debbie got home late the next afternoon and we went out for dinner. My cases stayed locked up in their cubbyholes and we spent some much-needed quality time together. We both wondered and worried about Joey but were at peace with it, at least for that night.

The next day, the phone calls started early. The first one was from an ex-husband of Melanie Folsom.

Melanie was a repeat customer and I was tired of seeing her name on my skip board. Her forfeiture was approaching its fifth month, and she had been as slippery as they come.

Frank was particularly irked by Melanie's case, too. She'd skipped on us before, and the bondsman who'd interviewed her in jail hadn't checked my records before he made her bond. By the time the bondsman discovered his error, it was too late—Melanie was long gone.

Repeat customers are harder to catch for a couple of reasons. First, if I've arrested them before, they're going to remember my face. Second, they usually learn from the experience of getting caught.

Melanie was a case in point. The first time she'd skipped, I'd tricked her into meeting me at the office, telling her all she had to do was show up and we'd get her bond reset. There was, of course, no such thing as resetting a bond. Melanie walked happily in our front door. She left unhappily in handcuffs. Melanie was no dummy by any stretch of the imagination. She wasn't likely to fall for the same trick or any variation on it again.

Melanie was from a well-to-do family who owned a large farm and was considered one of the pillars of the community. Her parents had several children and they'd built homes on the farm for them and their families. They'd put Melanie through college and, after receiving her master's degree, Melanie taught school and married an accountant. Melanie and her husband lived in a nice home on the farm, one her parents had given them as a wedding present. She'd been an honor student since grade school and was fervently active in the church.

Melanie continued to teach school until she had her first of two daughters and then stayed at home to be a full-time mother. It was the type of life she grew up dreaming about. She seemed to have everything a person could want.

Nobody knew where she met Lonnie. It could have been when she volunteered with the church to serve food at the shelters or in the course of her other charitable work. Maybe it was a chance meeting that was dictated by fate, but the results were devastating.

One day, she dropped the kids off at her parent's house and said she was going shopping. Her husband came home to find a note that read, "I've found somebody just like me. I'm leaving and won't be back."

At first, her husband tried to find her. He spent countless hours scouring the crack houses and back alleys. He couldn't understand what had happened to his bride.

For almost two years, the family's only contact with her was when she would occasionally call to talk to her daughters. According to her ex, her voice had changed and she spoke erratically. Melanie's father had died and no one knew where to reach her. Some blamed his death on the stress caused by his daughter.

The first time I arrested Melanie, she'd skipped out on a charge of possession of crack cocaine. When she was booked into jail, the officers removed from her purse soiled pictures of her daughters in their new Easter dresses. She hadn't seen them in over a year.

Lonnie, of course, had a long record of theft and drug charges. The two of them lived in cheap hotels and in the back of an old Buick. Her face was pale and drawn and clothes hung from her bony frame.

Lonnie got locked up again before Melanie was released and she made an attempt at straightening herself out, entering a rehab program. She made intermittent visits to see her daughters, but, as time went on, there were longer and longer periods of relapse. As soon as Lonnie got out of jail, the attempts at rehabilitation stopped and Lonnie and Melanie disappeared into the streets.

Melanie's ex had called to tell me that she'd dropped by a couple of hours ago to see the kids. She was high and got upset when he wouldn't let her see her daughters. She drove away with a man in a blue Ford Escort with a shattered back window and the ex thought it was Lonnie behind the wheel.

A short time later, Melanie's sister saw the same car parked at her mother's house. Someone—guess who?—had broken into the house. Cash as well as jewelry that had been in the family for generations were missing. The inside of the house had been wrecked, evidently by someone searching for more valuables.

After I hung up from talking to Melanie's ex, I glanced at my watch. I hadn't been working her case as hard as other cases, for a couple of reasons. First, her bond wasn't worth a lot of money compared to others on the skip board. Second, given her history, the odds of the cops picking her up again were pretty good. Still, I hate to see old cases on my board and things were falling into place.

It was about an hour from town to her family's farm. Figure another ten minutes or so for her to ransack her mom's house and another fifteen minutes tops to fence the goods. I might have just enough time to spot her car and hopefully catch her coming out of a crack house. There was not a doubt in my mind that's where they were going.

I knew that Melanie preferred the services of crack dealers that lived along the back streets of Magnolia Avenue to those in the housing projects. All of her and Lonnie's previous drug arrests had been in that area, and they were unlikely to change at this stage of the game.

Driving Frank's chase van, I cruised by the most popular crack establishments, up one alley and down another. Lookouts stood outside the crack houses watching for the cops as customers came and went. I turned up the alley that ran between Magnolia and Fifth Avenue. Just at the entrance was a church that housed a preschool that was letting out for the day. Parents were picking up the kids at the Fifth Avenue access, and traffic was being directed by an off-duty police officer who was working a second job as security.

Just as I turned up the alley, I spotted the Ford Escort. It was parked in the middle of the alley, flanked on the passenger side by a cinderblock wall and a chain-link fence on the other. An abandoned vehicle was parked at the alley entrance and blocked my approach.

There wasn't enough time for me to say "Shit" before Melanie and Lonnie walked out of a gate on the fenced side of the alley and headed for the Ford. I slipped out of the van and as quickly and stealthily as possible tried to slip up behind them. All they had to do to spot me was to turn and look. They did.

They made a mad dash for the Escort and I broke into a sprint and yelled for them to stop. I didn't really expect them to stop but it didn't hurt to try. Besides, this was one of those times that drawing attention to a situation might be helpful.

Melanie slammed the passenger door shut on the little Ford and locked it just as I grabbed the door handle. She was attempting to roll up the window while Lonnie stuck the key in the ignition.

I dove through the window over Melanie and tried unsuccessfully to grab the keys from Lonnie. The car started and we headed down the alley with me hanging halfway out of the vehicle. My feet dragged on the ground. When I picked them up, they skimmed down the cinderblock wall behind me. This wasn't good.

I stretched my left arm out and grabbed the steering wheel. I held it straight, preventing Lonnie from trying to veer into the cinderblock wall and scrape me off.

Melanie leaned forward and bit my outstretched arm. I probably would have shot both of them except that both my hands were otherwise occupied. My left hand was holding the steering wheel straight and my right hand fumbled for the keys, trying to turn the ignition off. Seeing my dilemma, Melanie chomped down harder.

A bit farther down the alley, my fingers closed on the keys. I turned the car off, jerked the keys out of the ignition, and lofted them out of Lonnie's window, skimming them just a few inches away from his nose.

With the car turned off, the steering wheel locked. Ignoring Lonnie's curses and threats for a moment, I slapped the shit out of Melanie, loosening her teeth from my forearm. (Hanging out of a window while being dragged down the road caused me to step out of my normal sensitive and compassionate role.)

Lonnie bailed out of the Escort, pausing only to grab a sawed-off baseball bat from behind his seat. His eyes were wild as he held the club high and started to run around the back of the car toward me. I quickly wrenched Melanie's arm out the window with a wristlock and cuffed her wrist to the outside door handle. Then I turned my attention to Lonnie.

Moving automatically, my right hand clicked the thumb break on my holster. I was in the process of drawing my gun when a loud voice boomed down the alley.

"Freeze!" The off-duty police officer from the preschool had run the fifty yards or so down the alley and had his gun out. He was out of breath and panting hard as he pointed the weapon back and forth at Lonnie and me.

"Drop the bat," the officer yelled. He was doing the right thing, by the book, taking no chances on approaching any closer until he had us disarmed.

Lonnie obeyed immediately, then quick as a weasel turned and jumped over the chain-link fence and ran off between a row of houses. Being an experienced felon, he knew the cop wouldn't shoot him in the back.

Melanie was starting to squirm in her seat. I started to turn to look at her, but the cop didn't like that even a little bit." Stay perfectly still and keep your hands up." He didn't have to tell me twice. I now had his undivided attention and was staring down the barrel of his Glock.

Just then, three police cruisers with sirens blaring came screaming down the alley. Two of them drove up behind me and the other stopped in front of the alley and blocked off the drive. The cops all jumped out of their cars and headed for us. Now there were *four* Glocks pointed at me. I stayed frozen like an ice sculpture until they ordered me to slowly place my hands on the hood of the Escort.

One of the cops recognized me but not before I was searched and disarmed. They kept their eyes on Melanie as she fidgeted in the front seat of the Ford and I cooled it in the backseat of a cruiser.

My arm was throbbing. Luckily, I'd worn a thick sweatshirt that day and her bite hadn't broken the skin. Even so, a large blood bruise was beginning to rise inside the tooth indentations that were halfway between my forearm and wrist.

After they verified my warrants, the cops released me and returned my gun. The off-duty officer told me he thought he was witnessing an attempted kidnapping. That would have made me the perpetrator. From a distance, it very likely could have looked that way. Just goes to show, things aren't always as they appear.

Lonnie was long gone by this time. The officers made a police report of the incident and told me to consider charging him with assault. Like I don't have enough to do. Besides, there was no money in it.

Melanie squirmed the whole way to jail. Her meaningless, repetitive movements were indicative of someone on a crack high. She fidgeted with the cuffs like she was trying to wiggle out of them, and then rocked back and forth. Then she'd break into uncontrollable sobbing, which ended as quickly as it had begun. Then she'd start the same sequence all over again, like a record needle stuck on a scratched track.

She happened to be in the middle of a crying jab when the correctional officers pulled her out of the car and led her back for booking. They were irritated and I couldn't say that I blamed them. Dealing with junkies detoxing was part of their daily life, usually the same people over and over again.

To say that Frank wasn't particularly amused at my report of Melanie's arrest would be an understatement. "Are you fucking crazy?" he asked. "What the hell were you doing, diving into a moving vehicle?"

"Well, it wasn't moving when I dove into it," I answered. It'd seemed quite a logical choice at the time. And, given the outcome, the right one.

"Not only that, but you could have very well gotten your ass shot."

I looked at him and smirked. "I seem to remember a couple of stories about a few of your chases. Let's see, how about the time…"

Frank interrupted me. "That was then, and this is now. Things are different these days." I wasn't buying it and he knew it. That's the problem with swapping war stories with somebody—they come back to bite you sometimes.

Frank gave up his attempted lecture with a sigh. "Aw, what the hell. Go on—get out of here and go home. See you tomorrow."

On my way home, my cell phone rang. It was Tamara Fields. "Snake has a map to the cave where Wiley hid before."

"Where did he get that?" I asked.

"He's been checking around and talked to some people"

I knew what that meant. "You mean he's been buying dope."

"I ain't saying. You wanna go with him or not? Snake says he's going by himself if you won't go."

I was getting impatient. "I'll meet him, but only if he's straight. He better not be high when we go or he *will* regret wasting my time."

"Okay," she said. "If he has to be straight, it might be a couple of days before he can call you."

"Fine," I said. "Give me at least a day's notice in case I'm into something when you call." I hung up and I turned the phone off.

# ten

The cell phone evidently bore a few ill feelings over being turned off so abruptly the day before. It powered up and then waited patiently until I'd settled into my normal morning stupor over a cup of coffee. Only when I was unprepared did it strike, chiming to inform me that I had a voice mail waiting for me. It must have picked up a few tricks from watching me stalk skips.

There was no point in trying to ignore it—it would only keep chiming and generally being obnoxious until I answered it. Like it or not, my day was going to start before it was supposed to.

There were two messages, one from Snake and the other from Ken Reynolds. Snake's slurred speech was so garbled that I couldn't figure out what he was trying to tell me. The cell phone politely informed me that he'd left his message at 2:00 A.M. It was undoubtedly a good thing for my relationship with Snake that my phone was turned off—and for the cell phone's good health, too.

Ken's message was only an hour old and was blessedly brief. He wanted me to call him at work.

When I returned the call, Ken himself answered. "That Snake fellow called me last night and was higher than a kite," he said in a hushed whisper. "He told me where Wiley might be hiding. Said he needed some expense money."

"What did you say?" I asked. I had a sinking feeling I knew what I was going to hear. This wasn't the best time of the day for me to explain once again the facts of life to Ken.

"Told him I needed to talk to you first. That thing with Bob taught me."

Slightly relieved, I laughed. Ken didn't get to where he was by being completely unteachable. Always a good thing when someone learns from experience—especially when it's my ass that's getting shot at. In a slightly more pleasant tone of voice, I said, "Good thinking, Ken. Snake told me he thought Wiley might be hiding in the same place he hid after killing his brother-in-law."

Ken's voice perked up. "I know where that's at. Me and my boys have hunted all over them woods. I know *exactly* where that cave is."

"Well, well," I said. I'd told Tamara that Snake had to be straight when he called me. Maybe I wouldn't have to wait for that unlikely occurrence after all. "I can be up there later this afternoon. Can we meet and you show me?"

"Sure can!" Ken bellowed. "It's about a two-mile walk in from the road. Or about a mile if we take a boat in from the lake, but I don't know if I can line up a boat by this afternoon or not."

"That's okay. Let's just walk in. If we get lucky and catch him, I'd rather walk him out."

He laughed out loud. "We ought to make the son of a gun swim."

Ken's voice was getting a little loud and I wasn't particularly pleased about the exuberance in his tone. Since I'm the one taking the risks, I'm the only one allowed to enjoy it. Providing vicarious thrills for other folks who want to pretend they're involved in a big case or that they're dangerous isn't part of my job description.

"Ken, don't get too excited," I warned, trying to dampen his enthusiasm. "This is a long shot at best. But first, understand me—don't tell a soul about this."

Ken promised not to tell anyone. We agreed to meet in the parking lot at the head of the trail.

It had been raining for the past couple of days and just that morning had tapered off to a cold drizzle. My ALICE pack was stuffed with a change of clothes, including two extra pairs of socks and rain gear. Preparing for this romp in the woods reminded of me of the many hunting trips I'd taken over the years. Somehow, after I'd experienced the rush of tracking down two-legged predators, stalking Bambi didn't provide quite the same thrill that it used to.

I filled the pockets of my black BDU's with protein bars and extra ammo. The cuffs bloused neatly at the top of my Gortex boots and a Velcro gun belt secured the pants at the waist. I was ready to go.

On the way to the meeting place, I decided to stop for a hot lunch at one of those family-owned restaurants where the sign reads, "Home Style Cooking." In this day of misleading advertising, it was good to see an establishment that lived up to its word.

The parking lot was proof positive that this was a favorite local eatery. It was full of pickup trucks with tagged deer carcasses in the beds. Inside the restaurant, there was enough camouflage clothing to equip a small militia. My veins hardened at the mere sight of the plates loaded with cholesterol.

My waitress delivered five plates in one trip to a group next to me and dished them out on the red-checkered tablecloth like a dealer at the blackjack table. That taken care of, she turned her attention to me. She seemed like a pleasant, helpful woman and looked like she ate here herself fairly often. Her apron strings strained to contain her well-nourished figure. "Whatcha having, hon?" she asked. Her double chin quadrupled as she looked down at her notepad and wrote down my order. She nodded in approval at my selections. "Going hunting?"

"Yeah," I answered. "Maybe this will be my lucky day."

There's something about the prospect of going into the woods on a cold rainy day that makes biscuits and gravy with country ham and eggs taste especially good. I was like a pig at the trough, along with all the other great white hunters in the room. Even though we'd never met, we shared the camaraderie of decadent consumption and the pursuit of quarry.

After wolfing down my yearly allotment of triglycerides, I hit the road again. The warm glow of the carbohydrates and protein filled me with optimism. Maybe we would find Wiley in the cave. Maybe he'd resist a bit. Maybe Ken had finally learned his lesson about talking to other people. Anything was possible, I thought.

The warm glow diminished the moment I pulled into the parking lot and saw Ken. He was standing next to his car talking to a younger man as I pulled up.

Ken and the other man approached my van together and their resemblance was unmistakable. Both had the same toothy, ear-to-ear grin and it immediately became apparent that Ken hadn't kept our meeting a total secret.

Ken didn't wait for me to raise the issue and interceded with an introduction. "Hi Joe. Meet my son, James. I know you said not to tell anyone, but James just got out of the Army and he grew up hunting in these woods. It makes me feel better knowing he's with us."

James and I shook hands. He was several inches taller than his father with the same strong jaw and firm handshake. His eyes looked straight into mine as he spoke. I could tell his down-to-earth demeanor was genuine.

"Nice to meet you Mr. Laney," he said, his voice polite. "I want to help you catch this guy. Just tell me, I'll do whatever you say."

While I was glad to meet James and he seemed like a trustworthy fellow, that wasn't the issue. I looked at Ken. "Where were you when you called James and asked him to help us?"

Ken looked puzzled. "I was at the office. I called him right after talking to you, about four or five hours ago."

"Who was with you?"

"Nobody knew we were coming up here, Joe. I was real careful."

Not exactly a direct answer to my question. James and Ken exchanged a puzzled look. I didn't know if they understood what I was getting at or whether Ken would understand how he'd breached security, but nothing was to be gained by berating them. What was done was done and we were going to be going after Wiley all the same.

"Well, let's just get going," I said. "It'll be dark before long."

Ken pulled a Bible out of his knapsack. "Joe, would you join James and me in a word of prayer before we leave?"

"Sure, Ken, I'd be glad to," I answered.

With heads bowed, we stood in a small circle as Ken led us in prayer. He prayed for our minds to be clear and our journey safe. There were words of praise for the Lord and blessings for the downtrodden. Ken even asked forgiveness for the man we were setting out to capture. The steady drizzle continued and we all muttered a hushed "Amen" when Ken finished the prayer. He put the Bible back in his knapsack and we prepared for the trail.

A familiar mechanical racking sound caused me to look over my shoulder. James had opened the action on a Bushmaster AR-15 and then quickly released it and chambered a round. He slung the rifle over a khaki tactical vest with multiple pouches that were filled with extra magazines. I took a moment to admire his preparations and equipment. In addition to the Bushmaster, he had an H&K USP stainless in a .45 caliber holstered on his belt along with spare clips. A hundred feet of rappelling rope was draped over his other shoulder. A canteen of water was attached to his belt in the back.

Ken walked up with a breached Weatherby over-and-under 12-gauge shotgun with a walnut stock and engraved receiver. A tanned leather pouch hung around his neck with extra shells. He looked for all the world like he was going duck hunting. There was no doubt these gentleman had good taste in firearms.

I threaded pouches for my extra 9mm clip and canteen of water onto my gun belt, and then hung a pair of field binoculars around my neck. The cell phones were in and out of coverage, and taking along some signal flares seemed like a good idea. Frank knew where I was going and was waiting to hear from me as soon as we got back to the vehicles, so if anything happened, at least there'd be somebody looking for us. The three of us—armed to the teeth and packing the King James version of the Bible—headed down the trailhead and into the woods.

The earth seemed to object to our mission from the very first. Each step sounded like a plumber's plunger as the soggy ground tried to suck our boots off our feet. The trail was nothing more than a series of small ponds, and avoiding them was an exercise in futility as the soggy soil around each one pulled at our feet like a noose. It was much easier to just plow through the ankle-high water and be thankful it wasn't deeper.

ATV tracks marked the trail like a tic-tac-toe board. Three- and four-wheeled vehicles had replaced horses and turned this wilderness into an off-road superhighway. Some tracks kept going up the path and others fanned out like a spider's web into the surrounding woods.

It wasn't raining hard enough to hear it falling on the trees, but the heavy blanket of mist hanging in the air made its own quiet noises. Finally, a bit of cooperation from Mother Nature; the leaves under our feet were wet and plastered together and masked the noises we made walking, far better for a covert approach than walking on dry, crisp leaves. Sounds travel further in denser air, however, and we all knew to keep our voices low and to whisper.

The trees were naked, stripped of their leaves by the oncoming winter. Beyond the bare trunks we could see deep into the forest and get the lay of the land that in most seasons was concealed by a thick cover of undergrowth. Our view of the terrain was limited only by the changes in elevation and the occasional evergreens that were the only splashes of color in the drab surroundings.

We plodded through the water and mud for about a mile before reaching a fork in the trail. The three of us stopped and huddled together at the split and James picked up a stick and carved a rough map into the wet ground.

"We turn off the trail about a mile past this fork," he said. "We'll come to a stand of locust trees at a bend in the path. There's a ridgeline a quarter mile into the woods with a fairly steep grade. The cave is another hundred yards up."

My skills as a scout were no match for James's knowledge of the area and he took the lead. Ken brought up the rear.

We were all keenly aware of the fact that Wiley could be just around the bend. James kept a sharp eye out ahead as Ken and I watched the woods to our sides for any movement. The trail split. The ATV drivers found both directions equally appealing, reducing the traffic along the branch we chose. Further on, tire ruts in the ground were even less numerous as they veered off the path, heading for destinations unknown. Eventually, they disappeared altogether.

Ken and I cued off James's movements. He would occasionally stop suddenly and look around, which caused a chain reaction in the two of us. The closer we got to the point where we would leave the trail, the more cautious our progress was. Finally, James turned and faced off to the right and raised his hand. Ken and I quietly approached him and I strained to hear his hushed whisper.

"We turn off the trail here," James said. "I'll lead up to the top of the ridge but I think we should fan out. If Wiley's watching for us up there, we'll be sitting ducks."

Testosterone hung heavy in the air, amped up with a double shot of adrenaline. James and Ken were experienced hunters, judging from their fine choice of firearms and woodcraft—now they were finding out what it was like to hunt prey that could shoot back.

The cocktail of hormones coursing through their bodies affected them individually in slightly different ways. Their nostrils flared with each breath and they steamed up the air like bulls pawing at the dirt. James was wide-eyed and excited, ready to explode into action. In contrast, Ken's eyes were squinted with determination. Ken looked years younger, his face alive with the hunt. For a moment, it was like looking at Ben and Lindo.

I know all too well the effects of that potent cocktail of hormones. The high was what kept me in the bail enforcement business. No other occupation gives me that kind of rush.

James started up the hill first. Ken and I spread out on the flanks and stayed about twenty yards behind him.

The closer we got to the ridgeline, the slower James moved. He occasionally flashed some type of hand signals that would have undoubtedly conveyed a great deal of information if I'd had the slightest idea what they meant. At one point, he pointed at me, did something with his fingers, and waited for some type of response. Unable to decipher his gestures and thus comply with his request, I did the next best thing—nothing. I stared back at him until a disgusted look came over his face and he moved on.

As we reached the ridgeline, a faint smell of smoke came and went with the changing of the wind. James squatted behind a log at the top of the hill and motioned us up. He pointed ahead at smoke rising from the ground. "It's coming from the cave."

It wasn't the steady billowing smoke a blazing fire produces but rather lazy puffs from smoldering embers that dissipated into the fickle wind that swirled about.

We crept up to the mouth of the cave and peered in. It looked like a large hole in the ground; opening into the earth, rather than what you'd normally think of as a cave. The smoke we had spotted earlier swirled out from the pit and worked its way out past us. Sets of ATV tracks rutted the ground down the other side of the ridge.

Along one side of the entrance was a steep muddy slope. A rope tied to a tree near the entrance led inside the cave.

I pointed at the ATV tracks and whispered to James. "What's in that direction?"

"The lake," he answered.

There were two things on my mind at that point. First, we were going to have to go into the cave. A section of it was out of view and there was no way of telling whether anyone was home without going in. Second, we couldn't all go. If Wiley had been here and left, he could be back at anytime and surprise us.

James flipped off the safety to his AR-15 and pointed it down the hole. Ken walked several yards into the woods, hid behind a tree, and watched for anybody that might approach us.

I grabbed the rope and descended down the side as James covered the entrance with his rifle. Not as easy at it sounds. The slope into the cave was greater than forty-five degrees and the dirt was as slick as glass. A spring bubbled out of the saturated ground near the entrance and formed a small stream that drained down the incline and into the crevice. It was like trying to walk downhill on roller skates, as the sides of my boots tried to dig into the soup. Controlling my descent required keeping both hands on the rope. It was up to James to handle any trouble coming from below me.

There was a large rock at the entrance to the cave itself and I appreciated the good footing. I entered the crevice with my gun and flashlight drawn. My light bounced off the damp walls and floor.

A small woodstove was just inside the entrance. The smoke we'd seen was coming out of a short flue that was pointed up and out. Even though the stove was small, it was made of iron and had to weigh at least a couple hundred pounds. It was no minor feat to have hauled that thing this deep into the woods and then maneuvered it down that slope and into the cave. Somebody went to a lot of trouble to set this up.

A meager woodpile was stacked next to the stove and a dome tent had been set up close enough to benefit from the heat. Its zippered flap was open and revealed an empty sleeping bag.

Rock ledges on the cave walls served as natural shelves and held an unappetizing assortment of canned food. The grocery list included pork and beans, Spam, and beanie weenies. A half empty, plastic five-gallon water jug sat next to the tent along with the lid to a tin of Copenhagen snuff.

I opened the door to the woodstove and peered in. The interior was full of ashes and smoldering coals. A fire hadn't been started since the last night or early that morning. Then I shone my light down into another small cavern that was below where I was standing. It had been used as a trash receptacle from above and its floor was littered with Wiley's brands of tobacco and beer cans. The whole area reflected those homey details I'd come to associate with anywhere Wiley lived.

I searched the tent, but found nothing of interest. There were no extra clothes in it and I didn't figure Wiley as the type to make a laundry run. Getting to this place was not particularly easy, even if Wiley had made such a radical change in his lifestyle as staying clean. No, he was gone for good—and I was pretty sure I knew why.

From what I could piece together, Wiley and his cronies ferried him and his supplies in from the lake. Once on solid ground, they'd used ATVs to haul Wiley and his gear up to the ridgeline and the cave.

We couldn't have missed Wiley by more than a day; probably it was just a matter of hours. Wiley was really starting to piss me off.

The fact that we had just missed him had to be more than a coincidence. I was pretty certain God wasn't looking out for him, so that left me with only one conclusion. Someone had tipped him off.

I looked up at the entrance of the cave. James and Ken were both looking back down at me. Shit.

I grabbed the rope and pulled myself back up the steep bank. Without looking at them directly, I said, "Somebody went to a lot of trouble to haul a woodstove and supplies up here."

Ken scratched his head. "Yeah, those ATV tracks lead down to the lake. Red has a pontoon boat that could carry all that."

"Well, he won't be back here." It was time to return to an earlier point I'd made that hadn't sunk in with Ken. "Ken, are you sure you didn't tell anybody about us coming here?"

"Yeah, I'm sure."

I looked over at James. "What about you? Did you mention coming up here to anybody?"

James shook his head. "Nope. Only person I talked to all day was Dad when he called me about this."

That's what I'd thought. So much for hoping Ken had learned his lesson on security. I turned back to Ken. "Where were you when you called James?"

"In my office. Why?"

"Was anybody in there with you?"

"Just some of my men."

James and I both shook our heads as we looked at him. James swore softly.

A look of disbelief crossed Ken's face. "You don't think one of my own men would tell Wiley, do you?"

I was too tired to get mad. Besides, ultimately, he was the one who stood to lose a lot of money. "Well, let's see. First of all, I don't think you can count on your hiring process to screen out all the questionable characters. After all, Wiley used to work for you, too, remember? Second, we're dealing with folks involved in drugs and money. Wiley was buddies with your men. Did it ever occur to you that they hang close so they can hear what's going on?"

Ken's face took on a real mean look. "I'll fire the whole bunch."

"That's like slamming the barn door after the horse gets out," I said. "Best thing to do is to keep them close. Maybe we can feed them information that will set Wiley up. In the meantime, don't talk to me unless you're alone and away from the office." I wasn't all that confident that he'd get the point even now.

It was a long walk out of the woods. I really missed the adrenaline rush that had accompanied us in. Disappointment and disgust wasn't nearly as much of a rush. The long walk also gave me time to think about Ken. I couldn't understand how somebody with so much business acumen and drive could be so naïve and stupid.

At the same time, I knew that Ken wasn't used to dealing with the same scum that I rubbed elbows with on a daily basis. He was doing the best he could and figured whatever happened was the will of God.

By the time we got back to the parking area, it was almost dark. The steady drizzle had turned into light snow. With heads bowed, we formed a circle for another word of prayer. Ken ended with a plea for forgiveness for all those who transgressed against him. Our solemn amen's were followed by the sounds of chambers being cleared from locked and loaded.

I started the van and let it warm up while I changed into dry clothes, stuffing my wet muddy garments into a plastic bag. Wiley had slipped through my fingers once again. The thought haunted me the whole way home.

The wet weather moved out the next day but it was windy and raw, taking with it my enthusiasm for physical exertion and braving the elements. With no current leads on Wiley, I decided to follow up on another old skip named Philip.

I was feeling less than completely gung ho, which influenced my choice of stakeout locations. Kicking back in the warmth and comfort of a public library beat sitting on a cold rock. Besides, it would give me an opportunity to catch up on my reading.

I wasn't really all that zealous about catching Philip. He was going to be an easy one. Or so I thought.

Philip was a male prostitute and he was no stranger to the annals of knowledge, i.e., the public library. Many of his colleagues also frequented this particular branch.

It wasn't that Philip was exactly a bookworm. I doubt he would have known the Dewey decimal system if Dewey himself had bitten him on the ass, but there's more to a library these days than a card catalog and row after row of stacks. There's technology.

The library served as sort of an office for a lot of streetwalkers. It was warm and had clean bathrooms as well as a bank of computers with internet access. Security guards were posted to prevent the homeless riffraff from entering, but the male prostitutes were usually dressed to kill and passed right through. They didn't cause any trouble and there was no reason for them to be denied entry.

Since I'd arrested Philip several years ago, he knew me. Although I could have gone looking for him outside or at his last place of residence, waiting for him at the library and trapping him inside would be a lot easier.

Philip, at five feet five inches and 145 pounds, was obviously not a large man and had never been known to be violent. He catered to clients who liked the young athletic type. He always wore tight blue jeans, and in cooler weather the blond curls of his wig fell down onto the shoulders of a high school letter jacket. The thirty-five-year-old could have passed through the doors of any senior prom.

Bail for a prostitution charge is usually low, so I'm not too eager to spend time chasing down hooker skips. But in this case, I had a couple of reasons to go after Philip.

This time, Philip had been arrested with one of his out-of-town clients just as they were in the act of consummating their transaction.

His customer heard from one of the jailers that Philip was HIV positive. We bonded him out before the poor guy could find out for sure if what the jailer told him was true. They both had the same court date and when Philip didn't show, his former customer was more than a little unhappy.

While we were both interested in locating Philip, I had far more lucrative cases on my skip board. His former customer didn't want to hear that I'd get around to Philip in a couple of weeks and upped the ante, offering a generous reward if Philip was captured sooner rather than later.

As it turned out, Philip's patron was married and a prominent businessman from Chattanooga, and he wanted the matter handled with the utmost discretion. He gave me his private cell phone number and asked me to call as soon as I caught Philip. I had no doubt that, given the delicacy of his position, he'd pay the reward.

Chasing skips who were HIV positive or infected with some other blood-borne pathogen such as hepatitis C was nothing new. I always assume that all skips are carrying some sort of disease and exercise caution in all cases, taking particular care not to be exposed to their bodily fluids. A lot of times, the subjects being arrested might not themselves be aware they had a transmissible condition.

Besides not getting beat up, one of the main benefits of martial arts training is the ability to do selective targeting. Faced with a skip resisting arrest, most bounty hunters bust him in the mouth or flatten his nose. For the most part, they simply don't know how to do anything else, although there are those who simply seem to enjoy it.

Bad moves. Both techniques are guaranteed to cause injuries that spew blood like Niagara Falls. These days, jails refuse to accept prisoners who are bleeding profusely. That means the bail enforcement agent who arrested them must sit with them at the ER until a doctor releases the skip for incarceration. A well-placed technique is not only important for the health-conscious bounty hunter, but it is also a valuable time-management tool.

The potential for legal repercussions is actually much greater for untrained bounty hunters—they leave so much more evidence. An old myth is that black belts must "register their hands" as deadly weapons with some sort of anatomy police somewhere. Who knows where that got started? The truth is that the faster you end the fight, the faster you can secure the arrest and prevent a confrontation from turning into a brawl. That's where good techniques come into play.

What's a good technique? In my book, it's one that leaves no witnesses and no visible injuries. A bad technique is one that gets videotaped and shown on the evening news.

No matter how justified the action might be, the sight of five cops beating the hell out of somebody isn't pretty and any similar behavior from a bounty hunter will certainly land the bounty hunter back in the courtroom, this time on the wrong side of the railing.

Now, things don't always go right, not even with the best training. But in a violent profession, good techniques hedge the bet. When you're dealing with people who might be carrying one type of virus or another, good techniques avoid making them leak.

Philip and his customer were arrested in a car in an area cops have nicknamed "Queer Corner." The rather politically-incorrect term refers to a park in the middle of downtown, where male homosexual prostitutes congregate. It's within easy walking distance of several downtown hotels and the public library. Philip's worried client, like many other patrons, stayed in one of the upscale hotels while he was in town on business and spent his free time on the wild side at the park.

One of the great things about our public library system is that it provides free internet access to its patrons. As I watched, a steady stream of people came in and out to check their internet mail.

After a few hours, Peter, one of Philip's buddies, came in the door. He went straight to a computer and sat down. I was pretty sure I knew what he was up to and his reaction to his e-mails removed all doubts.

For some of the male prostitutes, this was the only way they made dates. For those who had built up a faithful stable of customers, it was a lot safer than standing on a street corner all the time.

Not that Peter himself stood on many street corners—not these days. He was in the top echelon of his chosen profession and scheduled dates only by appointment. Although we'd bonded a few of his former companions out of jail, Peter seldom got into trouble himself. But when he did, our services were always fast and friendly, so he had a reason to be favorably disposed toward assisting me.

My eyes were strained from reading and boredom had started to settle in. It was time to take the direct approach. I put away my book and ambled over to stand behind Peter. When Peter logged off the terminal, he turned and saw me there.

Peter batted his eyes, as he looked me up and down. "Well, hello, Mister Bondsman. What brings you here?"

"Just working, Peter."

His voice was coy and playful. "Me, too. Can I do something for you?"

Being harsh with him wouldn't be helpful. I mustered up my compassionate understanding and exercised my capacity for accepting diversity in our modern culture. "I hope so. I'm looking for Philip. He might be sick and spreading it around." There was no need to explain the exact nature of Philip's possible ailment, not to Peter.

Peter's lips pursed and he shook his head in disapproval. "I've heard that rumor. Philip has turned into *such* trash. He doesn't care whom he's with. Sure, I can help you find him. But what's in it for me?" Peter's eyes batted again and he licked his lips.

The reward offered by Philip's former patron left plenty of room for me to offer some snitch money. "Tell you what. You help me find Philip and I'll pay you one hundred dollars, cash."

Peter cocked his head. "Oh, shucks. That's not exactly what I had in mind." He saw the look on my face and a bit of his playfulness disappeared. "But okay, I'll do it. Mainly because Philip should be stopped if he is going around unprotected. You wait here, Mister Bondsman. I bet finding him won't take long."

Well, I'd waited in much worse places, so I cruised the aisles and picked out another book to read. After about an hour, Peter returned and winked at me on his way back upstairs to the computer bank. A few minutes later, he came back down and told me that Philip was to meet him in a parking lot across from the Coliseum in two hours. A mutual friend was going to drop him off at the corner to meet Peter.

"How did you set this up?" I asked.

"Well, I don't want to get into any trouble. Let's just say I let some of his friends know I wanted to get something to smoke from Philip. He sells the stuff."

"I don't want to know anything about that," I said immediately. "If you get caught doing anything illegal, it's your ass." I knew as soon as the words left my mouth that they were poor choices.

He lowered his head and cut his eyes up at me flirtatiously. "Oh, Mister Bondsman, it's my ass every day."

Time to get off that subject. "Okay, you'll ride with me to within a couple of blocks of the parking lot. You'll get out and walk up to the corner. In a couple of minutes, I'll pull in and park close to some other cars. Watch where I park. When Philip gets there, tell him you want to get away from the street. Walk with him past my van and I'll do the rest. Be sure to walk as close to the back of the van as you can."

"I can do that," he said.

"Just one more thing. After I get him, you're on your own as far as getting back downtown."

"Not a problem. It's only a few blocks."

Peter left the library first and was to wait for me at the park. When I got there, he was leaning inside a blue Mercedes, apparently conducting a negotiation of some sort. The car drove off. Peter pranced a bit as he headed back to my van and got in.

I winced. There was no doubt that someone who didn't know what was going on could have easily misconstrued both my intentions and my relationship with Peter. Luckily, nobody I knew was in the area.

Peter leaned back in the seat and looked at me. "Sorry. Had to take care of some business. That'll be my ride back to town."

Peter got out a couple of blocks from the coliseum. When he got into position, I drove past him and into the parking lot. There were a few cars scattered about and I pulled into a space about fifty yards from where Peter was standing.

The large parking area was divided into sections by grassy medians that were contained by ankle-high concrete curbs. Peter was on the driver's side of the vehicle, and there was a large building several hundred feet away on the passenger side. If Peter could talk my quarry into going around to the back of the building, they would have to walk right past the back of my van. Easy enough.

I got in the back of the van. The tinted windows concealed my movement. I left the sliding side door slightly open to allow me to stealthily slip into pouncing position. With binoculars in hand and my feet propped up on a canvas bag full of shackles and handcuffs that Peter would have paid good money to play with, I waited.

Minutes passed and a red Mustang pulled up to the curb where Peter was standing. The passenger door opened and Philip stepped out, wearing a leather high school letter jacket. They stood and talked a while, then turned and headed my way.

I eased out the side door and bent down so they couldn't see my head over the top of the van. I felt like a tiger ready to pounce, listening intently as they approached.

Their voices got louder as they drew closer. When they were near enough for me to hear their feet scuff the asphalt and it was just going to be a matter of reaching out and snatching Philip right off his feet, my nostrils flared. Then they were dead even with the back of the van.

I waited for them to come into view, anticipating the moment, only to find that Peter had steered them wide. Philip was ten to fifteen yards away from the back of the van, too far for me to just reach out and grab him. As they passed the rear of the van, Philip lit a cigarette. Then he looked over and saw me. The recognition on his face was plain to see.

I didn't wait for him to recover from the shock of seeing me and sprinted toward him. The cigarette dropped from Philip's mouth. He spun around and ran.

His brief surprise at seeing me gave me a slight jump on him and I was in full stride while he was still accelerating. I shouted at him to stop. He ignored me. The chase was on.

After about fifty yards and just before we reached the street, I'd closed the gap between. With a burst of energy, I drew even closer, then reached out with my left hand and grabbed the back of his jacket collar.

We were stride for stride in an all-out run when I jerked him down from behind. Philip fell flat on his back in the grassy part of one of the medians. I tried to turn loose of him as he fell but my arm was fully extended and the hand was caught inside his collar. Instead of taking a dive on the grass, I landed on my left side across the concrete curb surrounding the grass, my body from the waist down sprawled out on the hard surface of the parking lot.

The impact knocked the wind out of me. I felt like my chest had been crushed. Long after the time I should have been able to breathe again, it was still impossible to catch my breath. If Philip had gotten up, there would have been no way to catch him. Luckily, the fall had knocked the breath out of him as well.

My left hand was still hung up in his collar and the arm was useless. Fortunately God gave us two of almost everything for moments just like this.

Philip turned his head and looked right at me, then tried to turn over and get up. The pain was excruciating but I was able to roll over far enough to deliver a hammer smash with my right hand.

The blow hit him at the jawline just below the ear, on or about meridian point known as Stomach 6. Philip immediately went limp and both of his eyes rolled back in his head. He remained out long enough for me to struggle to my knees and roll him over.

My left arm was still useless, but Philip was in no condition to offer any resistance. Hammer smashes do that to you. While he was still dazed, I cuffed him using only my right hand. I had a second pair of handcuffs on my belt and I managed to snap them on around his ankles. If Philip had been much larger, it would have taken shackles to restrain his feet. Restraining his feet was essential, given my condition. If he jumped up and took off, I would've been able to do little more than wave goodbye.

By the time the two of us were ready to attempt standing, Peter had long since disappeared. Once I got my feet under me, I found I could only stand if I braced my right hand on my thigh and slouched to the left. Taking a deep breath was out of the question—I was working up to short gasps and each one of those felt like somebody was twisting a knife in my chest.

The short trip back to the vehicle seemed like an eternity. I grabbed his hands, which were restrained behind his back, and used him like a crutch. This didn't slow him down any. Since handcuffs aren't really designed to restrain legs, Philip's ankles were chained a mere two inches or less apart. He hopped a foot or so with me hanging on while at the same time I stepped with my right, and then I would drag my left leg in to catch up. Hop, step, drag, this repeated over and over as we went at a snail's pace. I had to stay bent to the left or I couldn't breathe.

We finally got back to the van. The side door was still open. I couldn't push enough air out of my lungs to speak much above a whisper—actually, it sounded more like a low growl—when I said, "Hop your ass into the van and shut the fuck up."

Growl or whisper or whatever, it must have sounded sufficiently ominous and threatening to Philip. Or maybe it was echoes of the hammer smash still rattling around in his brain. Whatever the reason, he wasted no time in trying to hop his ass as directed. Come to think of it, it must have been the hammer smash still ringing his chimes, because it took him three tries to get in the back of the van.

Climbing into the driver's seat was an ordeal. It took me several minutes to negotiate the short step up. After I finally made it, I had to reach over and close the door with my right hand.

It was a long, quiet ride to the jail. Philip didn't utter a peep and I kept the radio off. I rested my head against the door where it met the side window and drove slumped over in the seat. I could barely see over the dashboard and navigated with only a sliver of a sideways view of the road and oncoming traffic. Making a left turn meant tilting my head back and mashing my nose against the window glass. I probably would've laughed at the situation except that even the thought of taking a deep breath made me wince.

Somehow, I made it to the jail. Evidently I looked fairly odd behind the wheel because the deputies in the sally port just stood there and stared at us.

Finally, curiosity got the better of one of them. The driver's side door opened. Only my seat belt kept me from falling out. A familiar face poked in and saw me slouched over. The deputy scratched his head and asked, "You all right?"

I tried to speak, but a low growl was I could muster. I tried again and what seemed to be somebody else's voice said, "Been better. Think I might have some busted ribs."

"Did he do it?" the deputy asked, pointing at Philip. "You want to charge him?"

"No. I fell. It's all right."

The deputy removed Philip from my van and took my paperwork. He handed me back both sets of handcuffs. Only then did he ask me if I needed an ambulance.

"No, I'll be all right," I said. "Thanks for the help. I appreciate it."

It got harder and harder to breath—no matter what I did, I couldn't get enough air. I got to the ER parking lot and fell out of the van onto my knees. Hitting the ground felt like being shot. It took several minutes before I could stand up.

My trek across the parking lot must have been a spectacle to behold. People stared at my step and drag walk. I was bent over almost completely to the left, doing my best imitation of Dr. Frankenstein's assistant, Igor. Nobody offered to help and somehow I made it to the admitting office on my own.

The triage nurse was taking my vitals when suddenly I felt like I was underwater and unable to breathe at all. She decided to move me to the head of the waiting list.

A torturous heave lifted me up on a gurney and they wheeled me back to X-ray. Each time the technician turned me over for another view I swore to myself to remember him. After being rolled back to a holding room and staring at the ceiling for an eternity, a doctor finally came in. A nurse pushing a cart followed him.

"Well, Mr. Laney," he said, after introducing himself, "you've managed to break ribs eight and nine and you have a collapsed left lung. We need to evacuate the air from the chest cavity and see if we can get the lung inflated again. The X-rays didn't look too bad and usually they inflate right up and stay there."

I was halfway expecting him to break out a sterilized bicycle tire pump wrapped in plastic. Later, I wound up wishing he had.

The doctor wiped a topical anesthetic on my side and told me to hold still. He took out a syringe that was as long as a sword and stuck it between my ribs. "It's going to hurt when it pops through the muscle," he said.

I looked up at him. "No shit?"

It really wasn't as bad as one might think. Ah, but don't underestimate the capabilities of modern medicine—little did I know that the best was yet to come.

The doctor taped the catheter to my side and then opened a valve at the back of the syringe. Air hissed as it escaped from my chest cavity.

All at once, relieved of the pressure inside the rib cage, my lung reinflated, air whooshing in through my mouth. I thought my ribs were going to jump right out of my chest. The sudden intake of air lifted me slightly off the table. If I'd had my gun, there would've been a mass killing.

Something of my desire to wipe out the entire hospital must have showed in my face, because a shot of Demerol appeared moments later. In my book, it could've come a lot sooner.

They left me there for several hours with the needle stuck in my side. Every once and a while the nurse came in and opened the valve to see if any more air came out. I woke up several hours later, when the feel-good shot started to wear off, to find the doctor removing the catheter.

The leak in the lung had sealed itself and the lung was staying inflated. They told me to take deep breaths, as pneumonia could be a problem with a collapsed lung if I yielded to the impulse to take shallow breaths.

Broken ribs are a pain that keeps on giving—you don't realize how many times each minute you breathe until the broken ends of your ribs grate together when you do.

It wasn't hard to tell when the Demerol had worn off: they let me go. My trip back out to my van didn't break any land-speed records and the step up into the driver's seat looked like Mount Everest. My gait wasn't quite as crooked, but each breath was torture.

Debbie wasn't amused that I hadn't called her from the hospital. Fortunately for me, she's a kind person. Once she realized how much pain I was in, she took pity on me and helped me into the bed.

Finding a comfortable sleeping position was impossible. I spent the entire night conscious of each breath, watching the numbers click over on the digital clock and devising particularly nasty tortures for Philip. Unfortunately, I wasn't entirely certain that he wouldn't enjoy anything I could think up, and that frustration contributed to my cheerful personality the next day.

# eleven

For the next few days, I lived in my recliner and spent most of my time figuring out how to get from one place to another with as little movement as possible. Every time I sneezed, it felt like somebody smacking me across the back with a baseball bat. Laughing was out of the question. The easiest way to sleep was to be angled back in my recliner. Cordless phone, cell, laptop, and TV remote along with a day's worth of food were all strategically placed within easy reach. Getting up to go to the bathroom was put off as long as possible, and my breaths were still little more than short, painful gasps.

Christmas was upon us but it didn't seem like the season to be jolly. Joey e-mailed us, saying only that he was leaving the ship and we probably wouldn't be hearing from him for at least a couple of months. He didn't have to fill in the details—those were readily available from CNN. I lay back in my chair and tried not to move, watching the news uneasily. Elements of the 15th Marine Expeditionary Unit were setting up Camp Rhino, the first base in Afghanistan.

Joey's second deployment was originally scheduled to end in January. I'd been planning to meet his ship in Honolulu and sail the final leg back with him on the ship to San Diego. The "Tiger Cruise," as it was called, would be at sea about a week once it left Hawaii before it arrived back in California. The events of September 11 changed all that, and the deployment was extended indefinitely.

After several days, the boredom became more painful than the physical discomfort and I began to resume a modified routine. Sparring duties in the dojo were delegated to my black belts, which was probably overdue anyway for their development. In a brief period of time my students had witnessed their instructor in a state that they trained hard to avoid. They realized my profession could be riskier than most, but they sometimes incorrectly assumed my invincibility. It might have been because it made them feel safer themselves that the person teaching them had been through so many altercations unscathed.

No matter how good you are, sooner or later the odds catch up with you. It was a warrior's life I chose and I wouldn't have it any other way.

My students understood that they were learning to avoid situations that I intentionally walked into. How better to learn to handle dire circumstances than to study from someone who embraces them? If somebody wants to learn how to fight, he or she better find a teacher who's been in more than one. Problem is, there aren't that many who have actually walked the walk.

The beauty of the martial arts is that there is never a plateau at the end of the learning curve. A runner will get to the point where his time for a distance run is the best he will do, and weight lifters will find the ultimate weight they can move. A dedicated martial artist is in a continuous state of growth and there is no level of stagnation. It is, truly, beautiful.

I learned something with each workout and everyday events correlated with the martial arts experience. Beginners in karate have taught me volumes and provided insight to lessons heard all my life. The fact that arresting such a small and nonviolent man caused an injury to me seemed on the surface to defy logic. After all, my fighting skills and physical training were designed to prevent physical harm to myself. A simple principle explained the reason for my vulnerability in that situation. It came down to the first phrase taught to me in the dojo. The words I heard many years ago were just now made clear: karate was for self-defense.

From the ancient origins of the martial arts came the lesson that karate was to be used for self-defense only. Most people, myself included, took that to mean we weren't to use our skills to bully or take advantage of other people. We trained to defend others and ourselves against bad people, and we were warriors for goodness. The goal was to reach purity of mind and spirit in the process of transforming our bodies into weapons.

All that is true. However, as with most things, the real meaning of the principle was much simpler and more practical than anything we read into it. The fact is karate would *only* work for self-defense. It has little to do with intent or motive as much as the actual physical application of the techniques.

If self-defense is the objective, common sense dictates that if a bad man is running away, you let him. It doesn't make much sense to run after trouble when trying to save your skin. The skills best suited for that are developed by cowboys with their lassos rather than martial arts training, which is designed to address someone coming *at* you.

Chasing down Philip had nothing to do with self-defense. Like much of my work, it was predatory.

Now, if he had stopped fleeing and turned to fight, things would have been different. Then I would have been defending myself. Like other countless lessons I've learned, the truth was much simpler than my complicated misinterpretations of it.

With Christmas coming next week, I wasn't going to let a little inconvenience like cracked ribs stop me from making some holiday money. Knowing exactly where a skip is going to be is too good an opportunity to pass up.

With Interstate 75, which connects Florida to cities up north, and I-40 stretching coast to coast, Knoxville is a crossroads for much of the country. That means that Frank's agents bond out not only locals but also folks who were just passing through when they got into trouble. As I've said, most of my fugitives find their way back home during this time of the year. Unfortunately, lots of the homes they go back to are out of state.

I've driven every mile of both those main arteries looking for skips. Since road trips are a part of the job I dislike the most, it makes sense to go after skips when you know where they're going to be.

Most of Frank's out-of-state clients come back to take care of their legal troubles, but some don't. Even those who don't return voluntarily don't always require a road trip. Sometimes I can trick them into driving back themselves.

Other times, I can avoid a road trip by convincing an unreliable out-of-state client to send the bonding company hold money. "Hold money" is used to pay off the court if our clients don't show up for their court dates. We "hold" the money until the forfeiture is final. If the client does, in fact, decide to appear, he gets his money back.

Our clients like the "hold money" option. They know if they skip and stick us with the bond, I'll come looking for them, even if the law won't come looking for them or will refuse to extradite except for serious felonies. With hold money on their account, they generally don't have anything to worry about. Sure, there's still a warrant out for them, but the state isn't going to go after them unless it's a serious felony, and getting an extradition order is even less likely.

Frank loves hold money because my fee is always included in the amount and it doesn't come out of his pocket. In the case of hold money, I'm more like a collections agent than anything else. The difference is that if a skip misses a payment, I repo their ass.

I have a large map of the United States hanging over my desk. Pink or blue pushpins, designating gender, dot the map where skips had been located. Each pin has a tag stuck on it with the skip's name and bond amount.

When there are enough pins stuck in a general area or on the way to other pickups, it's time to hit the road. My roundups have netted as many as four fugitives in a single trip.

Richard Phelps, however, was worth a trip to pick just him up. He was from the Detroit area and he'd stiffed us on a $15,000 bond.

Richard was arrested in a county north of Knoxville on his way back to Michigan. Passing motorists had called police to the scene of a man by the side of the road attacking a woman with some type of object. Richard had pulled his car over to the shoulder and dragged his wife out by the hair. According to her statement, he was beating her with a flashlight because she refused to perform oral sex on him.

Deputies in rural Tennessee counties take a dim view of that type of behavior, especially since there were two small children in the backseat. Phelps was also highly intoxicated, which might explain why he fell down multiple times during the arrest and suffered injuries that required several stitches. He was charged with aggravated assault, domestic violence, DUI, and reckless endangerment of a child, two counts.

After getting stitched up herself, Ms. Phelps drove back to Michigan with her two children and left Richard sitting in jail. His one phone call was to dear old dad in Detroit, who immediately made the nine-hour trip down to bail his son out and then turned around and drove him back home. That was four months ago.

Richard's father owned a large landscaping business north of Detroit. As part of my groundwork, I'd been in contact with him. He had promised to either deliver Richard to court or pay the hold money, but he had done neither.

My patience had long since worn thin when Richard's ex–mother-in-law called me. Her daughter had divorced Richard and orders of protection were issued to prevent him from being in contact with her.

Those pesky little court papers didn't deter Richard and he continued to stalk and harass his ex-wife. The ex–mother-in-law complained that the police weren't doing anything about it. She was more than anxious for me to remove Richard's person from Michigan. It was time for a trip.

My last trip to the Motor City was to a quaint little neighborhood in the 8 Mile Road vicinity. I also have family who live north of the city but had not had time on recent trips to stop and visit. Even though my brother-in-law is most hospitable, he wouldn't welcome the caliber of houseguests I'd be traveling with.

I usually take my time on the outgoing leg of a road trip and try to rest up. The return trip, with a skip in custody, is normally nonstop, so I try to arrive in good shape. Sometimes circumstances prevent this. On one trip, I left Knoxville on a Monday morning, drove to Denver, and returned to Knoxville with my prisoner in the afternoon on Wednesday. I'm getting too old for that anymore.

Back in the good old days, I could drop off my prisoner at a local jail and grab a night's sleep at a motel. They would let me pick him back up the next morning, and in return they were paid the thirty dollars or so for a night of housing my prisoner.

That's no longer allowed because of liability issues. That means my skip stays in my custody all the way back home. I've tried getting a room and chaining them down to the bed next to me, but a body just doesn't sleep well under those conditions. Every time they toss and turn, they rattle their chains. Even when they're quiet, I've got one eye open, watching for trouble, and that just makes for a long night. It's just as easy to come on back and pull over for a quick catnap or two.

That's why it's important to get as much rest as possible on the outgoing leg of the trip.

Richard was known to spend the night in his Ford F-150 Lariat Super Cab after a hard night of drinking (which was almost every night). He would park the red truck in front of his father's business and sleep in the back of the extended cab. My briefcase contained maps to the landscaping company, daddy's house, and the local sheriff's department, since I planned to check in with local law enforcement when I arrived.

I tilted the seat back, turned the cruise control on, and headed up I–75. The first part of the trip took me over Jellico Mountain and into Kentucky. That's when my flavor of radio stations always faded out. I was just pulling out my first CD of the trip when my cell phone rang. It was Ken Philips.

"Joe, I've got some news," he said. "There was an explosion. Red Crawford's drug lab blew up and it burned him real bad. They flew him by helicopter to the burn center at Erlanger Medical Center in Chattanooga."

I had a hard time feeling too sorry for somebody who tried to have me shot. The bad news was that this meant if Wiley was still hiding out with Red, Wiley would probably run.

I hung up the phone with Ken and slid *Eat a Peach*, by the Allman Brother's Band, in the CD player. My mind drifted into the world of the white lines as "Mountain Jam" played on.

Two stops, thousands of white lines, and several CDs later, I pulled into the sheriff's department parking lot in the county north of Detroit proper. I knew it would be a lot colder than it was in Knoxville, but I wasn't prepared for the frigid air that pried its way into my lungs. It felt like an icicle jabbed between my ribs. I hadn't given my ribs time to heal completely and they were still tender. I still took short, shallow breaths, and I'd developed an irritating cough that didn't help them feel any better.

My heavy, green camouflage jacket repelled some of the frigid north wind. My insulated boots crunched on the hard-frozen ground as I made my way toward the lobby of the jail. The pockets in my BDUs were filled with cough drops and tissue paper. A black wool cap topped my head.

It wasn't enough. The short walk to the front door made all my warm clothing seem grossly inadequate.

The sergeant sitting at the front desk was a large black man with arms the size of stovepipes. His high and tight haircut accentuated his square jaw and stern expression. He looked up at me from his paperwork and seemed somewhat puzzled by my attire.

The shortness of breath made my pronounced Southern accent evident to even me as it drew out my syllables more than normal. "Hello, I'm Joe, from Tennessee."

"No shit," he said. "What can I do for you?"

I showed him my warrants and gun permit and asked for directions to the nearest auto salvage yard. Local police were helpful most of the time. Even when they're not, the risk of not telling them I'm working in their jurisdiction far outweighed any benefits. The vast majority of them tried to help, but others had been known to impede my progress for one reason or another. The last thing anybody needed was for me to wind up in jail, and if checking in with the local law blew my case, so be it. After all, this was about money and there's nothing profitable about getting locked up.

The sergeant turned out to be one of the helpful ones. He told dispatch to advise patrols in my surveillance area that I was going to be there. That way, if neighbors started calling in reports about a suspicious black van lurking in the area, the deputies would know what was up. The last thing I needed while I was trying to be inconspicuous was a police cruiser pulling up next to me.

A quick stop by the junkyard provided me with an expired Michigan license plate. Richard felt safe on his turf, but if he spotted a van hanging around with a Tennessee tag, it might spook him. My fleetness of foot had fled. This would be, by necessity, an operation of extreme stealth.

But the license plate on my van wasn't the only thing that gave away my origins. The sergeant's reaction to my Southern drawl didn't go unnoticed. I stuck the question of how to conceal my enunciation in one of the cubbyholes in the back of my brain, counting on my subconscious to figure something out.

The terrain in this area was flat as a billiard table. No hills and few curves. Roads were long and straight and the one that led to the landscaping business turned into dirt about a mile off the main intersection. Good if you want to watch someone—not so good if you want to avoid being seen.

I drove by and Richard's truck was nowhere to be seen. After a couple more passes, I spotted a grove of trees next to an old barn about a quarter-mile from the business. If I parked there, I'd have a good view of the landscaping business while keeping concealed.

Since it was still early, I thought I'd check out good old dad's house and a few of Richard's favorite social establishments before settling in to watch for his van. His ex–mother-in-law had been kind enough to provide a detailed list of addresses.

A few hours later, after I'd checked out all the other places, I returned to my stakeout site close to the landscaping business and backed the van into the grove of trees next to the barn. It was cloudy and almost dark. The only light came from the windows of a farmhouse a good distance down the road. The trees hid the van from any vehicles that would have approached from either direction of the road. It was time to settle in and wait.

Wiley was on my mind. The way he'd slipped through my fingers grated on my nerves. Since I was just killing time until Richard showed up, I figured I might as well follow up on a couple of long shots at locating Wiley.

I rummaged through my briefcase and pulled out the cell phone that belonged to Mountain Man. After all, maybe I could find a number that would allow me to return it to him. My laptop was connected to the internet via my own cell phone, so I ran a trace on each of the numbers in Mountain Man's cell phone address book.

Once I had the location of each traced phone call, I called the local police department in that area to see if they'd come across one Wiley Lee Kent. Most of my skips have difficulty staying out of trouble and quite often the local police departments will know where they are. Sometimes I'd find out they were sitting in a jail somewhere just waiting for me to pick them up. Or, they were arrested but released, and the local law sometimes knew where to locate them.

I didn't try calling the folks in Mountain Man's directory myself. I doubted they would be too sympathetic to my cause, and chances were that word would get back to Wiley and spook him. It's always better to know more than your prey thinks you do.

About halfway down the directory, a number jumped out at me. It was the same number displayed in Mountain Man's outgoing call list about the time of the attempted assassination. The number traced to a residence in Hastings, Florida.

The officer in the satellite office of the sheriff's department down there told me he'd cited a Wiley Kent a couple a days back for public intoxication. My heart jumped through my chest. I described Wiley to the deputy—a perfect match. I was just about to say to hell with my current stakeout and head straight for Hastings, Florida, when the deputy told me the rest of the story.

Wiley had been given a simple citation. He wasn't taken into custody. He hadn't been fingerprinted and they hadn't checked for outstanding warrants. In short—they'd had him and they'd let him go.

The longing to drive straight to the traced number in Hastings was almost unbearable. I squirmed in the seat as the adrenaline coursed through my veins.

Wiley Kent was probably basking on a sunny beach in Florida, laughing at the deputy who'd let him go. I was freezing my ass off in Michigan looking for an idiot who beat his wife with a flashlight. Life was not fair.

I made up my mind right then—the van was about to rack up some serious miles on it. As soon as I delivered Richard to Tennessee, I was heading straight for scenic Hastings, Florida.

But for now, Wiley would have to wait. I stuck Wiley back in his cubbyhole and focused on the task at hand.

The sun had long since set. I'd thought it was cold earlier—I'd been mistaken. It was cold now. I could see my breath crystallize in front of me. It was time to start the van and turn up the heat.

That established a routine I would follow most of the night as I watched and waited. A few minutes of glorious heat pouring out of the vents, defrosting my extremities and brain, air that I could breathe with far less pain. Then turning off the engine, watching the frost creep back across the windows and my exhalations become not only more audible but visible as well.

Periodic protein bar snacks and sips of bottled water finally took their toll and I was forced to risk permanent injury from frostbite and venture outside. I'd already disabled the inside light to prevent it from giving me away when the door opened. That might have been the least of my worries since I damn near screamed when the frigid outside air invaded my lungs. I performed the necessary bodily functions as quickly as possible, trying to minimize how long my lungs and other sensitive areas were exposed to the elements. I was starting to really hate Michigan.

Suddenly, headlights appeared off in the distance, getting brighter as the vehicle approached. A truck matching the description of Richard's passed my stakeout location and pulled into the front parking lot of the landscaping business. The driver turned off the headlights and the engine. My watch told me it was 3:00 A.M.

The red truck just sat there. There was no indication that the driver intended to exit it, so I watched and waited, counting the hours that passed, turning on the heater more and more often as the bone-chilling early morning air cooled down the van faster. The nagging cough helped to keep me awake as each spasm felt like a well-placed punch to my ribs.

Finally, at 6:30 A.M., the red Ford started up and pulled around the side of the building next to the office door. I picked up my binoculars, tweaking them into focus, and finding the driver's side door. Sure enough, Richard stepped out. The information I'd been given was correct, as he had spent what was left of the night in his truck. At least he didn't have far to go to get to work in the morning. I wished I could say the same.

I started the van and drove up the dirt road to the business. All at once, I flashed on the big sergeant's reaction to my accent and a solution popped out of the same cubbyhole.

It's funny how often cubbyholing something works for me. If I shelve something instead of concentrating on it, the answer often comes just when I need it. Your subconscious is far better at multitasking than your conscious mind is and it works pretty much nonstop.

My subconscious understood the problem completely and in very straightforward terms. The first words out of my mouth would tell Richard I was from somewhere a lot warmer than Michigan. He would get spooked and run. With my hacking lungs and tender ribs, I wouldn't be able to catch him. He would get away and I would have spent a night freezing my ass off for nothing.

The way to prevent that whole sequence of events from happening, my subconscious informed me, was pretty simple: don't talk. More specifically, be a person who doesn't talk.

Richard had walked around to the other side of his truck and was standing at the open passenger door when I pulled up. His face was slack, his eyes bleary, and his hair was sticking up in all directions. He looked just like what he was—a guy who'd gotten drunk and slept it off in his truck. He had a shaving kit in his hands. He turned to face me with the distant gaze that often accompanies a rather serious hangover. No wonder he hadn't been turning on his truck every few minutes for warmth—the alcohol in his body had undoubtedly acted like antifreeze.

I stepped out the van and waved, putting on a friendly and slightly confused look. I held both hands up in front of me and started moving my fingers rapidly in what looked to me like meaningful combinations. Confidence, I told myself.

It was a good thing Richard didn't know sign language because he would've known I was a fake.

"Can I help you?" he asked.

My fingers slowed down from their meaningless tirade long enough to point at my ears. I shook my head, an apologetic expression on my face.

Richard got the message that a deaf person was standing in front of him. He threw up his hands as if to communicate that he was at a loss as to what to do. Naturally, as a deaf-mute, I had experienced this reaction before. I made scribbling gestures on the palm of my hand to indicate that I wanted to write something down.

Richard was fairly sharp for someone with a serious hangover. It only took two or three repetitions for him to figure out what I meant. His eyes widened as understanding dawned on him. He made pronounced movements with his mouth while speaking and pointing to the side door. I guess he assumed I was blind as well as deaf. Then, speaking loudly and enunciating clearly, perhaps on the off-chance that I could lip-read, he said, "Okay. Follow me into the office."

Richard unlocked the door and we went inside. The concrete floor had a thick layer of dirt on it and plant material was scattered about.

There weren't any other exits. Finally, a break—he was hemmed in, which was exactly what this not deaf but otherwise pretty disabled bounty hunter needed.

Richard walked ahead of me. I followed and shut the door behind me. The second it closed, I had my gun out of the holster.

"Get on the fucking floor. Now!" I screamed.

Richard spun around with a look of horror on his face, caught completely off-guard by the abrupt change in the universe as he understood it. A deaf-mute was screaming at him. Not only that, he was staring down the barrel of a gun. It was a lot to take in even when you're sober. Maybe it was easier being half-awake and hung-over.

Fortunately, the sudden alteration of reality as he understood it didn't affect his reflexes. As requested, he hit the floor instantly. He landed sprawled out and face down so fast that clouds of dust flew up around him. I stuck the muzzle of my gun on the back of his head. That was all the encouragement he needed to immediately place his hands behind his back for cuffing.

Once I'd patted him down for weapons, I rolled Richard over onto his back. The once-dusty floor underneath him had turned into mud. You spend all night at a beer joint, there are going to be certain metabolic consequences and by-products. For just a moment, I wished he'd risked frostbite when he'd pulled up a few hours ago rather than waiting until now to take care of them.

Well, there was no way I was going to drive all the way back to Tennessee with the van stinking of beer urine. For a moment, I was tempted to strip him and take him outside and hose him off. But the air was still pretty cold and I didn't want to have to breathe unheated air any more than I had to. Instead, I cuffed him to one of the steel posts supporting the roof while I retrieved some dry clothes from his truck.

Richard's dad drove up just as I finished securing his son in the van. He had time to do little more than wave goodbye. Once we were on the road and headed south, we stopped only for dire rest room breaks, gas, and to go through drive-through fast-food lanes.

I called Frank on the way and told him about the tip on Wiley from Florida. It was hardly a sure thing, maybe not sufficient standing alone to warrant the trip (although Frank would have had a hell of a time talking me out of it). However, my pushpins on the map saved the day.

We had two more skips in the same area. Standing alone, they hardly warranted a trip, but they looked a lot more profitable if you stacked up the possibility of nabbing Wiley next to them. At the very least, even if we missed Wiley, we would defray some of the expenses by picking up the two smaller cases. Either way, it wouldn't be a complete waste of time.

My next call was to Debbie. I asked her to lay out some fresh clothes for me and to call my senior black belt to let him know he was in charge of the dojo for the next few days. Eight hours after Richard waved goodbye to his dad, we were back in Knoxville.

I was starting to feel like Federal Express. I dropped Richard off at the jail, grabbed the files on the other two Florida skips from my office, and stopped off at home just long enough to take a quick shower and toss clean clothes into my duffel bag. Eighteen hours after leaving Michigan, I crossed the Georgia state line into Florida.

I checked into a motel just off the interstate. I hadn't had any real sleep in more than forty hours and it was getting too dangerous to drive. I was out as soon as my head hit the pillow.

No matter how tired I am, I can never sleep very long when I'm on a hunt. A little over four hours after lying down, I was back in the van, heading south.

By then, I'd reached a state of being I'm all too familiar with. My mind was numb and dull, and my world consisted of the van and the white lines of the highway streaming past my glazed stare. I was safer than I'd been four hours earlier, but not by a lot.

When I do a multiple-skip road trip, I usually plan out picking up the skips that are located farthest away, then getting the others on the way back. This minimized the amount of time that I would be transporting more than one prisoner and made things easier. I set things up differently this time, though. My other two runners were further south, but I wanted Wiley real bad. I was going after him first.

The sign at the Hastings city limits read "Potato Capital of Florida." The entire community was built around the potato industry and huge farms that produced the spuds were sprawled out for miles. Migrant camps that provided workers for the fields were everywhere. The foremen who drove the men to the farms each morning to work also operated the camps. The foremen were paid daily. They then paid the workers, deducting a percentage of the worker's wages as a commission as well as rent for staying in the camps. Rarely did a property owner know the names of the workers, as they dealt only with the camp foremen. It was the perfect place for somebody to hide. Nobody asked for proof of your identity and everybody was paid in cash every day.

A visit to the satellite office of the sheriff's department didn't tell me much more than I already knew except that the name and address of my phone trace belonged to the owner of one of the smaller migrant camps. The officer who'd arrested Wiley was not on duty. Several of the local grocery and beer store clerks made a positive ID on Wiley from his picture. He was a regular and stopped in with the farm bus every evening after work to pick up his Natural Ice beer and Copenhagen tobacco. His habitual purchase of those items, in addition to being white, made him stand out.

Migrant workers often come and go unnoticed in a community, but one of the store clerks was from Tennessee and remembered talking to Wiley about the Volunteer State. She remembered his first coming into the store a few weeks ago, but she hadn't seen him for three or four days. That made sense—that would have been about the time Wiley picked up the public intoxication citation. Everyone I talked to said the same thing—they hadn't seen him in three or four days. This wasn't sounding good.

When lunchtime rolled around, busloads of migrant workers came into town to eat. They got their food and the foremen would pay the bill and deduct it from the workers' pay at the end of the day.

A clerk pointed out the foreman in charge of my suspected skip. He knew my man as Wiley Lee and stated that he and another worker had left several days ago. The foreman's wife looked after the migrant camp, and he gave me her name and said she would tell me everything she knew. Her name was Isabella.

The camp was a square, cinder-block structure with no windows or doors on the outer walls. An unlocked chain-link gate led into a courtyard encircled by thirty or so rooms. Most of the doors were open. As I walked in, elderly faces stared at me from the gloom of their rooms. Children ran through the courtyard and played barefooted in the sandy soil. A dog lay stretched out under the meager shade of a stunted tree in the middle of the quad.

Isabella stopped folding her laundry and showed me the room where Wiley had been staying with a roommate. Her English was broken but somehow we were able to communicate.

Wiley and his friend had hitchhiked to a truck stop and were going to catch a ride out west from there. They had been gone for several days and nobody had seen them since. Their room had yet to be reoccupied, and she pointed it out to me. A brief inspection revealed garbage bags full of Wiley's favorite beverage and smokeless tobacco scattered about.

Wiley was really starting to get to me. He had to be the luckiest skip I'd ever chased. The man was a drunken, filthy, nasty, perverted sack of shit. That a man with the IQ of a slug kept slipping through my fingers was almost more than I could stand. It was almost like divine intervention, but I knew there was no way God would protect him. If Wiley was the recipient of supernatural help, it surely came from below.

I know better than to let a case get to me like that. I reminded myself it was only a job.

It was time for Wiley to slither back into his cubbyhole. I had two more skips to pick up in Florida and there was no way I was going to ride back to Tennessee empty-handed.

First things first. My fuel supply of adrenaline had gone dry; I had had only four hours of sleep since leaving Michigan and that nagging cough had turned into a deep-chested hack. I needed a good night's sleep before I headed further south.

The next morning was the beginning of a long trek down I–95 to a section of Miami called Liberty City. This quaint little community was the home of one Jeffrey Ray. He'd had the misfortune of getting pulled over in Tennessee and found to be in possession of a small amount of crack cocaine and a .38 caliber revolver. My man worked as an auto mechanic and he listed a phone number for his place of employment on the bond application.

White people are definitely not a majority in this part of Miami, so I asked a black friend of mine in the bonding business to place a call to the garage. He asked for Jeffrey specifically and, after a short wait, my man came to the phone. Jeffrey was more than helpful and gave my friend a quick estimate on some automotive repair work and told him he was at work everyday from 8:00 A.M. until 4:30 P.M.

I got into Miami about noon and checked in with the local law. They told me I was crazy to consider going into that section of town alone. I thanked them for their concern and headed into that section of town alone.

Just a few blocks off the interstate, the surroundings reminded me of downtown Beirut. Burned-out cars sat in vacant lots and just about every square inch of standing concrete was covered with graffiti. Any businesses that remained in the area had their property barricaded with razor wire.

The garage was not much more than a cinder-block building with cars parked in the yard. The front of the lot was small and a ride around the block showed more cars in the back. I figured that was where most of the work was done.

I parked the van a block away from the garage and got out my binoculars. It was like doing recon in the middle of a war zone.

I heard a *squeak, squeak, squeak* and looked in the rearview mirror. A large black man weighing every bit of 300 pounds-plus was riding up to the van on what looked like a child's bicycle. He could have carried it far more easily than ridden it. For a moment, I wondered if it was some sort of clown circus act.

The man rode right up and tapped on my window. I rolled it down and stared into a broad, friendly smile. "Hello brother," he said, reaching in a satchel slung across his shoulder. I tensed a bit, but there was nothing threatening in his posture or his voice. "Read the word of God," he said, his voice deep and resonant, as he pulled out a miniature Bible. He passed it to me through the window. Then, with one final smile and nod, he started squeaking his way on down the road. I watched as he weaved in and out of the parade of drug dealers and prostitutes on his way to wherever. It was completely surreal. The thought crossed my mind that an angel might have just paid me a visit.

I was past the point of fatigue when a series of not-too-distant gunshots reminded me to stay alert. The ground vibrated with the loud *thump* of a heavy bass from a car stereo as what looked like a brown 1979 Chevy Malibu approached. My pistol was already in my hand and resting on my lap.

Right before the car pulled even with my van, it slowed to a crawl. The music died abruptly. The Malibu crept past as I made hard eye contact with the driver. Four black males were inside and they all gave me the "stare" as they drove slowly by. I'd just been warned, I guess, that I was on someone else's turf.

A younger guy in coveralls came out of the garage and walked toward one of the cars parked in the yard. Its hood was already up and it looked to be next on his list of jobs for the day. My trusty binoculars confirmed what I suspected—it was my man, Jeffrey.

Jeffrey leaned over the front of the car and began working on the engine. It didn't require any complicated brainwork to figure out how to approach him. I simply got out of the van and walked up behind him. He never even knew anybody was behind him until the hood of the car he was working on slammed down hard on his back.

The impact straightened Jeffrey's body out like a plank. His legs stuck straight out, presenting his ankles perfectly for my leg shackles.

Jeffrey was quite vocal about the discomfort his position entailed. When I lifted the hood off his back, he ignored my advice to make no sudden movements. He tried to come after me, but his chained ankles took him facedown to the ground.

I reached between his legs and squeezed both of his testicles. Getting him to put his hands behind his back and submit to handcuffing was not a problem.

Two of Jeffrey's fellow mechanics must have heard his screams and came running out brandishing tire tools. Something in my expression must have told them that I'd long since passed the point of caring about how I dealt with interference, because they stopped as soon as we locked gazes. They just stood there as Jeffrey was led off. No one said a word, not me, not the mechanics.

The Chevy Malibu I'd seen before had rounded the block and had crept back to the van. It was stopped in the road and waiting for us. Again, I was past the point of caring and stormed straight for them with Jeffrey hopping in tow. Whatever the mechanics had seen in my face must have still been there. The Malibu occupants all looked at one another and seemed to arrive at the same conclusion—that it was time to leave. Good move.

I loaded Jeffrey into the van, then left Liberty City, heading north. My next pickup was on the way back, just east of Orlando.

Once on the road, Jeffrey was resigned to his fate. Like many others, he seemed relieved that the running was over. "I'm glad it's over," he kept saying. "I got myself straight and been working hard to get my little girl out of that place. At least now there won't be no looking over my shoulder. Once I got ahead, I was going to turn myself in, I swear."

We struck up a conversation about bounty hunting and he started to get pumped about riding along on another chase with me, even though his attendance wasn't exactly voluntary. "Hand them maps back to me," he said. "I'll read off directions when we get closer."

Paul Franklin was the next skip on my list. He'd run a red light while driving under the influence and broadsided a car driven by a sixty-two-year-old woman. Paul was also charged with leaving the scene of an accident. Police found his car in a ditch about five miles away from the collision. His victim, the grandmother of three, was in the hospital for weeks and now used a wheelchair. Doctors were uncertain if she would ever walk again.

"Man, that's wrong, that's just wrong," Jeffrey said, after hearing the story. A concerned look crossed his face. "Hey man, you all right? You're looking awful tired."

"I'll be all right," I said with more conviction than I felt. "Listen, if you see me nodding off, kick the seat or something, okay?"

Jeffrey's eyes got wide. "Don't worry, man. I'll keep you awake. I got to get back to my little girl."

We made a restroom stop, grabbed some food at a drive-through, and arrived in Orlando about four hours after we'd left Miami.

"This is the exit," Jeffrey announced. He'd been watching both the mileage markers and my eyes, making sure I stayed awake. "Get off here and take a right off the ramp. How'd you find this guy, anyway?"

"He lives down here with his mother," I said. "She denied it over the phone but a neighbor verified that he was staying there. His cell phone bills are sent to his mom's house and he charges gas at stations in that area. He's there."

"Man, that's slick," Jeffrey said. "So you got his cell number?"

"Yep. I even talked to him. He told me he was living in Tampa and wasn't coming back to Tennessee and that I'd never catch him."

"Shit man," he said. "That must be one dumb motherfucker. You don't piss off the man like that."

"Yeah." I didn't bother pointing out the irony of Jeffrey's take on the situation. I've had worse company on long drives and at least he could read a map.

I checked in with the local law and then followed Jeffrey's directions to the house belonging to Paul's mother. We pulled right up into the driveway that circled part of the way around the brick rancher.

The drapes on the front plate-glass window were open and revealed a lit Christmas tree. Two people looked out as we drove up. A third person pulled the curtains shut in a bedroom facing the driveway. I parked the van nose in so the license plate was not visible from the house.

As I walked up the bricked path, the front door opened. A woman around fifty years old, with heavily sprayed graying hair, greeted me. She was wearing a cashmere sweater and was draped in pearls. Baggy suede pants hung down to the tops of Gucci shoes that matched her sweater. Little Christmas tree earrings dangled from her earlobes. A thin, small-framed man with solid gray hair who was dressed in a jogging suit stood behind her.

"May I help you?" she asked cheerfully.

It took a concentrated effort to hold back a looming siege of coughs and my answer came out almost like a bark. "I'm looking for Paul Franklin. I'm his bondsman from Tennessee."

Her face suddenly drew up tight and she answered with a snarl. "I told you he doesn't live here. Now get—"

The honk of a car horn cut off her next words, which was just as well. I wasn't in the mood for more lies. She followed me around to the side of the house.

Jeffrey was leaning over the front seat and mashing on the horn. When he saw me, he stopped and yelled, "Hey, man. Your boy just stuck his head out the back door. I recognized him from the picture. He ran back inside when I blew the horn."

Ms. Franklin looked inside the van and saw Jeffrey. "Get that nigger off my property," she said. "I won't have it." She turned to her male companion and screamed at him to call the police. He ran inside, probably as much to get away from her as to follow her orders. I didn't blame him—she looked like she was on the brink of exploding.

I walked around to the other side of the house and stood off from a corner so I could see both the front and the back doors. There was no doubt that Jeffrey had the other side covered.

The police arrived about five minutes later. Two officers, one white and one black, got out of the car. Ms. Franklin ran up to the white cop in a tirade. "I want that black son-of-a-bitch off my property."

The two officers looked at each other and then they walked up to me. They checked my paperwork on Jeffrey and then verified my warrants for Paul. The black cop walked up to Ms. Franklin. "Your boy was positively identified as being in the residence. This bondsman has the right to go in and search. If you interfere you could be charged with obstruction of justice." He then turned and looked at me. "My partner will watch the backdoor and I'll make sure he doesn't come out the front. Search all you want."

This left her speechless and she followed me inside, staying behind me like a shadow. It was a large house and my patience for hide-and-seek was nonexistent. Then I remembered an old technique I'd used in the past.

I stood in the middle of the house and dialed Paul's cell number. After that, it was simply a matter of following the rings. Within moments, I was standing at the door to the laundry room, listening to the phone ring and smiling politely at my angry shadow.

Ms. Franklin just stood there as I opened the door to the washer. Paul was inside, twisted up like a pretzel to wedge his frame into the small space. The contortions required to hide in a washing machine weren't at all compatible with reaching his cell phone and turning it off. As painful as the position looked, I was sure it was far more comfortable than the daily life of the grandmother he'd hit.

For just a second, I contemplated turning on the rinse cycle. But then my better judgment intervened. The presence of witnesses had absolutely nothing to do with my decision not to.

It took a bit of work, but Paul finally managed to extricate himself from the washing machine. As soon as he was out, I clamped on leg shackles and handcuffs. Ms. Franklin remained silent, but there was yet more to come.

She followed us out to the van and her expression turned to pure horror as she watched me chain her precious little contortionist to Jeffrey.

I watched, then felt compelled to reassure her that I am an equal opportunity kidnapper. "They're going to be like Siamese twins all the way back to Tennessee," I said. "Tell you the truth, I feel sorry for Jeffrey."

The trip back took a little less than nine hours. Jeffrey helped keep me awake with jokes and his intentional aggravation of Paul. Each one had to be deposited at different jails, and by the time I got home I was coughing nonstop. My skin felt like I'd been sandpapered and the pounding in my head grew louder and louder. But sleep deprivation won out over pain, and sleep came the moment my head hit the pillow.

# twelve

Twelve hours later, I gradually came to. Debbie had figured I needed to sleep and had slipped out quietly to work. The night was a vague memory of heavy coughing, shivers, and on-again, off-again, deep sleep. My skin was on fire and taking a breath was like sucking hard on a clogged straw. It felt like someone was sitting on my chest. Violent coughing sieges brought up gobs of green phlegm. I lay in bed, awake, but not willing to move.

Debbie called home about noon. After she'd interrogated me and listened long-distance to one of my coughing spells, she threatened to come home and drag me to the doctor. I held her off by promising to call him myself.

My regular doctor was not working that day and the nurse instructed me to go to the ER. The same doctor who'd been working the floor the night of my collapsed lung was on duty again. He shook his head as he listened to my lungs. My body temperature was a touch over 103.

"I told you this could happen with a collapsed lung," he said.

A chest X-ray confirmed his diagnosis of pneumonia. He sent me home with a handful of antibiotics and a prescription for more. "If your temperature doesn't come down by tomorrow or if it goes higher, call your doctor. He'll need to put your ass in the hospital," he warned.

Debbie and I spent Christmas glued in front of the TV, hoping to catch a glimpse of Joey. Some of the networks had reporters embedded with the troops and they were letting them send back holiday messages.

Even if Joey didn't get tapped to tape a message, maybe we could catch a glimpse of him in the crowd.

No such luck. His face never popped up on the screen at all. We had heard not a word from him since before Thanksgiving.

I needed to heal up. In addition to the antibiotics and other regimes prescribed by the doctor, I had my own ways of dealing with my damaged lungs. Twice a day, I spent a few minutes on the deep breathing exercises that were part of my Isshinryu training.

I started by standing in a relaxed seisan stance. Then I took in a long deep inhalation through my nose, filling the lower portion of my lungs first, which forced my abdomen to protrude. Initially, each attempt ended in a sudden and violent coughing spell that brought up buckets of phlegm. After several attempts, with my lungs a little clearer, I was able to continue inhaling, filling my lungs from the bottom up like a glass of water. The inhalation continued until the top portions of my lungs were completely inflated and my chest was expanded like a tight balloon.

The exhalation began by forcing out the air in the top of the lungs through my open mouth (tough to do with it closed) with a loud rushing sound. I continued tightening my muscles to expel the air in the reverse order it was taken in until it felt as though every last bit of air was forced out the bottom lobes by my retracted stomach. Each cycle began and ended the same way, with my concentration focused on my "one point" or energy source just below the navel. I finished off each session with a glass of orange juice and 750 mg of Augmentin. Other than an occasional trip to the bathroom or a trek from the bed to the sofa, that was the extent of my physical activity.

A few nights later, I woke up drenched in sweat. My fever had broken. By the time New Year's Day rolled around, I was really tired of being in bed. My breathing was less congested and I was starting to get restless, even though I didn't yet have the energy to do much.

I had just settled in to watch a full day of college bowl games when I heard Debbie squeal from back in the office. "It's Joey!" she said. "He's back on the ship. We got an e-mail from him!" His e-mail contained the welcome news that he'd been in the desert for about six weeks and that his unit was now rotating back home.

Over the next several days, we received several e-mails from him. The Tiger Cruise was still on, but at a later date. His ship was scheduled to leave Hawaii and head back to California on February 23. Debbie began to make travel arrangements for me to meet him in Honolulu and sail back aboard the USS *Peleliu* to San Diego.

As my strength began to return, I stepped up the intensity of the breathing exercises, adding the other movements that intensified the breathing portions of the routine. Before the inhalation, I would step forward with my right foot, setting it down with toes turned in at about a forty-five degree angle. Then I'd tuck my butt under and tilt my pelvis forward, which caused my feet to grip the floor. Then, pulling my left hand back to the side of my pectoral muscle, I'd begin the inhalation.

The violence of the transition from yin to yang coincided with the beginning of the exhalation, which began as I slowly extended my left hand in a twisting punch. During the exhalation, my toe-in stance and pelvic tilt, combined with tension applied to my leg muscles, locked my legs in place. As my arm moved forward in a slow-motion twisting punch, I applied dynamic tension to my upper body, timing the final moments of the exhalation to coincide with full tension in all my muscle groups.

At first, I used only mild breathing and light muscle tension while performing *Sanchin* kata. Even with easy practice, it was evident that my ki was disrupted. I could feel how both the antibiotics and the disease they were fighting disrupted my energy flow.

As the days passed, I increased the intensity. By the time the prescribed medication had run its course, I was running the kata at full bore. The transition of opposites felt like an explosion and my body was a conduit for a surge of energy that was generated from the core. I was back.

My lungs weren't the only things that had been clogged up. If anything, my in-basket was in even worse shape. The two-week hiatus resulted in a logjam of cases and armloads of forfeitures from the courthouse. In just a short period of time, my almost-cleared chase board was almost full.

Frank told me to take all the time I needed, but the number of skips had grown to the point that he had a serious amount of money at risk. Not only that, but in a little over a month I would be on vacation for a couple of weeks with a trip to Hawaii and the Tiger Cruise back with Joey. My goal was to wipe the board clean before leaving.

It was the month of the cell-block express as I rounded up skips and herded them off to jail. Between the short road trips and arrests across county lines, not to mention the ones inside Knox County, I generated a huge backlog of paperwork. With the hoosegow shuttle operating at full tilt, I was wearing out my eraser wiping names off the chase board.

Time flew by. Before I knew it, my trip was only a week away. I had no new solid leads on Wiley, which bothered me, but every lead on his whereabouts turned into a dead end. Besides Wiley, there was only one other big case on my chase board. At least it was starting to break open.

Wayne Ballenger wasn't your ordinary sort of burglar and thief. He was an entrepreneur, one who believed in finding a need and filling it. His business model was built around developing a "wish list." Wayne would collect a list of items that people were in the market for and, when the list got fat enough, he would go steal the merchandise and sell it at a fraction of the legitimate cost. That way, all his items were pre-sold and he wasn't bothered with the inconvenience of finding a fence or the risk of going to a pawnshop.

The enterprising entrepreneur also believed in networking. A business associate of his named Barry had a wife who worked as a housecleaner for a resort rental company. She would let Wayne know when the remote chalets were scheduled to be vacant. She'd clean them up—then Wayne would clean them out. Since his pre-orders consisted of everything from TVs and VCRs to beds and other furniture, it was actually quite an efficient operation with no fuss, muss, or waste. Well, at least until he got caught and then failed to appear in circuit court on charges of burglary and theft.

As luck would have it, Barry got busted while in possession of fifty pounds of marijuana. Frank made his bond, but while Barry was out, Barry picked up another drug charge. We could have revoked his original bond just for that, but Barry was in poor health and not considered a flight risk. Besides, in return for our gracious benevolence, Barry agreed to drop a dime on Wayne.

There was something about Wayne's file that bugged me and I couldn't put my finger on it. He was married to a girl named Kim and I was pretty sure the couple had fled to somewhere in Georgia. Barry said Wayne was in trouble with some drug dealers down there and was headed up to hide out at his grandmother's house on the Cumberland

Plateau. Barry called a couple of days later and told me that Wayne had made it back and was holed up at Granny's.

The weather can be tricky up on the plateau during that time of year, but the forecast called for fair skies. I went home to pick up some warmer clothes and placed more arrest folders in my basket to be entered into the database. The stack of folders had grown large, and I wasn't looking forward to tackling them.

There was still something bugging me about Wayne's file. I ran a query on all the names and phone numbers on his application through my database but no matches turned up. Then I printed out a map to his grandmother's house. It was about an hour and a half west on I–40 up the long grade to the plateau and then another hour or so along winding two-lane highways. I still couldn't pinpoint whatever it was that I ought to be noticing about Wayne's file, so finally I gave up. Maybe an answer would turn up while I was on the way.

Once I got up on the plateau, I stopped to check in with the local law. As luck would have it, a bondsman friend of mine named Scotty Spence was at the jail taking care of some business. Even though Scotty worked for another company, we readily shared information and at times assisted each other when we found ourselves on the other's turf. Scotty knew all the back roads and hollows on the plateau and was generous about sharing his knowledge. Similarly, he looked me up when his work brought him to the housing projects in Knoxville.

After exchanging greetings and catching up a bit, Scotty told me to call him if I needed anything and introduced me to the shift sergeant on duty. The deputy made a note in his logbook and said he would have cars in the area in case of trouble. They all knew Wayne, but there weren't any local warrants out on him.

Wayne was supposed to be driving a red, two-door, 1984 Cadillac Coupe DeVille. My snitch, Barry, told me that Wayne and Kim sometimes slept in the car, and the trunk and backseat were loaded with sleeping bags and camping gear when they weren't hauling stolen loot.

Granny's house was right off the highway. I cruised by it and Wayne's car was nowhere to be seen. Several more passes by the house revealed little and the only vehicle in the driveway was an old Ford pickup. Nobody was outside the white-framed house and a steady stream of smoke plumed from the brick chimney. An empty porch swing hung to one side of the front door that was still decorated with a Christmas wreath wrapped in a large red bow.

I drove by the house one last time and then continued up the highway. Granny's house was the only residence around for a couple of miles in either direction. It was surrounded by woods. A five-strand barbed wire fence that ran for several miles between the road and a cow pasture lined the other side of the highway. There was no place to sit and watch her house, absolutely no decent spot to set up surveillance.

After about five miles or so, the highway I was on intersected another state thoroughfare. A yellow caution light blinked over the crossroads and a convenience store sat at the corner. I decided to pull in and think over my next move, maybe have a cup of coffee.

Talk about luck. Just as I pulled into the parking lot, I saw the red Cadillac sitting at the gas pumps. It was the only vehicle parked at the pumps and there was no way to block it in. There was a male sitting in the passenger side of the vehicle but his face was turned away from me.

I felt the adrenaline surge through my system. My mind raced. I pulled the van into a space in front of the store, then adjusted the rearview mirror so I could watch the passenger in the Cadillac, silently willing him to turn toward me so I could see if it was Wayne. The pumps were between our vehicles and my gaze stayed fixed on the mirror. My gut already knew it was—but my mind demanded at least one decent visual.

Unfortunately, I'm evidently not too telepathic, because for several minutes the passenger refused to give me a good look at him. Finally, the passenger made some movements that looked like he was adjusting the radio. Slowly, his head turned and I got a good look at his profile. It was Wayne, no doubt about it.

Then the glass door of the store swung open and another familiar face headed for Wayne's car. It suddenly became clear what had been bothering me about Wayne's file.

I knew the woman as Kim Sloane and hadn't made the connection with her name change to Ballenger after she married Wayne. She'd skipped on a shoplifting charge a couple of years ago and I'd chased her down to Georgia, arrested her, and hauled her back to Tennessee.

We made eye contact. Kim immediately stiffened and then walked briskly past my van.

No need to play it cool—she'd made me.

Kim figured it the same way. She dropped her bag of groceries and ran screaming toward the Cadillac.

I got out of the van and ran toward them but she jumped in the car and had it started before I reached the pumps. They peeled out of the parking lot. I ran back to the van, threw it in reverse, then pulled around and took off down the road after them. The chase was on.

In its day, the red Coupe DeVille would have left my Ford Windstar in the dust. Fortunately, that day had been many years and a few missed oil changes ago. The Coupe DeVille no longer had the advantage.

We sped down the highway and passed Granny's house without so much as slowing down. I caught up with them and eased out to the side and tried to pass. Kim swerved across the centerline to keep me from getting next to them. At the last second, we both veered back into our lane to avoid an oncoming dump truck. Whenever the road was clear, we were all over it, bouncing back and forth between the blurred white lines on the edge, me attempting to pull up next to them, Kim trying to run me off the road.

We approached another intersection and a country store. The brake lights on the Cadillac came on and it slowed down. Kim whipped the car into the gravel parking lot of the store and fishtailed around it, throwing rocks in every direction. I cut in behind them, duplicating the maneuver, throwing even more gravel into the air. I regained control and followed the Coupe DeVille around to the back of the store.

The passenger door of the Cadillac swung open and Wayne bailed out, coughing as he breathed in the thick dust we'd kicked up. I slid the van sideways to a halt, jumped out, and took off after him on foot.

Behind the parking lot was an open dirt area that looked like it'd been graded for construction. Past that were woods that looked like they might go on a fair piece.

Wayne had about a fifty-yard lead on me and reached a tree line while I was running across open area. He disappeared into the woods. Suddenly, a loud *crack* ripped through the air. Dirt spurted up from the ground, peppering me with small pebbles.

No cover. I slammed face-first down onto the hard-packed earth to minimize the target, drawing my gun as I fell. Rounds slammed into the ground on either side of me, but the flashes that accompanied each shot showed me which tree Wayne was using as cover.

I returned fire. Bark flew off Wayne's tree as my rounds hit it. Wayne stopped shooting and fled deeper into the woods.

I got up on one knee, scanning the woods for any sign of Wayne. I'd instinctively emptied my lungs of air before hitting the ground, so I hadn't gotten my breath knocked out of me, but my ribs were screaming protests at their treatment.

In the distance, I could hear a police siren, and it grew louder every moment. No doubt where they were headed. I holstered my gun and walked back to the store. The chase had to be called off for the time being but it was far from over.

Two sheriff's cruisers had blocked off the Cadillac and a highway patrol car came screeching into the parking lot, followed shortly by a detective in his unmarked unit. The store owner had initially called to report the car chase and then reported back that shots had been fired.

People from inside the store spilled out into the parking area and watched the excitement. I raise my hands as two officers approached me with their guns drawn. One of them removed my pistol from the holster, dropped the magazine, and cleared the chamber. He put the magazine and ejected round in his jacket pocket and carried my gun in his hand as we walked back toward the vehicles.

Flashing blue lights surrounded the Cadillac and both its doors were wide open. Kim had been handcuffed and placed into the back of a police car. She was screaming obscenities and bounced up and down.

Out of curiosity, I took a quick look in the backseat of the Cadillac. Nothing could have prepared me for what I saw there, surrounded by piles of clothes and blankets and strapped into a car seat: a baby.

I felt like somebody had punched me in the stomach. I immediately turned around and puked. The crowd of spectators got more than they bargained for. Luckily there was nobody standing behind me.

My knees felt weak and sudden uncontrolled shaking took over my hands. I began to breathe slowly and deeply and gradually regained power over my emotion. The same internal focus that helped to heal me physically brought my feelings almost under control.

Almost. Just as my composure was beginning to return, I felt a wave of intense anger sweep over me.

The detective came over to me and we sat in the front seat of his car. "Did you know there was a baby in the car," he asked.

"No," I said. "There's no way I would've chased after them had I known. That's no excuse and one thing is for sure, that was the last car chase I'll ever be in. The fact is, you can never be sure and nothing in this world is worth it. If that baby had been hurt, I don't know if I could have lived with it."

The detective sighed. "Well, I know how you must feel. But one thing's for sure: those sorry excuses for parents knew that baby was in the car when they decided to run. They intentionally put that child into a dangerous situation. Somebody from the Department of Human Services is on the way down to take the baby into state custody for the time being. Kim is going to jail for reckless endangerment of a child. I need for you to come to the office and make a statement about this whole incident. You can drive down there yourself."

They called a tow truck to haul the Cadillac to the county lot after somebody from the state arrived for the child.

My buddy, Scotty, was in the lobby making a bond when we arrived at the jail. By now he'd heard the whole story. "An assistant attorney general is in the interview room," he said. I saw a trace of sympathy in his eyes.

I shook my head. "Don't go anywhere. I might be needing you."

Maybe I should have asked for a lawyer and refused to give a statement until the local equivalent of Sherman Sikes showed up. But even though I'd had no idea a child was in the car, I couldn't help feeling guilty for the child having been at risk, and I was going through that gut-wrenching experience of having one's priorities realigned.

I tried to tell myself something good could come out of it, that an innocent baby would be removed from such insanely reckless parents. Maybe it was just my way of rationalizing my part in it or maybe it was true. Either way, my days of high-speed car chases were over.

The assistant D.A. and detective listened to my story from start to finish. They counted how many rounds were left in my pistol and we reconstructed the gunfight. The interview lasted about an hour, and then the two men walked out and left me sitting alone in the room. I fully expected them to return and place me under arrest.

Instead, the detective returned alone. He handed me my gun back. "You're free to go. But we need for you to sign warrants against Wayne for attempted murder and aggravated assault. Kim is already in jail and the child is in state custody."

"I'll sign the warrants on Wayne," I said. "But not until after I take him in to jail myself. He has a date in another county first."

The detective laughed. "Haven't you had enough for one day?"

I wasn't about to fill him in on the plan that was already forming in my mind. Instead, I said, "I'm just getting started," and left it at that.

My rage at Wayne and Kim for endangering the baby and the adrenaline from getting shot at combined to create an intense burning in my gut. The breathing techniques helped me maintain focus, but there was only one way to bring some balance back into what had happened, and that was through my own brand of applied justice.

Scotty was waiting for me in the lobby. "How much is your bond?" he asked. "I'll make it whatever it is."

"Thanks, buddy," I said. "I wasn't charged, but I have another favor to ask of you."

Scotty's eyes widened. "You mean they're not locking you up?"

"Nope."

"Then what do you need me for?"

I moved closer to him and whispered, "I want you to bail Kim out of jail."

Scotty's disbelief changed to shock. "What the hell?"

I smiled a bit. Scotty stepped back.

"Just where do you think she'll go when she gets out of here?" I asked.

I saw the light dawn in his eyes. "Probably straight to that no good son of a bitch, Wayne," Scotty answered.

"That's right. And associating with fugitives will be a violation of the terms of the bond you're going to write her. I would be more than happy to act as your agent if she meets him. You can immediately revoke her bond and I'll arrest her along with Wayne. No charge, of course. Just returning a favor."

"You're serious?" I could tell Scotty appreciated the rather elegant solution to the problem of locating Wayne. He studied my face for a moment, then said, "Yeah, I guess you are. Okay, I'll do it."

"Here," I said, shoving a wad of bills at him. "Take this money, pay the impound fee on the Cadillac so she can get it out. But don't tell her anything about it."

"Are you going to try to follow…?" Wayne stopped himself. "Never mind. I don't want to know. It'll take about forty-five minutes to make her bond and get her released. Whatever you do, don't let her skip on me."

"Don't worry, buddy," I said. "I'll be on her like a fly on shit."

The impound lot was an open gravel area across the street from the jail. I walked across the street to the Cadillac. It was unlocked and I crawled into the backseat and lay on the floorboard, my head on the passenger side of the Coupe DeVille and my knees against the back of the driver's seat. I pulled the piles of blankets and clothes over me. My own van was parked out of sight, so I was hoping she'd figure I'd left.

After what seemed like an eternity, I heard footsteps approaching the car, scuffing the gravel in the lot. The driver's side door creaked as it opened. Kim sat down and her weight pressed through the seat against my legs. The DeVille peeled out of the lot, kicking up gravel that splattered against the floorboard just inches from my face. Kim drove for about half an hour, fiddling with the radio and occasionally swearing or banging on the dashboard. Finally, the car slowed and turned up a gravel drive. Although I had no way of seeing where we were going, it sounded like we were pulling up to somebody's house. Kim shut off the car and got out, slamming the door behind her. I stayed where I was, silent and unmoving.

About an hour later, I heard another car pull up the drive. Its headlights lit up the inside of the Cadillac as it approached, then it veered to the side and parked next to it. I heard the engine die and then the sound of two male voices. They slammed the car doors and walked away from the vehicles.

Several minutes passed and then I heard footsteps approaching. Both of the DeVille's doors opened and the seats sagged as two people got in. I froze, hardly breathing, careful to make no sound. Both doors slammed shut, the car started up and backed out of the driveway. Still I waited, knowing it was almost time to spring my trap.

Neither occupant spoke until they were clear of the driveway and back on the highway. Then I heard Kim's voice say, "We can't go back to your grandmother's. They'll be looking for us there."

A familiar voice answered. "That bounty hunter won't be looking for us anymore. I scared the shit out of him. He won't be back." I think I smiled at that, although I doubt it was a pleasant sight. Wayne continued with, "We'll camp out anyway, though, in case the law is looking for us. Then we'll hit the road tomorrow and get the hell out of here." He was silent for a moment, as though waiting for an answer, but evidently Kim was nodding her agreement. Wayne said, "I need some cigarettes. Drive to the store just across the county line and get me some. We'll camp over there somewhere tonight."

Not a word about their child. Not a question about where the baby was, how he was doing, much less any recognition of what they'd risked by running from me. I was finding it harder and harder to hold still, but the promise of settling this on my own terms made me patient.

The Caddy rumbled on for a while and slowed before it turned into a well-lit area. Kim turned off the car and got out, leaving Wayne sitting in the passenger seat.

I slid my fingers quietly to the edges of the blankets, took a firm grip, and then suddenly threw them aside. In the same instant, I unfolded from my hiding place and popped up behind Wayne.

Wayne didn't even have time to take a full breath before I slid my right arm around his neck and grabbed the inside of my left elbow with my right hand. Then I balled up my left hand into a fist and placed it at the base of Wayne's skull. I felt him reach with his right hand to try to dislodge me before he went totally limp.

The sleeper hold would keep him out for around ten seconds, more than enough time for me to jump into the front seat with him and open the passenger's side door. Wayne's right hand was clutched around a .45 semi-automatic wedged in his waistband. I took it away from him and tucked it into my own belt before pushing him out the door and face down on the pavement. I had him cuffed and shackled before Kim even came out of the store. The keys to the car were in my pocket, and I was damned sure she couldn't outrun me.

I dragged Wayne, facedown on the sidewalk, around to the front of the car. When Kim walked out of the store, she saw me sitting on the hood of the Cadillac with my foot in the middle of Wayne's back, smiling at her.

Kim screamed and charged me, arms flailing. I sidestepped her initial swing, then caught the follow-up with an X-block, twisting the block into a wristlock. I felt like tearing her head off but settled for applying pressure to her wrist and forcing her facedown on the DeVille's hood.

Just a little bit more pressure and she quickly relented to being cuffed. The physical restraint had no effect on her mouth and she continued to spout a string of profanities. After having listened to her in the car earlier, I realized she had a somewhat limited vocabulary of them.

Just then, Wayne finally started to stir, but my foot on the chain of the leg shackles prevented him from getting up. I forced Kim down on the sidewalk next to him and linked their handcuffs together. Kim was still being uncooperative, so I placed my foot lightly on Wayne's testicles from behind, pinning them to the sidewalk. Wayne froze, completely silent until Kim tried to twist away again. The handcuffs that connected them made Wayne twist, too, and he found that a far more unpleasant sensation than she did. I applied a little pressure and Wayne screamed at Kim to hold still. A little pressure was all it took and one foot controlled them both.

With the situation stabilized, I called Scotty on my cell phone. He agreed to come pick us up. I unloaded Wayne's gun and placed it under the seat, then locked the car. The store clerk had already called the law and they could handle that end of it. Scotty drove us back to the jail. He'd already revoked Kim's bond so she went back inside, this time to stay.

Wayne hobbled to my van and we made the long ride back to the county where he was wanted. While we were en route, Scotty called and said the Cadillac had again been impounded and the gun registration number came back as belonging to a stolen handgun. The number of jurisdictions that were interested in talking to Wayne was quickly growing. That wasn't a problem; Wayne was going to be easy to find for quite some time.

No job is done until the paperwork is complete. My trip to Hawaii was in two days, but before I could concentrate on the final travel arrangements, the packing, and the sheer anticipation, I had to get caught up on data entry. A stack of chase folders threatened to spill off my desk. I sighed, pulled out my chair, and sat down to catch up.

I worked for about an hour, made a substantial dent in the stack and had just entered arrest number nine hundred ninety in the computer when my cell phone rang. It was the lead detective in the Wiley Kent case, Detective Finchum. He had bad news. Wiley had slipped through again.

The railroad police had arrested our boy, Wiley, for hopping boxcars in Oregon. Wiley had been cited for trespassing and they'd taken his fingerprints. Unfortunately, through some snafu, the railroad police had released Wiley before the routine check of fingerprints had come back. By the time they'd realized they had an honest to God criminal in their hands, Wiley was long gone.

"Damn," I said, as Finchum finished his story. I could tell the detective was as annoyed as I was. It just didn't seem fair for a stupid scumbag to keep running into so much luck.

"Yeah, I know, I know," Finchum said. "But sooner or later, his luck will run out."

I knew Finchum was right. It's trite, but true: you can't run forever. Still, the sheer magnitude of Wiley's dumb luck was seriously testing my faith in old adages.

Wayne was the last skip I had to enter in the computer. When I called up a fresh record, I saw that he was arrest number one thousand. Even though I set more store by not getting cut or shot at more often than I do, it was a landmark nevertheless. When I got home, I'd tell Debbie. Maybe this was a good excuse for a small celebration.

But Wiley was still out there somewhere. Okay, maybe no celebration—I'd save that for the day his luck finally ran out.

I erased the last name off my chase board and put away the paper files. Then I backed up my files and shut down the computer. I closed the door to my office and took one long look around the bail office. It was empty now, but it would be business as usual tomorrow. There would be more Waynes, Kims, and TCs calling the office or sending their families in while I was gone. There would be more prostitutes making bail, snitches wanting a bit of cash, and internet con men pleading for bonds. My chase board might be empty now, but that wouldn't last. Crime was, unfortunately, a growth industry.

I locked the office door behind me, setting the alarm at the same time I shoved Wiley Kent far back into his designated cubbyhole in my mind. As far as I was concerned, he would cease to exist for the next two weeks. When I got back, maybe there would be new leads. Maybe he'd be tripped up somewhere, arrested, or perhaps even run out of luck. Whatever was going to happen would happen and I would deal with it when I returned.

I slammed the cubbyhole door tight and locked and bolted it. I was going to Hawaii to be reunited with my son, and that was all that mattered.

The End

# about the authors

Joseph Laney makes his living as a bail enforcement agent and a certified trainer of police officers. He was formerly a sergeant in the drug enforcement unit of the Sevier County, Tennessee, sheriff's department. He is an eighth-degree black belt and master instructor in Isshinryu karate. His website is steelhanddojo.com.

Cyn Mobley is a retired Naval Reserve commander specializing in surface and antisubmarine warfare and a former criminal defense attorney. She is the author of twenty-three books, including *Rites of War, Rules of Command, Code of Conduct,* and *Complete Idiot's Guide to Aircraft Carriers.* She devotes much of her time to the rescue and rehabilitation of discarded racing greyhounds and owns a small publishing house that raises money for canine rescue groups. Her articles have appeared in *Navy Times,* the *San Diego Union Tribune,* and *Celebrating Greyhounds* magazine. Her website is dogbooks.org.